S0-ATM-322

Learning to be Deaf

Contributions to the Sociology of Language

43

Editor
Joshua A. Fishman

Mouton de Gruyter
Berlin · New York · Amsterdam

Learning to be Deaf

by

A. Donald Evans
William W. Falk

Mouton de Gruyter
Berlin · New York · Amsterdam

Mouton de Gruyter (formely Mouton, The Hague)
is a Division of Walter de Gruyter & Co., Berlin.

CIP-Kurztitelaufnahme der Deutschen Bibliothek

Evans, A. Donald:
Learning to be deaf / A. Donald Evans ; William W. Falk. –
Berlin ; New York ; Amsterdam : Mouton de Gruyter, 1986.
(Contributions to the sociology of language ; 43)
ISBN 3-11-010637-X
NE: Falk, William W.:; GT

Library of Congress Cataloging in Publication Data:

Learning to be deaf
(Contributions to the sociology of language ; 43)
Bibliography: p.
Includes Index.
1. Children, Deaf – United States – Language. 2. Children, Deaf – Education – United States. 3. Sociolinguistics – United States, I. Evans, A. Donald, 1934 – II. Falk, William W. III. Series,
HV 2545. L43 1986 362.4′285 86–12838
ISBN 0-89925-161-7 (U.S. : alk. paper)

Printed on acid free paper.

Typesetting: Arthur Collignon GmbH, Berlin. – Printing: Druckerei Gerike, Berlin.
Binding: Dieter Mikolai, Berlin. Printed in Germany.

Foreword

Now that it has been done; now that two sociologists have given us a detailed picture of the sociolinguistic impact of a residential school for the deaf – it seems like such an obvious thing to do that one wonders why it had not been done before. Even more so than for the hearing child, the residential school is the very heart and soul, the veritable center, of the social experience of deaf children. No wonder then that it is there that "sign" is entrenched as both a co-creator and byproduct of an authentic ethnocultural identity and tradition. Evans and Falk show us "sign" is *indexically* related to the culture of the residential school, how it is *symbolically* related to the culture of the residential school, and, finally, how it is *part and parcel* of the culture of the school.

As with other utterly powerless and peripheral minorities, the question has been posed whether deaf children "belong" to their own culture or whether they "belong" to the hearing culture that surrounds them and controls them, particularly in their after-school years. If the latter option is favored, then the culture of the residential school may not provide the best corridor to the mainstream world, nor are its cognitive and other accomplishments more than pitifully inadequate by the standards of that world. However, if the graduates of such schools may be said to constitute a speech community of their own, with a repertoire of varieties, each with indigenous norms, then the residential school for the deaf can also be endonormatively evaluated and its language viewed relative to the socio-cultural desiderata of its own culture. Both of these options are explored by Evans and Falk. Their ethnography is as much an ethnography of the language-in-culture type as those we have become accustomed to in connection with hearing children.

However, it is more sociologically informed than most of the foregoing and, therefore, brings into play an entire literature that is enriching for the sociolinguistic enterprise. Unfortunately, although minority cultures may be studied and understood as if they were self-contained and self-validated units, they are nevertheless frequently far from being such operationally. The ambiguity in connection with "whom the deaf child belongs to" is, therefore, repeated in connection with the deaf school itself and deaf culture as a whole. Evans and Falk highlight this double or triple ambiguity. As a result, no one can read their book without becoming aware of the burdens and complications that characterize the life of the deaf child, burdens and complications that the child's language reflects and that the school briefly compensates for, but life-long burdens and complications after all. For making all of this clear to us from a sociolinguistic perspective we owe a tremendous debt of gratitude to this book and to its authors.

Joshua A. Fishman
Ferkauf Graduate School of Psychology
Yeshiva University

Contents

DEDICATION

We dedicate this book to our wives,
Barbara D. Evans and Geraldine Falk.

Acknowledgements

As in all projects such as this, persons too numerous to mention have been helpful. For Evans, foremost among these is the deaf community itself whose members helped me know their language and their culture. And, in particular, deaf students at SSD (a state school for the deaf where our study was conducted) helped make our discovery of new knowledge possible. I "wave the handkerchief" to them with much gratitude. At SSD the principal (and his staff in general) could have offered nothing more to facilitate the study.

Mercer University supported the initial work by providing time off to conduct the field work and more time off for writing. It also recruited extra clerical workers who seemed to work endlessly on our several versions of the manuscript. Vince Leitch, who also writes on language, read parts of the manuscript, met with me several times and gave very constructive feedback. And Al Bond frequently read parts of the manuscript, spent hours querying, debating, and challenging some of our ideas.

JoAnna Watson never stopped encouraging the work and was, for me, a source of inspiration and pride. Gene Bell definitely helped facilitate the production process. In the sociology department Mabel Edmiston typed and re-typed chapters, and, with pride, spoke of "our book." I am very grateful to all these Mercerians.

At home, Barbara Evans, my wife and best friend, kept saying the extra hours of work were well spent.

For Falk, several individuals and institutions must be mentioned. First, Louisiana State University provided a sabbitic leave during which much of the initial organization of the book was undertaken. Second, Andy Deseran at LSU and Peter Mills at the University of Leeds (in England) read drafts of chapters and shared many coffees/teas/lunches to converse about the book; my sincere thanks to them both. Third, the secretarial staff at Leeds, and later at LSU never complained about typing and retyping drafts of our work; to the contrary, Carol Peaker and Lynn Kelly at Leeds, and Reba Rosenbach at LSU were continuously interested in the book.

Also I have had the steadfast support of my assistant, Cathy Olivier. Finally, my wife, Geraldine Falk, read drafts of some chapters and helped point out redundancies and "wordy sociologisms"; furthermore, her own continuing interest in the deaf aided my outsider's view.

Preface

This book is about deaf children and their everyday lives in a state residential school. Our study of these children's lives documents just how crucial language is – for these individuals are deprived of language as most people think of it. To be understood, these children must talk with their hands; i.e., they must physically sign what they wish to "say." And, as we show, for them this is their natural language, just as spoken language seems "natural" to persons in the hearing world.

The children in our study experience the world very differently from other children. Their group is more like a tribal or oral society than a literate one where the written word is so important. In the sign language, or tribal-talking society, reality is daily encountered and affirmed through the hands of others. This experience is quite unlike that of Marshal McLuhan's (1967) literate-alphabetic man whose reality largely gets defined, established and sustained by linear sequentially printed words.

In the symbolic universe which we call SSD, a state school for the deaf, the sign language experience is much more iconic and ideographic than the alphabetic syllabic, or arbitrary word, culture of the conventional speech community. Signs at SSD resemble those used by early human beings who graphically represented salient parts of their local reality by means of holistic ideographs in the form of cave paintings and rock engravings. In a similar way American sign language (ASL) is a pictographic language "written" in the air by human hands. It is a unique language that tends to reify significant objects found within a local situation (see Collins, 1985:73). In this book we consider how language influences the way we think. Thus, consciousness for these deaf signers tends to involve molar-macroscopic interpretations, divisions and taxonomies of the world in sharp contrast to the more molecular-microscopic cogitations of speech users which reduce global phenomena to more elementaristic components. As in nonliterate societies, there is for the deaf more "directness of relationship between symbol and referent" at SSD (Goody and Watt, 1972:313).

In deaf and in non-literate societies knowledge systems, including legends, myths, and cultural doctrines, are mediated orally. Similarly,

SSD is a talking society where high school student members list in the yearbook "talking" with signs as their "hobby." And deaf people in general have been compared to "ancients" in that both "stand on common ground" in terms of mythical world views (Russo, 1975:107,200). This world and its fund of knowledge is relatively closed, local and concrete. In fact, when asked "Why Columbus did not use an airplane to discover America?" some students at SSD cannot respond correctly. Why? A top administrator thinks they cannot because "the past is abstract and not experienced ..." The adventures of Columbus were not local.

At SSD we encounter a homogeneous social world quite removed from Max Weber's modern process of bureaucratization, which involves the rationalization of institutions and transition from small to large group life, from mythical to scientific world views. For Weber such changes caused the "disenchantment of the world." But SSD, linguistically and socially isolated, remains more nearly a magical, mystical world. Indeed, we find some teens who think that Superman is real and that he actually flies. Here, then, is an interesting homogeneous social world characterized by holistic language and thought, its own peculiar fund of knowledge.

Drawing on the sociological perspective called symbolic interactionism, and other sociological views that we discuss, we accord great importance to the role that everyday interaction plays in people's lives – for it is from such interaction that much of our sense of the world is derived. The world is experienced and learned as one interacts with those around him. The uniqueness of any culture is the product of the interactive experience that its members have and the shared history that is passed along from one generation to another.

Our book, then, is about language, symbols, knowledge, consciousness, and world views. It is much more than a mere description of handicapped children. It is both an exploration of and a statement about the connection of human life and language. And in this work we are forced to speculate, to theorize, and to confront the fundamental question of what is meant by social scientists when they speak of "human" as opposed to "animal" behavior. Of course, human beings *are* animals, but what, specifically, makes a Homo sapiens creature "human"? We answer this by presenting a story about the amazing journey of symbolically disadvantaged children who grope from stimuli to symbols, from *animal* to *human-animal*. Our narrative recounts Helen Keller type miracle stories that occur frequently and ones which can be observed in deaf schools all across America.

This is also, to our knowledge, the first ethnographic report on a state residential school for the deaf ever conducted in the United States. In it our immediate task was to enter, observe, participate in, and chronicle the everyday interactions of a unique linguistic group. Oddly, this is a group of children who learn to "speak" a foreign language – ASL – generally unknown by their own parents, neighbors, and the society in which they live. Metaphorically, they occupy a small island inside, but apart from, the mainland's conventional language, culture, and social interaction.

The general plan of our ethnographic work was to produce a "picture" of this island – its norms, values, symbols, language(s), and patterns of interaction. But we also knew that we had to investigate the mind-self-society (Mead, 1977) nexus because sign language systems really constitute something very *new* and unusual for researchers in this domain. Something "new" because traditional research and theory have almost completely ignored non-verbal, manual-gestural-spatial-holistic languages such as formal sign systems and *their* roles in and connections to the language-consciousness-reality complex mentioned above. Interestingly, it was the Gardners (Fleming, 1979) and their studies of ape sign language usage in the 1960s that first attracted the attention of a few members of the scientific community to this extremely different way of communicating.

Many of the ideas, questions, and issues addressed within this book have evolved over a span of years, beginning with Evans' Master's Thesis (1971) entitled *Differential Socialization of the Deaf in a Residential School.* In 1972, at another residential school for the deaf in a different state, Evans collected both qualitative and quantitative data that focussed on experiential deprivation within a school for the deaf. For 15 years he has taught a course at Mercer University called, "The Sociology of Language With Emphasis on the Deaf," as well as advanced sign language courses. In addition to teaching he has formed and directed many theatrical productions using signs. Thus, many provocative questions and issues raised in this book have been tested with hundreds of university students, many of whom have gone on to become teachers of the deaf.

Evans, himself hard-of-hearing, and Falk met at Louisiana State University where Falk teaches courses on the sociology of education.

At the graduate level, these courses give considerable emphasis to what has been called the "new sociology of education" (Karabel and Halsey, 1977), with its intellectual roots in Europe and its organization in England. This "new sociology" developed from the activities of a network of researchers who focus directly on microlevel problems such as the organization and *content* of education, the curriculum, and the internal dynamics of schools.

Evans, with fifteen years of interest in language, symbols, and deafness, the quintessential obstacle to symboling, was immediately attracted to the interactive and Marxian emphasis in the 'new sociology' and to the work, in particular, of Basil Bernstein. Bernstein has related linguistic processes and development to the social class-based nature of most schooling. Thus, for Bernstein, teachers make initial and continuing assessments of children based, in part, on their ability to use certain codes of language. To oversimplify, Bernstein conceptualizes language codes as being either "restricted" or "elaborated" with the latter having a more complex conceptual hierarchy and the one least likely to be found in poorer, working class (and for us, deaf) children.

From this first contact with the new sociology of education, many subsequent discussions between Evans and Falk occurred – Evans with his focus on the sociology of language, on the fate of the deaf, and on symbolic interaction theory, Falk with his own educational research grounded in the 'new sociology of education.' Over a two-year span, the project that evolved into this book was formulated. Subsequently, Evans lived at the State School for the Deaf (SSD) that was the main study site. He and Falk conferred frequently while he was at SSD, talking about where the research was going, which paths were productive, which were not, and which new paths should be pursued. The initial work was reported in Evans' dissertation (1981). Since completing that, countless hours have been spent reorganizing, rethinking, and extending the study to produce this book.

From the time of Plato great minds have made claims for the powerful role of language and its causal relationship to cognition, consciousness, knowledge, self, and world view. It is surprising then that so little attention has been directed to those without hearing and their prodigious language-symboling problem! Obviously, social scientists need not wait for bizarre discoveries of ferals or isolates in order to study the effects of linguistic and cultural deprivation. There is no need to wait because young deaf children are accessible and can be easily found in families and in residential, public and private schools. The interesting (and tragic) thing is that they initially live *outside*, primarily *outside*, the human symbolic universe and remain outside so much longer than children who can hear.

Indeed, if we consider this extraordinary socialization quandary in terms of Herbert Blumer's (1969) two worlds – the so-called physical universe and the symbolic universe – then we are led to consider a fundamental question, "Where are deaf children who have no language at all (no signs, no words)?" Are they experientially trapped in the non-symbolic world of all other non-human animals? Are the physical objects of their world ever experienced as phenomenological essences independent of the immediate experience of a thing itself?

To explore this question further we incorporate two or three other binary concepts that help represent different facets of reality. Marx, for example, neatly divides existence into substructure/superstructure (*Unterbau/Ueberbau*; see Berger and Luckmann, 1967:6). The substructure refers to human beings interacting, working, relating, and talking. Significantly, they are *talking*. It is this frequent conversational activity that produces a "superstructure," a world, i.e., a culture.

But what about deaf children who cannot talk to each other? What superstructure exists for/is produced by them? Is theirs a partial, ragged, fragmented, and gapped skeleton of a world? No more burning question emerges from our study than this: To what extent, if any, can a languageless deaf child symbolically communicate? What is an example of such symboling? Is one limited, in George Herbert Mead's parlance, to a "conversation of gestures"? As Peter Berger and Thomas Luckmann say, the dog cannot be separated from his snarl as the dancer can be separated from his dance. What, then, of the deaf person signing versus the oral person speaking? These are difficult questions not easily answered but it is important to ask them, to raise the theoretical issues they imply. For example, can a child observe a mother's usage of an automobile ignition key and, days later, lead her to the keys on the table as if to say, "Let's go for a ride?" If so, are these acts composed of mere signs or of symbols?

To continue this intriguing line of thought, we integrate the concepts of two German writers, Uexkull and Heidegger (See Percy, 1983:86fn), who distinguish between the human experience of *Welt* (world), into which the social self may be flung, and *Umwelt* (environment). Again, we pose disturbing questions. Is a deaf child who has no language primarily dwelling in the *Umwelt*? Is it a world of stimuli instead of symbols? Can much social knowledge be learned visually? Is this a world primarily of physical, not social, objects?

Where does a four or even a ten-year-old languageless deaf child think he is on the first day of school when parents unload him from the car and drive away? Can this child displace without language? That is, can he think of objects not immediately present? Is he able to think of his parents and wonder where they are? Did they abandon me forever? (How can a teacher even begin to explain that the parent will return in two weeks?) Who are these strangers? Why am I here? Look at their moving hands! What are they doing? When and where can I eat? [How could one even think *these* questions without language?]

Fundamental epistemological questions are rampant here. What social and cultural knowledge, (distinctively *human* knowledge), can be acquired without language? Are deaf children virtual *tabulae rasae*? What happens inside their heads? Without words, or signs, how do they think? How do they talk to themselves? How can they have an "inner voice?" Is their interior universe a profound cranial silence where unsegmented reality is experienced as a mental set of dancing images/pictures-wholes? To what degree can they have ideas as to "who" they are (You're "Jeremy," a "boy", a "Georgian," a "student," my "son")? How can a *social* self develop if language is absent or extremely limited? How can collective definitions, meanings, and valuations be assigned to and internalized by a child who cannot hear nor understand them?

In this book we emphasize that, above all, human social life is symbolic interaction. But, unlike nearly all other symbolic interactionists we explicitly state that "symbolic interaction" means that two or more people are languaging. For us the *human* world is a languaging world. Conversely, the non-human animal world is one of signs and signals. We understand, of course, that non-verbal symbols are important, but they pale in significance before languaging. Deaf children without language actually play "together" without engaging in symbolic behavior and, therefore, do not experience the *human* world – not, at least, in any significant way. Obviously, this proposition opens up yet another complex set of questions about Mead's claims for role playing, symboling, playing, and conversation of gestures.

For us, views of the world are of central importance. And much of the book is spent trying to explore certain aspects of deaf children's world views. One of our "domain assumptions" (Gouldner, 1970) is that languages, symbols, and world views arise from and reflect particular social contexts. We have attempted to observe and to discover how sign language, residential school life (the interactional context), and world views might be related. What, if any, usual or unusual definitions of reality might be confirmed or constructed?

Language helps us create reality and, dialectically, it helps shape our inner realities, our consciousness. Given that Eskimos produce many terms for snow, Arabs many terms for camels, and Americans many classifications for automobiles, we wondered what salient social objects and processes will be labeled in the restricted residential existence of deaf students? And equally as interesting is an opposing question, "What major and common social objects, structures and processes for the outside world go unnamed within the deaf student world?" That is, what important symbolic and linguistic gaps exist within this closed society? If language is likened to a map, are this society's maps relatively barren of grids, graphics, and markers except for those within its own locale? In fact, is the larger "map" understandable at all to any appreciable degree or is the deaf child's world truly that – i.e., *his* entire world?

This raises another fundamental question: How do such children define/understand/evaluate their own deafness? Are their concepts of self identity well formed or different compared to those of hearing children? And if language acquisition is late and vocabulary development is relatively restricted, how is self development affected? Will the initially assertive, egotistical, individualistic "I" be eventually buried by the weighty, conformist, tribal-like, linguistically-dependent "We" (i.e., community of deaf students)? Is competition or cooperation the hallmark of this group?

Ethnographers have historically travelled to distant exotic places to document strange and unusual cultures. Conversely, we attempt to provide a close-up, "colorful" view of student culture in a residential school for the deaf, a *local* linguistic group generally ignored by social scientists.

The site for our study was a large residential school for deaf children located in a Southeastern state. The superintendent, who was well known by one of the researchers, agreed to let the research be conducted with much latitude at SSD. At this institution significant demographic changes have recently occurred. During the 1960s the student population reached 600. But in 1981, during our study, it had dropped to less than 350 with an ever-increasing proportion of black, poor, and multi-handicapped students. The rubella epidemic of the 1960s that caused deafness was over and the mainstreaming in education movement was on.

In the fieldwork we attempted to follow a general strategy outlined by Glaser and Strauss (1967) and given greater structure by Lofland (1971). Research began with as few preconceptions as possible. Thus, any theoretical ideas we had were to grow out of and fit with our observations rather than the other way around.

Generally, our interviews were in the form of guided conversations where we sought, in the words of Strong (1943), to discover the participants' "axes of life," their frames of reference within which meaning was located. The first days of work began in the lower school among very young children (the "babies") and their teachers in order to see first language experiences. Overall our time was fairly equally divided between lower, middle, and high schools for the four months duration of the study.

Classroom observations were made for one week at a time, and the lower and middle schools allowed Evans to observe interaction from behind one-way mirrors. At night and on weekends observations were also made in dormitories, play grounds, field trips, and snack bars. Teachers were interviewed in classrooms during their free hour and/ by appointment after school hours, sometimes in the privacy of their own homes. Houseparents were generally cooperative and gave interviews after students were in bed.

Most in-depth interviews and conversations lasted about one-and-one-half hours with a few five hour sessions. In all cases, some form of note-taking occurred and, when appropriate, a small pocket-size dictaphone was used. (A deaf person's signed responses were verbalized into the recorder). Many of these literal renditions of sign talk appear throughout the book and will surely seem choppy and cryptic to the reader.

Throughout the study Evans lived in the school's infirmary adjacent to two dormitories. His own hearing loss and wearing of two hearing aids *plus* his fluent use of sign language gave him a certain insider status that might otherwise have been more difficult to obtain.

Before turning to the text, one final thing must be mentioned. The field of deaf education is currently embroiled in a major controvery

– a controversy shared by all educators dealing with "handicapped" children. At issue is whether these children should be kept separate, attending schools of their own or included in local schools. While we do not directly address this issue, our study clearly has implications for this debate. It remains for the reader to draw his own conclusions about what should be done. Whether in local, special or residential schools, problems will abound for deaf children, only their context will change. As will soon be abundantly clear, it is not just language that is crucial to function in our society, but a particular type of language – acceptably spoken, written, understood English. In the absence of this, a type of paralysis occurs that renders the individual helpless. The degree to which the deaf can overcome this obstacle and the educational setting where it can be best achieved remains open to debate.

Chapter I

Deafness, Community, and Sign Language

> Only a very small proportion of deaf people ... can learn how to be culturally deaf in their parental homes; they must learn to be the adults they become from others, in other places, and often without their parents' knowledge or approval. This strange and melancholy circumstance reverberates through the entire life and history of deaf people all over the world.
>
> Beryl Lieff Benderly

> I must confess that my conversation with my family is very limited. I am much happier with the other deaf. I have more freedom in talking. I can talk all I want with the deaf.
>
> Mr. Marquez

This is a book about deaf children and the daily situations within which they find themselves. This is also a book about deaf people more generally, a group of people who have a most unusual minority group handicapped status – they are invisible. The very attribute which makes them "minority" persons is not readily detectible by either their parents or in large groups of people. What eventually makes a deaf person known to the general public is that they must "show" themselves if they wish to communicate; they must exhibit their unique language[1]. It is a language which is largely alien to non-deaf people, a language whose ideas can only be conveyed by physical signs. Above all else it is this visible, signed language which sets deaf people apart from the general population.

Although not specifically referring to deaf people, Goffman's (1963:5) general description of the stigmatized individual is of especial relevance here:

> (A)n individual who might have been received easily in ordinary social intercourse possesses a trait that can obstrude itself upon attention and turn those of us whom he meets away from him, breaking the claim that his other attributes have on us. He possesses a stigma, an undesired differentness from what we had anticipated (p. 5).

Clearly, deaf persons can be conceptualized in Goffman's framework as "stigmatized;" they are different and "normal" people may turn away from them. This is but one cost to being different. Other costs are experienced early-on in the educational experiences of young, deaf children. Depending on their degreee of hearing loss, they may have difficulty understanding teachers and peers; and if regular schooling is sufficiently difficult for them, they may eventually attend some type of special education program, possibly a school for the deaf.

When children are sent to a school for the deaf, and especially if they are to be residents there, there is little difference between their social status and that of any other group which is confined. In some sense of the term, they are "institutionalized" – which is simply a societal euphemism for being intentionally kept apart. But unlike some other institutional groups, they have *done* nothing to earn their institutionalized status – it is purely ascriptive. Similar to sex and race, one is born into it (although some are deafened by disease or accidents); but unlike them, with deafness one may be forcibly set apart for differential treatment. In this way, of course, the beginnings of a possible self-fulfilling prophecy are set up wherein a type of labelling occurs: if deaf are different, and I am deaf, then – ipso facto – I must be different. And it is critically important to be mindful of the role that language plays in this for it is from the absence of language (in its oral form) that one's status and possibly stigmatized existence arise. Even among members of the speech community the proper use of English is valued and distinctions are made between "correct," "good" speech (*Hochdeutsch*) and "bad," "incorrect" speech (Hertzler, 1965:368). Likewise, the use of standard linguistic forms is associated with middle-class, upwardly mobile persons, either white or black" (Nash and Nash, 1981:33).

An Introduction to Deafness

It is necessary to make clear at the outset that there is considerable variance among deaf people (i.e. not all deaf people are equally "deaf"). Some are born deaf (prelingual deafness) while others lose their hearing later (postlingual deafness). The simple axiom which prevails is: the longer one has had hearing capacities, *ceteris paribus*, the greater the probability that one has a more nearly normative vocabulary and use of the society's language. One's language disadvantage, then, corresponds to the degree (moderate, severe or profound) to which one has been or is currently deaf *and* to age of onset of deafness.

It is important to take note of this variability among deaf people because, in this study, the ability to "talk" is given much emphasis insofar as it is related to the individual's ability to comprehend the world around him. Reality construction and knowledge acquisition are directly related to hearing capabilities. Also, the forms of talk among deaf people are varied, there is not simply one aural-oral language. Instead, aural-oral language may be supplanted or even replaced by sign language, a purely physical language. Fant (1972:iii) notes that there are several sign languages (and, as we shall see in Chapter Four, there are several sign systems used at the State School for the Deaf [hereafter called SSD]). In the United States there is American Indian sign language and two other sign languages which are used by most deaf Americans – these are signed English and American Sign Language (ASL; Fant calls these "Siglish" and "Ameslan"). Fingerspelling would seem to be another sign language but according to Fant is not; that is, "fingerspelling is nothing more than the presence of spoken English in a visual-manual medium ..." (p. iii). For us this distinction is important. Fingerspelling is alphabetic, sign language is primarily ideographic and these two systems symbolically represent objects and events in different ways. Another extremely important point (discussed in Chapter Three), for us, has to do with the fact that users of ASL constantly switch back and forth between ASL and fingerspelling. That is, a signer constantly uses fingerspelled English words along with his/her signs. While it is true, perhaps, that *all* languages borrow lexical items from others, what other language finds it necessary to flip-flop back and forth between two different languages in order to converse? The point here is that ASL is a language whose lexicon is very undeveloped (and thus is very limited) much like that of, say, a tribal language which attempts to function/operate within a very complex high-tech society.

American Sign Language (hereafter called ASL) is the most common language among deaf people (Fant, 1972:v; Furth, 1966:15) and is used by them as their primary language (Schlesinger and Meadow, 1972:31; Jacobs, 1974:34). Furthermore, most deaf people feel that ASL is the "natural" language for them (see Cicourel and Boese, 1972; also Northern and Downs, 1974:253). Given the widespread use and importance of ASL, it is important to briefly state some of its characteristics.

First of all, ASL is a real language which seems "restrictive" to English speakers because, among other reasons, it has "many fewer synonyms" and a relatively small vocabulary (Benderly, 1980). It is said to perform poorly in making "intellectual distinctions" so easily made in English, to outperform English, however, on emotion conveyance (p. 59). ASL has an estimated lexicon of only 25,000 signs (Moores, 1978:173) compared to one-million words for the English language. Not long ago it was held that ASL was a "loose collection" of primitive, home-made gestures without any grammar. Klima and Bellugi (1979:30) represent the current position of most linguists today:

> Far from being a loose collection of gestures, ASL is a language with a complex grammar, both at the level of internal structures of the sign and at the level of operations that signs can undergo as they are modulated for special meaning within ASL sentences. None of these operations derive from those of English; the principles on which they are based are directly suited to a visual-manual rather than auditory-vocal language.

Finally, Cicourel (1973:131) says the power of sign language is clearly limited by a lack of "detailed standardization found in oral languages." He also points out that, for language, a normative system of rules is a "powerful way of generating abstract meanings and doing complicated reference."

So ASL, then, is a language separate from *all* other languages. So separate is it that many writers on language make claims which simply do not fit nor apply to ASL. For example, many writers, perhaps most, define language in terms of sound: "Language is regarded as a set of rules enabling speakers to translate information from the outside world into sound" (Gumperz and Hymes, 1972:14). Again, "Not only are words symbols, but without words other symbols would not exist" (Charon, 1979:43). Finally,

> ... no language system ever discovered is so primitive that its speakers must rely heavily upon gestures as substitutes for words. Nor does any known language lack a highly organized system of sounds .... All languages possess pronouns ... and the capacity for full aesthetic and intellectual expression (Farb, 1973:11).

But ASL *does* rely heavily on formalized gestures (signs) and has neither words nor sounds. Even more differences are mentioned below. It is not a dialect of English nor does it derive from English. It is a "complexly structured language with a highly articulated grammar" (Klima and Bellugi, 1979:4). Therefore, ASL is viewed as a foreign language and most deaf students are considered to be bilingual and bicultural people (see Vernon and Koh, 1974:38). In a peculiar way deaf children are most often users of a language foreign to their own family members, neighbors and society at large. On the other hand, English is basically a foreign (or at best second) language for the deaf person (Cicourel and Boese, 1972). Thus we have a paradox: on the one hand, linguists and members of the deaf community – now more sensitive than ever to cultural pluralism – declare ASL to be an independent and functional language of its own. Any pejorative statements which claim it to be inferior are characterized as ethnocentric. ASL is defended as our "native" language; English is "your" language. However, while these deaf people live in a word-based society (an alphabetic/syllabic society) dominated by the use of written and spoken English, their English language proficiency is thought to be very poor (Moores, 1978:223). After all, in their world they "hear" with their eyes and "talk" with their hands.

Another unique characteristic to ASL (and for that matter, sign languages more generally) is its non-aural-oral quality. Furthermore, as a visual-gestural-spatial language it differs from some of the commonly accepted universal characteristics posited for language: "that language is based on speech and the vocal apparatus; that linguistic symbols are essentially arbitrary, the form of a symbol bearing no relation to the form of its referent" (Klima and Bellugi, 1979:3). ASL is pervaded at all levels by iconicity (being relatively representational, mimetic) and is global in character; it is a concept, not word-based language. Many of ASL's symbols are mimetic (pictoral) representations of objects or events, hence globally iconic. In this unique language, pantomime and non-conventional gestures are often interspersed among the more standard signs. As some have said, signers "sculpt their messages," they paint pictures of them (Benderly, 1980). ASL is truly a dramatical system of communication where "each signer puts on a small play ..." (p. 55).

There has been considerable debate around the iconicity of ASL with recent reports holding that ASL is not very iconic at all. While ASL is not a system of transparent pictures, it is a language whose symbols for objects and events are far more iconic than *any* spoken language (although it includes arbitrary signs too). While some writers (see Friedman's comments, 1977) feel that users of ASL are "culturally and cognitively deprived," the current trend among researchers seems to be away from that position. Moores (1978), for example, objects to equating ASL with Basil Bernstein's (1977) concept of a restricted code of communication (more will be said about this and Bernstein, more generally, shortly). For Moores and others sharing his position, ASL is capable of being expressed in both restricted and (another Bernstein concept) elaborated codes (these allowing for greater detail and abstraction).

Our own position is much like that of Cicourel and Boese in that sign language is very much context-bound or situated in space and time (see also Fant, 1972:24). Thus if one is not witness to some event, a full understanding of its signed description may yield a very truncated understanding of what took place. As Cicourel and Boese comment: "a sign used by two persons and embellished while developing their conversation carries more meaning than would be available to a third party who came in late in the conversation ..." (1972:39–40; see also Cicourel, 1973:131). This is an important point and we shall return to it at several subsequent points in our own analysis. Conceptually and empirically, we wonder how much effect reliance on a strictly physically produced language has on one's view of the world. How does a ten year old child "see" (viz., understand, comprehend, apprehend) the world in the absence of language and vocabulary? How is "reality" apprehended? In what sense does "social structure" exist?

Among deaf people it is possible to see crude homemade signs and more complex sign systems being used to convey meaning. On a crude-to-complex symboling continuum, the question arises: If a deaf person possesses very few or no significant symbols (i. e., no words [or signs] as such), no formal signing system, how does his/her mental experience of the world differ greatly from chimps or dogs who also lack a language? Mightn't he primarily inhabit the *Umwelt* (environment of physical objects which have no socially shared meanings/definitions) of all other animals but not the *Welt* (symbolic world of social objects) of man? Would his physical (animal) reality basically be continuous, unstructured and not at all dissected by categories and typifications? As Capra (1983:301) the physicist, reminds us, "Pictures of separate objects exist only in our inner world of symbols, concepts, and ideas." The reality around us, he says, is something continuous and not segmented (and "visual memory is organized like a hologram"). Would a languageless person "see" hills and mountains as animals do – as continuous terrain unbroken by terminological divisions? After all, "Reality, for the individual, depends on the words used to look" (Charon, 1979:3). If perspectives and conceptual frameworks (and reality) are "made up of words" (or signs) where, then, is a languageless child?

Cicourel's study of sign language led him to develop a two-level model of interpretive procedure (in contrast to traditional ethnomethodologists' one *verbal* world). One of these operates non-verbally in ways which enable an individual to perceive what others are doing and thus to sense a social structure (see Collins, 1975: 110). At the other level is verbal language or "surface rules." Both of these refer to symbolic realms of meaning. The anthropologist, Leslie White, claims that the symbol (with its intended meaning) is the "universe of humanity" (1949). With the symbol, an infant or person with no language at all cannot be human for "human behavior is (above all) symbolic behavior." But would a languageless deaf person learn a significant repertoire of human behavior by a lifetime of social interaction – if no language was known to him? Suppose a seven-year-old deaf boy with no language observes a parent's use of, say, an automobile ignition key (place it in a slot, twist it and bingo! the car moves). Would he not be able to bring the key to the parent (next week) to signify that he wants to ride? Is the key now a symbol for him or is it merely a *sign* which points to something else?

The "Natural" Acquisition of Language

Since most people have the ability to hear, language is acquired in a very natural, and for the most part, non-problematic way. Our knowledge of the world – conveyed by language – comes to us with little seeking on our parts. For small children, the taken-for-grantedness of things is so overwhelming that one's circumstances are accepted as *the* world (Berger and Luckmann); that is, there is no consideration of one's circumstances comprising one world of many but rather this world is the only one. At least for the young child, one's parents are surrogates for the society's culture. Things are a certain way and they can be no other. Little "thought," as such, is required to learn language and the knowledge that accompanies it.

One's knowledge of the world, then, is language-bound. In fact we could say that knowledge and language are two sides to the same coin and that one is a corollary of the other. Knowledge can only expand as our language expands; as we have new thoughts which give rise to new conceptualizations of things, we must at the same time have words to capture those things. Thus concepts or words are a symbolic shorthand representing larger ideas. And language and knowledge are always socially-situated in space and time. In this way they are structurally determined inasmuch as their tranferral from one person to another (as in socialization practices which constitute an inter-generational process of passing language and knowledge along) is based on some systemic regularities. As Luckmann (1975) says:

> The very emergence of language presupposes ... a certain regularity of human behaviour. Human conduct is based on the reciprocality of face-to-face relations which permits the development of stable social typifications ... one can hardly conceive of human society, individual sociality and the existence of social structures without language. The socialization of individual consciousness and the social molding of personality are largely determined by language. In fact, both processess occur concretely within a historical social structure and, at the same time, within a specific historical language (p. 7).

For most of us, then, language becomes the glasses through which society is seen; language is the "window of the world" (Farb, 1973:192). Too, it is primarily through language as a social phenomenon that our sense of the world occurs. Through language the world begins to take shape. It has meaning for us precisely because as our language and consequently knowledge about it increases, its workings (although not always understood) are more well known to us. We need not always know why (the motivation) our parents punish us when we engage in certain acts (a parental behavior found in a certain situation) but we slowly come to know that if we do certain things and are found out, then we can expect certain reactions from our parents. And this is as natural as the language we acquire which helps to give words to the acts of both ourselves and our parents. We learn that striking a match will produce a fire and that in the hands of a small child this is an undesirable thing.

Now this example is especially appropriate to begin a discussion which more specifically deals with the deaf, since it may not be the case that hearing is required to understand the relationship between our own act (striking the match) and that of our parents punishing us. While we may have no words to describe what happens, we nonetheless learn that one thing leads inevitably to another. At a primitive level, then, assuming for the moment that the child does not yet understand the meaning attached to particular words, we can say that learning has occurred. But what if no words ever shall be heard? What happens when the effectiveness of oral language is absent? How can one become the most transituational of all animals, how can the individual be abstracted from concrete situations? How does the deaf person learn and get socialized into the ways of the world? How truncated is his/her life experience versus that of a hearing person? How much can be known through a physical signing of one person to another? Can one study medicine via ASL? Can signs transmit complex medical science? In a child's world of few or no signs do other human beings remain mere *physical* objects and not *social* objects: (mom, dad)?

Sign Language as "Natural"

For most of us, hearing is a "normal" thing, and with the evolution of man, crude gestures were eventually replaced by more adaptive and sophisticated symboling systems, in particular oral speech. For those without hearing, however, it can be argued that their "natural" language is signing – that is, physical gestures which convey meaning. Cicourel and Boese (1972) very strongly argue that for deaf children, signing is the natural language. This is especially true where both parents are deaf so that the child very early on learns of his world via signs *only*; thus no words are ever spoken or heard and when words are heard as spoken by others, they may be regarded as oddities (for a good fictional account of such a thing, see Auel's book, 1980; *Clan of the Cave Bear*). But even where the parents of a deaf child are not deaf (by far the most common situation), the fit between the deaf and an oral language may be a poor one.

> Even if the deaf child had never been exposed to any kind of signing … we would still argue that the use of an oral method would not constitute a deaf child's native language. Our argument is based on the hypothesis that a deaf child, because he does not have access to a monitoring system whereby he has continual feedback from his own output, and therefore can recursively monitor that output in such a way as to make changes in it over the course of a conversation, cannot acquire oral language as a native … Indeed, the oral language must remain a strange phenomenon for the deaf child because nativeness (as in spontaneous oral language acquisition) apparently is lost unless there is some kind of reflexive feedback (Cicourel and Boese, 1972:40–41).

It is spontaneity which is essential in language acquisition and subsequent usage. To "converse" is to engage in a give-and-take relationship in which one person responds to the other. If hearing is absent and oral ability is consequently impaired, then normal conversational spontaneity is lost. As Cicourel and Boese note, 'a deaf child ... cannot acquire oral language as a native'.

Clearly the absence of the language of one's culture is a severely disruptive force in the deaf child's early learning. It would be difficult to make the case that societally "normative" socialization can occur when language is absent. As Scott and Lyman (1975:171) comment: "Talk is the fundamental material of human relations." Berger and Luckmann use the term "symbolic universe" to refer to the largest constellation within which meaning can occur (a concept meant to capture all world views which obtain for any individual). But what relevance can this have for the young deaf child who is technically "in" but not "of" his historically, temporally bound situation? His universe is a much more restricted one – one cut off from the scheme of things which must remain quite unfathomable to him.

Community Among the Deaf

The deaf world is a localized, Gemeinschaft one. Higgins (1980) goes so far as to call the deaf "outsiders" – people *in* but not completely *of* the culture in which they were born. While it is similar to the larger culture by its conferring status based on age, sex, education and ethnicity (Benderly, 1980), at the same time its "face-to-faceness" makes it in some ways unique. Thus preferred modes of communication (e.g., signing, speaking and lip-reading) and proficiency in them take on importance for community members. The following quote attributed to Galloway illustrates the unique and non-unique sides to the "typical" deaf person (in this case, a white male):

> (He is) a stable, productive, relatively well adjusted, and quite provisional member of the lower middle or working class. He supports his deaf wife and hearing children with a steady manual job, often skilled work that requires little communication with co-workers. He owns his own home in an average or slightly better neighborhood. He attended a state residential school and finished with a fifth-grade reading level. As a young man he participated in athletics at his local deaf club, and as he grew older he

moved into club leadership. The club, or perhaps a deaf church, is his main social connection (Benderly 1980:15).

We see, then, the likelihood for a deaf person to marry a deaf person, to have a manual job requiring little commuication and to use a local deaf-oriented voluntary association for 'his main social connection'. Not unlike other social groups, an ascriptive quality is a form of identification and social solidarity.

Of course, it is the use of a visible manual language which serves as the most obvious basis for stigmatization. It is that which sensitizes hearing people to the differentness of the deaf. As Higgins says. "Deafness as indicated primarily by signing is the master status for these outsiders" (p. 131). Individual attributes may pale, then, alongside of an ascriptive quality. The non-outsiders monopolize the definitions of who is and is not an outsider. For people who cannot hear, it is the hearing world which stigmatizes them and defines them as tainted. Even their own hearing children may be embarrassed to sign to them in public and their relations with them may be poor (Higgins, p. 66ff.).

For deaf people (and those hard-of-hearing) life is a series of constant minor irritations composed of stupid mistakes, dependency on others for routine needs, and small unkindnesses. In response to daily blunders and pains these subordinate people develop certain interactional tactics to "hold the powerful at bay" such as shuffling, head-bobbing, forelock-tugging and grinning (Benderly, 1980:66). They recognize that they belong to a particular group, that they are in opposition: "to be deaf is to be not hearing; it is to be one of us and not one of them" (Benderly, p. 229).

Nearly twenty years ago Sussman called for a sociological analysis of the deaf, an analysis focusing on the concepts of deviance and stigma, marginality, social movements, and the family. As stated by Sussman, and still true today, we may not know or sociologically understand much about the deaf because our frame of reference is fitted to those in a hearing world.

> We are intent with our preoccupation to do the right thing without seriously attempting to find out what deaf people really want. We do not hesitate to tell them what they should have. *The control* over the deaf by the nondeaf is so pervasive that those who are 'socialized into it' in reality become products of the system even against their own will (1965: 47; emphasis added).

The Role of the Residential School

For many deaf children, socialization into the society's ways is experienced *away from* rather than *in* one's home with one's own family. The place of this socialization is a residential school, where deaf children as young as four years may be sent to live and learn. Thus the family is replaced as the main agent of primary socialization; its role as surrogate culture or "culture bearer" (as some introductory texts may phrase it) is, instead, taken up by the residential school. This is especially likely with deaf children since most often their parents cannot speak the native language of deaf people. Thus the normal parental monopoly of influence on the child is broken. The vast influence of the family is replaced by the vast influence of the residential school.

This is a sociologically unique situation for investigation. It renders highly problematic our usual theorizing about how status advantages accrue to some people rather than others. It renders them problematic because they are removed and made irrelevant (although not completely so, something we show and comment upon in our analysis). Black and white, rich and poor, all are thrown together in one place – truly a kind of melting pot experience. For these children, the school serves as a comprehensive or total institution. It is, in the legal sense of the term, *en loco parentis*, the legal guardian of the child and affectively his parents during his stay at the school. Here we see a patent form of social determinism: the determinism of the situation and the linguistic-act by the social structure (Luckmann, 1975). However, unlike most discussions of total institutions as restricting one's sense of self (Goffman's "mortifications") and giving rise to a new culture (Goffman's "disculturation"), residential schools offer deaf children total "enculturation". The construction – not the mortification – of a first self will eventuate. Total enculturation – not disculturation – will be the norm.

Goffman (1961:xiii) defines the total institution as

> A place of residence and work where a large number of like-situated individuals, cut off from the wider society for an appreciable period of time, together lead an enclosed, formally administered round of life.

Clearly, Goffman's definition is applicable to a residential school for the deaf. It is a "place of residence and work" for "like-situated individuals" who are "cut off from the wider society for an appreciable period of time" and who "lead an enclosed, formally administered round of life."

For many of these near languageless children, the institution will structure the self, the mind and its stock of knowledge, and one's place in it. It will also provide the children with a language, an argot unfamiliar and unknown to most family members and others in the society at large. Objectified in a unique visible language (signing) is a configuration of meanings – a culture – which defines the world for the deaf child. For an extended period of time (all of one's schooling), very few people outside the residential school will have linguistic-symbolic access to the child, to his definitions of reality. Thus school peers and staff members have a near monopoly over the structural definitions of the world which the child may experience. The child's very existence is grounded in the school's womblike effect. It is this ontological process which is of especial interest to us in this study.

The Residential School in an Era of Change

In recent years the residential school population has changed considerably. Schildroth (1980) reports that there has been a national decline in the number of white, hearing impaired children attending residential schools. This is the result, in part, of a faster growing black population, especially in the age group under 14 (p. 90), but disproportionately more poor deaf children (regardless of race) are attending residential schools while disproportionately more children from affluent families are attending regular schools (Benderly, 1980:254). Too, there has been an increase in the percentage of students whose handicap is not only deafness (i. e. a greater percentage of multi-handicapped children; see Office of Demographic Studies, 1977). There has also been a national movement toward deaf children attending regular, neighborhood schools; a practice called "mainstreaming," given legitimation through Public Law 94–142 (the Education for All Handicapped Children Act of 1975).

A principle concern of residential school critics is that a type of experiential deprivation may occur if the deaf child is not around hearing children. This could result in a truncated socialization process and the learning of institutional norms and values versus societal ones (Benderly, 1980; Evans, 1975). One's personality may be negatively affected as evinced by immaturity, egocentricity, distorted perception, lacking empathy, more dependency on others and deficiency in intellectual functioning (Meadows, 1968: 29–30).

The role which the residential school has had to play has not been an easy one. Since most deaf children cannot grow up to be like their (hearing) parents, someone or some agency must help them to learn the culture's ways – and that role usually falls to the residential school. Traditionally (and increasingly even more so), they have received the hardest cases. Their students have been those with the greatest hearing loss. Thus the residential school, with its *en loco parentis* status, has been the home away from home for profoundly deaf students. Odd, then, that the language-culture of the school and that of the children should differ, but that has often been the case.

> Most adults who were deaf as children can describe the same experience – the frustration, anger, and loneliness of home; arrival at school; the sudden dawning of community and relationships. Of all adult cultures in the world, this is one of the very few handed down generation after generation from child to child (Benderly, 1980:228).

Over time the schools gave in to rising demands for the use of signs for it was this form of communication that was so unique to the children but troublesome to the schools. It was the children who refused to adapt to their deaf circumstances through a hearing-spoken-oral language (something desired by the school as much as possible). However it was not until the late 1960's that any school in America actually taught sign language. The school, as Benderly says, finally accepted it as a *fait accompli.* (Even today older deaf people harbor a "bottomless fury" [Benderly's term] over what was done to them by hearing people who had tried to make deaf children become hearing children.)

The residential school is home for many children who quite literally "visit" their hearing parents on holidays and summers. "The school became home because it was where the heart was, and vacations were interruptions to be dreaded, even resisted" (Benderly, p. 229). Joshua Fishman (1982: 12ff.) has referred to the "mismatch" and the "intrafamilial grief" which results between deaf child and hearing parents. Because the school is the major socializer and reference group, because it forsters deaf culture and deaf identity, this is "tantamount to taking children away from their (hearing) parents and that involves not only socialization ... but rejection, generation gap, guilt and conflict."

Deaf people belong to a language community, a sociological phenomenon unlike any other handicapped group, and many of them first developed a sense of this community at a residential school; it was "there they learned to be deaf" (Benderly, p. 229). Among the deaf it is language and communication which defines deaf social networks "much more so than most mainstream (or even other minority sidestream) networks in the USA" (Fishman, 1982:9). For these people, acquisition and use of a hearing-aid might increase their hearing but destroy their social world, their active involvement with deaf people and their institutions. It is their linguistic adaption to their deafness which makes them such a cohesive minority group.

Mainstreaming – the inclusion of deaf children in regular, hearing schools – is a new and formidable threat to state residential schools. It is not only a threat to their educational programs and practices but to the children's "native language" (i.e. signing) as well. Public Law 94–142 calls for "the least restrictive environment" and touches the idea that separate cannot be equal. The oralist (speaking) camp hailed the new law as a move toward social justice while the manualist (signing) camp worried not only about individual children but also about the future of the institution it had taken so long to build. The manualists doubt that local schools will have the expert knowledge and materials needed for deaf children and doubt that they will spend the necessary funds on so few students. They also believe that the public school would be a lonely world for the isolated deaf child and thus not be the "least restrictive environment" at all. This approach is described as "criminal idiocy," "ridiculous," "ethically wrong," and "insensitive" to the needs of deaf children (Vernon and Prickett, 1976). What would be sacrificed would be the hidden curriculum of friendships, camaraderie, sports and activities – things whose importance rival the more formal curriculum. These critics of mainstreaming say it is true that deaf people must live with the hearing but it is also true that they must live among themselves. Further they dislike the implication within the law that "normal" is preferable; that normal equals success, thereby implying that being handicapped must mean failure. In short, "the residential schools stand in increased danger of stigma, at the time that the country believes itself becoming more open to the handicapped" (Benderly, p. 253).

Of particular concern is that more mainstreaming and a more disadvantaged student body at residential schools may produce a decline in the increasing sophistication of sign language. As we noted earlier, Cicourel and Boese (1972) have described signing as the "natural" or "native" language of the deaf. While is possible for a hearing person to learn signs well, it is seldom possible for a deaf person to become a skilled ("native") speaker of an oral language. The deaf person in the hearing world is trapped by language – he/she is always on the inside looking out. What remains as pedagogically and politically problematic are the trade-offs between mainstreaming (where English is paradigmatically superior) and attending residential schools (where signing is superior). Is the child better off with a fragmented, limited and often faulty English or a grammatically unique (and limited) sign language?

The Deaf as an Object of Inquiry

The deaf truly provide a unique focus for sociological inquiry. They are people whose "ethnographic setting is basically a pictoral or iconic kind of environment" (Cicourel and Boese, 1972: 47). Unlike many other minority groups, the deaf (and handicapped people more generally) have only recently begun to be analyzed by social researchers. Thus little is known about them to influence our own theorizing. Instead we have been guided by a more general commitment to a dialectical view of the world with little attention paid to any one theoretical view. Lacking a testable theory about social organization of deaf people, we have drawn upon a wide range of sociological views. But always with the dialectic in mind. The broadest objectives to the present study may be phrased as questions:

1. How do deaf children get socialized into the world?
2. Once socialized, how do they muddle their way through a word-based world?

Each of these questions is cast against a backdrop of other relevant research questions, each with its own theoretical orientation.

3. How do deaf children acquire and use language?
4. How is a deaf child's sense of self bound up in his language?
5. How is life organized and maintained in a total institutional setting occupied by deaf children?

The sociology of language has no one theoretical view to which all must subscribe. Instead, it is a rather eclectic collection of ideas drawn from a number of sociologies. So, too, with our own work.

In particular we have drawn upon an interactionist view of the world but mindful of the important role played by structure, thus our use of a concept such as "total institution" which takes as *a priori* the existence of norms for organizing social life. If anything, this might be described as a study in the "new sociology of education" (see Karabel and Halsey, 1977, for a good overview of this area) for like that area, we find certain tenets of phenomenology, Marxist sociology, and other – not always popular – sociologies useful.

Having concluded this introductory section, we next turn to a brief statement about our methodological approach. This is followed by a fairly brief exposition of the sociology of language including sections on social class, deafness and sign language. We provide a compact and unique glimpse into the lives of languageless children whose mental activities ("thinking") occur via pictures, children whose encounter with first language and *world* building is in a collective, non-familial residential institution where symbolic experiences and repertoires are limited to the extent that the institution is closed (segregated). The core of our ethnographic analysis is presented as five separable, but inter-related sections: children without language, signing as language, official culture, student culture, and deafness and the self; having read one section may provide some useful information for understanding the next section. Lastly, we develop a series of theoretical statements grounded in our qualitative, empirical research akin to the strategy suggested by Glaser and Strauss (1967) but developed in a very formalized, philosophy of science framework. For those who wish to get to the heart of the matter, they can safely skip to Chapter 3, where our "story" begins.

A Note on Methods[2]

The site for this study was a rural area in a Southern state which, in 1981, was home to more than three hundred deaf children, a place we call SSD (State School for the Deaf). SSD contains grades at all levels, even including preschoolers (a factor which was of especial interest to us for examining the learning of language). At SSD these grades are contained on two separate campuses, one for elementary and the other for secondary grades.

The superintendent agreed to let Don live on campus for one semester (August – December 1981) to observe and collect data. This constituted the main part of the field work. Subsequent trips were also made to the campus to collect additional data as field notes were being written into the analyses. However, extensive field notes were taken all during the four months spent on the campus and the current report represents only some of that material.

The study is almost completely an ethnography. From the outset it was based on a commitment to doing first-hand observations of deaf children and the adults with whom they have regular contact. This was made possible by Don's actually living on campus squarely in the flux of everyday life and operations at SSD. It was an attempt to do sociological work "up close," to "know" (rather than to "know about") deaf students and their world (see Lofland, 1971 and Richer, 1975 who call for such qualitative work).

By using empathetic strategies (i.e., by trying to take the role of the other, to see the world through the eyes of the other) we sought to enter the "life world" (or *Lebenswelt*; see Schutz, 1964) of this tight-knit linguistic group. We wanted to discover the participants' "axes of life," (Strong, 1943), to "penetrate their minds" and to ascertain their frames of reference within which meaning is located.

Chapter II

Sociologies of Language, Schooling and the Deaf

> "In the Word was the Beginning. ... the beginning of Man and of Culture."
> Leslie White

> "Extremely recently in the history of the Cosmos ... there occurred an event different in kind from all preceding events in the Cosmos. It cannot be understood as a dyadic interaction or a complexus of dyadic interactions.
>
> It has been called variously triadic behavior, thirdness, the Delta factor, man's discovery of the sign (including symbols, language, art).
> Walker Percy

Language as an Organizing Framework

This book is written within a broad sociological view of the world. It is at once concerned with the sociology of language but at the same time (and we would argue unavoidably) concerned with sociologies of knowledge, education, symbolic interaction, phenomenological sociology, ethnomethodology, and so on. Like Berger and Luckmann (1967), we believe that language, as a sociological phenomenon, can only be understood in dialectical terms (see Israel, 1979, for an excellent extended discussion on this). For us, it is axiomatic that language arises out of interaction and is subsequently maintained and altered via interaction. Language has both structural, predetermined qualities and an emergent, situated, subjectively experienced side. It is our view that one can only be understood in light of the other – hence the dialectical emphasis. We agree with Becker's observation that we create words and they create us (1975:62).

In adopting a dialectic view, we are consciously refusing to accept any monocausal, predetermined view of how the social world evolves, is maintained and alters over time. Instead we argue that social life is characterized by a give-and-take, ebb-and-flow quality within which individual actors play an important role. And above all else, as individuals are Shakespearian actors upon the stage of life, it is communication by language which allows them to play their parts.

It is their use of language which makes their parts understandable as that term is used in its everyday context. That is, the actor's intended meaning is clear to us by his/her portrayal of a part. Thus via certain gestures and words (phrased in particular ways and in particular contexts) we come to "understand" what the actors are about. As Mow (1974) says, "Communication is the father of human relationships."

Given the importance of language, given that in our daily lives we could not understand nor be understood without language in one form or another, it seems odd, indeed, that language has been largely overlooked as a topic sociological inquiry (see Percy, 1983:163). It is only in very recent years that sociologists have begun to redress this analytical oversight (and even then the general area of the sociology of language could hardly be described as a hotbed of sociological writing and research. This is something to which we shall return at the end of this book). To date, however, most of the work in this area has been theoretical with few empirical studies to be found in sociology proper.

The theoretical work which has been done has, in some cases, been widely read and had a significant impact. No work of this genre is better known than that of Peter Berger and Thomas Luckmann, *The Social Construction of Reality*. Although their book's subtitle proffers it as a "treatise in the sociology of knowledge," a reading of the book makes clear that this includes much emphasis on and discussion about language. And just as we stated at the outset that our work has been influenced by a number of sociological (and non-sociological) perspectives, so, too, is this the case for Berger and Luckmann. Indeed, they state in their first chapter that they have been influenced in particular by Marx, Durkheim, Weber, Mead and Schutz. The dilemma they address is, much like ours, a dialectic one: man produces society but society also produces man. Thus there are objective and subjective sides to social reality. Some sociologists have expressed this as the micro (subjective, individualistic) and macro (objective, structural) sides of life. Or as Berger (1963) has phrased it, there is "man in society" and "society in man."

Marx, of course, provided the first general statements about a possible sociology of knowledge; an epistemological inquiry into thought itself and how knowledge is always bound to social circumstances. Axiomatically, then, knowledge is always socio-historically situated and *what is known* at some point in time may largely determine *what can be known.* While Durkheim's sociology is of a much different stripe than Marx's (for a penetrating discussion of where they may be similar on certain points, see Bourdieu,), he did argue that man existed because of society and that society existed because of man; one was only possible because of the other. It is especially from Durkheim that Berger and Luckmann adopt the idea of society as *sui generis*; in Durkheim's words, it is a social fact which exists external to and coercive upon its members. Clearly, then, from Marx and Durkheim one sees a structural emphasis mindful of individual constituents.

Weber and Mead are particularly evident in the work of Schutz (one of Berger's teachers), for it is Schutz who synthetically draws upon both of them. While we need not go into much detail about this here, it is important to mention certain concepts which Schutz borrowed from each. From Weber he got the notion of the social act and in particular the idea of intersubjectivity. Thus there is an emphasis on how individuals *jointly* create meaning ("intersubjectivity" being literally shared meaning). The prototypical example of this is the face-to-face encounter (Mead's social act). From Mead came the ideas of gesture and especially symbolic communication. Social psychologically, then, our "self" is the repository of gestures given off by others whose actions toward us are considered to be important. Our social selves are in large measure that part of us which behaves as we believe others wish us to behave (much akin to Cooley's "looking glass self" or Riesman's "other-directed" man). Schutz's contribution to this was primarily with his notion of the "taken-for-grantedness" of things. What Schutz was sensitive to was that when we act, when we engage others in social intercourse, we always assume a good many things. For example, when we speak with someone, we do not stop to define every word used. Instead we assume that the other person speaks the same language as us and the intended meaning of our words can be fairly easily apprehended by them. Whenever this becomes problematic the other person may ask us to "explain" ourselves, in short, to clarify the intended meaning of some statement we made.

A few years ago the American Council on Education sponsored a national campaign to focus attention on the importance of reading skills. Their logo suggested that "word power" led to "mind power". Although it is doubtful that they intended this to be a sociological principle, that is, in fact, what it is. Indeed, higher levels of cognition or thought are made possible by the accumulation of "meaningful gestures," where it is the meaning conveyed by something and not the thing itself which is important. Words, then, whether spoken or written take the form of a symbolic shorthand. They are compressed versions or maps of some larger reality which they partially represent. One might say that the more words we know, the larger is our sense of the world (to wit, the more our minds have been expanded). This idea is superbly contained by Wittgenstein's (1973) aphorism: "The limits of my language mean the limits of my world." One's vocabulary then is a "word-board," an "intellectual checking account" which may vary in size, depth and variety (Hertzler, 1965:46). Words help us categorize reality, they facilitate more precise analysis and "aid in the comparison of one portion of experiential data with other portions" (p41). Each culture, then, "classifies its surroundings into discrete categories of environment" (home, church, public square, classroom, etc.; Gumperz and Hymes, 1972). It follows that a speech (or sign) community and its corpus of shared knowledge will depend on intensity of contact and on communications networks (p. 16).

Now in all of this, there is a taken-for-grantedness about language itself. A language must exist; it must be possible to convey it from one person to another; and there must be individuals who are capable of learning this language. For all of this to happen language must have certain rules which give it a logic of its own; that is, there must be a syntactical structure which language users follow in a more-or-less consistent way thus allowing themselves to be understood. For all modern languages, or for that matter languages which require speech in an oral form, it is generally necessary for individuals to be able to both speak and hear. When either of these is absent (especially hearing), the formation of "mind" as we commonly think of it is rendered extremely problematic.

Now it may seem that thought is impossible without language. As Furth (1966) says, a common assumption is "that language faithfully mirrors thinking, that language is almost the only important symbol system, and that language, symbols, and thinking are necessarily, even inseparably linked" (p. 4). The same point is reiterated in one way or another by nearly all sociologists since one's environment is conceptualized as necessary for one's existence. As Furth also notes, however, in support of his own position, there is a second possibility: "namely, to expect no difference in cognitive structure between the hearing and the deaf" (p. 4). And this, in fact, is what he concludes:

> (L)ogical, intelligent thinking does not need the support of a symbolic *system*, as it exists in the living language of a society. Thinking is undoubtedly an internal system, a hierarchical ordering within the person of his interaction with the world. The symbol system of language mirrors and in a certain way expresses that internal organization. However, the internal organization of intelligence is not dependent on the language system; on the contrary, comprehension and use of the ready-made language is dependent on the structure of intelligence (p. 228).

These comments by Furth are especially important for our own study because Furth, like us, set out to investigate the deaf. And while we fundamentally disagree with some of Furth's analysis and theorizing, his work is critical because of the host of questions it raises about deaf versus non-deaf individuals as they use language in their everyday lives. We have no quarrel with Furth's basic premise that *intelligence* (innate capacity to learn) is not dependent on language. Our position, however, is that the acquisition of complex *knowledge* is certainly dependent on language. The more limited one's language, the more limited one's knowledge of the physical and the social world.

Language and Communication

It is the concept of language which is crucial here. As used in this study, language must be distinguished from the concept of communication; one is not the same as the other. Language is defined, by us, as a formal system of verbal and/or gestural (i. e., signs used by deaf people) symbols which have rules of syntax and grammar that specify the order and manner in which these symbols are to be used.

Communication, on the other hand, refers to the act (or process) of transmitting information/meaning, however done. Both animals and humans are able to communicate certain kinds of information with growls, whistles, cries, or grunts, groans, facial expressions, body postures, odors, colors, and so on. While it is possible to communicate certain information with gestures of one sort or another, conveying the full range of meanings (a quantitative dimension) and more sophisticated, precise information (the qualitative dimension to meaning) is better accomplished by standard spoken (or, possibly, signed) language. Again, there are many ways to communicate, there are many channels of communication but in the words of de Saussure (1970:46), "Signs that are wholly arbitrary realize better than the others [i. e., "natural signs" such as pantomime] the ideal of the semilogical process." We agree that language is the "most complex and universal of all systems of expression" (p. 46); that it is the "paramount, all-inclusive medium of communication in human societies" without which there would be "no possibility of precise messages" (Hertzler, 1965:20).

Language enables the child to master the experience of prior generations, to form higher, conscious mental activity (see Ashworth, 1979:49). Nonverbal means of communication (with the exception of formal sign languages) such as color, odors, or facial expressions can help attain neither of these.

There are, however, other more inclusive definitions of language (although a remarkable number of authors fail to define the concept). Some suggest, for example, that Edward Sapir's definition may still be the most useful one (Howell and Vetter, 1976;50): "Language is a purely human and noninstinctive method of communicating ideas, emotions, and desires by means of a system of voluntarily produced symbols [p. 8].

Randall Collins (1975:986ff.), a sociologist of considerable stature, distinguishes language from *symbolization.* (For us, his 'language' means communication; his symbolization means language). He boldly asserts that "Other animals, in fact, have language too" (p. 96). Since they make "vocal noises" and "gestures" birds, bees, insects, and mammals use language which is "strikingly similar to human rituals" (i. e., their language is stereotyped, social, communicative and emotionally charged). "The language differences between humans and other animals are not so great," he goes on. Like other animals we humans also make noises (upon which language is based, he says) – cries, pleas, snarls, demands, coos – "It is not language at all that makes us distinctively human, but symbolization, which changes the meaning of our animal noises ..." (p. 97).

So the *only* difference (for Collins) between human ritual and animal language is "a symbolic significance or *naming* quality that lifts its meaning to levels more remote from immediate experience" (p. 97). Much animal communication is "probably" learned and passed on which, Collins finally adds, means that "animals may very well have a culture"[3] [p. 97].

Obviously ASL is a language which uses no speech and no sound. There are no tones nor pitches of voice to add meaning to spoken words. Instead, body movement (speed and intensity of a sign; especially facial expressions) replaces these verbal meaning carriers (modifiers) and functions as they do.

Deficit Theories versus Situational Theories

It is very important for us to keep in mind the controversial nature of our problem: "Perhaps no issue in socialization is more controversial, with as little consensus on theory and findings, as the nature of poverty socialization" (Burr et. al., 1979). The core of the debate centers around the question of whether or not poor people (and, for us, deaf people) possess certain social, cognitive, and linguistic *"deficits"* resulting from conditions of poverty or, on the other hand, whether their subcultural patterns are *situational* adaptations to various physical deprivations and social structural circumstances of their existence (p. 390).

Deficit theorists say that the lifeways of the poor must be changed; the other side, however, argues for elimination of the physical conditions of poverty. For the former, the problem to be attacked lies under the skin (within the poor themselves); for the latter, the problem is an external, structural matter. As Burr (1979:390) puts it: "The myth of verbal deprivation is particularly dangerous because it diverts attention from real defects of our educational system to imaginary defects of the child. ..." Accompanying this is a second "myth": "that lower-class Negro children are nonverbal ... that middle-class language is in itself better suited for dealing with abstract, logically complex and hypothetical questions" (Labov, 1972b:243). For the anti-deficit theorists, one dialect (or language) is equal to another. No language is thought to have an inherent advantage over any other.

But in all of the polemics surrounding better or worse language and the schools in which it occurs, one over-riding assumption prevails – "language" is verbal and occurs in a verbal context. No language "pluralist" has addressed the degree to which their polemics apply to non-verbal language. No one has asked if a visual-gestural, (not-necessarily-sequential) idea-based (not word-based) language is equal to spoken languages (or to each other). Or whether or not such a language (which defies traditional definitions of "language") is more or less abstract, has codes, dialects, and so on. These are the kinds of issues which our study addresses.

To us, the manual signing of language is a type of deprivation; we do not say that it is inherently worse than any other languaging system but we do say that its use *may* deprive one of thought at its most abstract levels. As Jacobs notes: "Culture, as it is commonly conceived, is foreign to the short-changed deaf adult" (1974:64). For Jacobs, this is partially explained by the "unpleasant experiences with the traditional schooling methods" (p. 64). In particular the type of language one learns may be problematic in the larger society. Sign language is said to be "limited in scope and expressive power ... bound to the concrete, and limited in expression of abstractions, metaphor, irony, and humor" (Northern and Downs, 1974). Figurative language is "a nearly indigestible item on the language menu of the deaf adolescent" whose literalism seems to reflect something of a stall at Piaget's concrete operational level where he makes "direct use of visual and sensory data and moves little beyond it" (Russo, 1975:198–199).

Language "Codes"

The conceptualization of more-or-less concrete forms of language is given great emphasis in the work of Basil Bernstein. Bernstein is particularly interested in the relationship between symbolic orders and social structure, how the class system acts upon the forms of communication, and how speech codes may be differentially distributed by family types (something in the province of the sociology of knowledge). His theoretical framework integrates ideas from Durkheim, Cassirer, Sapir, Whorf, Mead and Marx but goes far beyond any one of them. He agrees with Marx that to understand institutionalization and the change of symbolic orders, one must understand "society's productive system and the power relationship to which the productive system gives rise" (1977:475). Not only is economic capital subject to appropriation, manipulation and exploitation, but so, too, are symbolic systems: thus we have cultural capital and not everyone has equal access to "the creative act which is language".

Bernstein's sociolinguistic thesis is clearly dialectic, examining how symbolic systems (speech, in this case) "are both realizations and regulators of the structure of social relationships" (p. 474). In contrast to Whorf, Bernstein posits that distinct linguistic forms and fashions of speaking will emerge within the larger dominant language and these styles will "induce in their speakers different ways of relating to objects and persons" (1977:204). He insists that no language or speech style is superior to another, yet he expresses the idea that a particular form of social relation acts selectively on both *what* is said and *how* it is said; again, the speech system (syntactical and lexical options) is both a consequence and a quality of the social structure. Fishman and Leuders-Salmon (1972:77–78) discuss verbal repertoires in a similar way:

> American teachers are still largely innocent of this elementary fact of the sociology of language, namely, that speech communities characteristically exhibit verbal repertoires and that the varieties in these repertoires are functionally differentiated ... in accord with societally established and reinforced norms of communicative appropriateness.

For a child, it is his experience with the social structure which forms his speech (or sign language) acts. A child is oriented by the socialization process toward what Basil Bernstein calls "codes of communication": (1) *elaborated codes* whose (middle class) speakers are oriented toward universalistic meanings and (2) *restricted codes* whose (working class) speakers are oriented toward particularistic meanings. As Bernstein says, the codes themselves are functions of, "a consequence of" a particular form of social relationship or, are more generally, "qualities of a social structure" (1977:476).

Central to these codes is the class system for it is from there, in the 'social structure,' that these codes emanate. The class system is produced and reproduced in such a way that the forms of language (i. e., codes are styles of speech) are differentially distributed (again indicating a predilection for Marx's position about the relationship between mode of consciousness and class location). In general the restricted codes are used by the working class. Some characteristics of this speech variant are outlined here:

1. Since a common history (among the users) exists the intent of the other is taken for granted.
2. With a common background, group members need not raise meanings to the level of explicitness (i. e., need not elaborate).
3. A strong metaphoric element is likely to typify the speech forms (something which is not true for users of sign language; see Russo, 1975).
4. The speech form is context-bound. Unless one shares the common history of a relationship one may not be able to understand the speech encounter. Social relations affect meanings, the syntactic and lexical choices (egocentrism is greater, grammar is relatively unimportant).

5. The communication acts utilize condensed symbolic forms (more cryptic than expansive).

6. Speakers occupy communalized roles based upon restricted social relationships.

Again, what are some of the consequences, the "net effect" of these code and contextual constraints? First, potential linguistic ability is depressed, the concrete and descriptive response is more probable and context-free generalization abilities are inhibited. Additionally, "... the different focusing of experience through a restricted code creates a major problem of educability only where the school produces discontinuity between its symbolic orders and those of the child. Our schools are not made for these children; why should the children respond?" (1977:483)

In a kind of summary fashion, we can say that restricted codes do (as an active accomplishment) two things. First, they yield a certain type of linguistic ability. Second, those characterized by this type of ability coalesce in generally small, localistic groups with their own idiomatic expressions, condensed symbols, and unique ways of phrasing events in the world. In short, the style of speech (or signs) and the users of it lead to a particular view of the world unique to them and this view is one with little ambiguity to it. Things *are* a certain way. In Adorno's scheme, this is much like an "authoritarian" view of the world with little room for debate and tolerance of diverse positions. This, of course, merely says that lexical items are socially situated, that small isolated (and nearly closed) groups like SSD generate vocabularies, concepts and language systems appropriate to, adaptive to their everyday needs and experiences. If there is relatively less daily need for more highly abstract concepts (as in science, technology, medicine, etc.), then few may emerge. Such a small isolated group will have a language sufficient for its particular reality – but their linguistic system (categories, lexical items) may falter when they enter the wider linguistic group (the hearing world).

The second code of communication, the "elaborated code," is concerned with

> logical, temporal and spatial relationships between objects and ideas. Therefore, it has greater potentials for the complex organization and analysis of experience. Restricted language use is more mundane; it is the language of subjective observation rather than analysis (Kerkhoff, 1972:48).

In the social world of the elaborated code, individualism is emphasized over communality, the "I" prevails over the "we" (Gecas, 1979:385). In a Durkheimian way, Bernstein posits that restricted codes reflect a type of mechanical solidarity (which we have alluded to above); in the signing community deaf people find a place of refuge, a chance to achieve intersubjective meanings (Nash and Nash 1981:64); i. e., mechanical solidarity. While this position may be somewhat problematic (see Gecas, p. 385), the larger point remains – language is grounded in social relations and relates its speakers to one another and to the world they live in (Farb, 1973:17). What is especially important is that the language to which the child is first exposed is that of his immediate family. His language is in the same form as their's. He speaks (and, at the same time, understands the world) as they speak. The language he learns, then, is predicated, in large measure, on the family-role system of his home; and working class homes, ostensibly (and empirically, again see Gecas) provide a different language-nurturant environment than do middle class homes. As Boocock (1980) expresses it:

> In middle-class homes, children learn the kind of 'elaborated' linguistic code (one that is based on abstract general principles that apply to any situation) that is congruent with the conventional classroom situation, while working-class children acquire a more 'restricted' code, which reflects their own limited life situation (p. 44).

Thus classrooms become reflections of the social class dynamics of the socio-geographic areas in which they are located. Social relations in the larger society (i. e., class relations) get brought into the classroom and may make a sham of any notion of equality and meritocracy. In the family-school-economy relationship, then, school may be nothing more than a holding ground for young people prior to taking their already determined places in the economy.

The Language-Schooling Nexus

Although not specifically addressing language and schooling, no one has provided a better account of in-school processes than Philip Jackson (1968). From his observations in California schools, Jackson noted the repetitious regimented quality of school life, referring to it as "the daily grind." That striking description refers to the humdrum and trivia, the cyclic and ritualistic quality of events which occur at school. The school is an institution, a bureaucracy, and the essence of a bureaucracy is rules. In school the major activities of everyday life follow rules, day-by-day, week-by-week, year-by-year. In a way which is highly similar to prisons and mental hospitals, life's daily activities are regimented. Activities are scheduled and "school is a place where things often happen not because students want them to, but because it is time for them to occur" (p. 12). In this situation, the greatest virtue is patience. One must learn to suffer in silence, to control but not abandon his/her impulses. And while sitting near many other people, the student must not communicate with them: one must learn to be alone in a crowd[4].

Students, like inmates or mental patients, are in a particular place whether they like it or not, their attendance is compulsory (Jackson, 1968; Boocock, 1980). As Jackson comments, school is "a place in which the division between the meek and the powerful is drawn" (p. 10). Whereas life at home is generally intimate and personal, upon entering the school the child finds him/herself with a stranger who exercises control in a relatively impersonal way (Jackson, p. 30). Parental authority at home is mostly restrictive but the teacher's authority is as much prescriptive as restrictive. The teacher makes the plan of action and prescribes (dictates) the work for the newcomer. In short, the teacher is the student's first boss and the student is not free to quit working just because the work may be distasteful. At school, as at work, the student learns to conform (Scherer and Slawski, 1979:148).

To guage performance, the student is continually evaluated. Since schools are reward-oriented systems, the student must learn to behave in ways that insure the chance of reward and praise, and reduce the likelihood of punishment; this is akin to Goffman's cynical actor who makes a great effort to avoid censure to win praise. The dramaturgical quality of this is nicely illustrated by Jackson's comment: "Learning how to make it in school involves, in part, learning how to falsify our behavior" (p. 27). You behave as others want, not as you might wish to.

Schools help to assure their desired outcomes by ability teaching, a practice highly correlated with student's race and socioeconomic status (Boocock, 1980; also see Sullivan, 1979). These structural considerations are learned by the student outside of school and brought into school as a basis for sorting. This, of course, sets up a potential self-sorting, self-fulfilling prophecy (discussed by Rosenthal and Jacobson, 1966). This is abetted as "students use linguistic labels to reinforce the image and to establish social boundaries" (Sullivan, 1979:237). Sullivan has referred to this system and the categorical differentiation associated with it as "sorting," the ways in which high school students form cliques and personal friendship networks.

The stratified side to life in school has long interested social researchers. Coleman (1961) saw a direct parallel between society-at-large and the social organization to student life in school. As he put it, "(I)ndustrial society has made of high school a social system of adolescents" (p. 74), what Coleman called an "adolescent society." James Rosenbaum (1976) examined this 'society,' especially to assess the relationship between the track structure of a school and the structure of its adolescent society. He found that students are, indeed, tracked into separate societies, with those in the college track more likely to be in places of leadership and positions of influence. Unbeknownst to the adolescent society is that these "lackluster" students (unadulated non-athletes, non-cheerleaders, etc.) who control student activities and organizations are the ones bound for social mobility. Rosenbaum states that:

> The adolescent society restricts individuals' access to friendship groups, activities, and leadership positions in a pattern analagous to the social discrimination in adult society. Only the elite are allowed into the best social groups, activities, and leadership positions (p. 171).

To the winners go the spoils. For the losers, life can be much like Garfinkel (1972) has described as "status degradation ceremonies." Rosenbaum discusses this as the "multitude of insults and deprivations that lower track students experience" (p. 182). Track placement, then, influences not only school success but self-concept and general feelings of worth and interest.

To a large degree Sullivan's (1979) ethnography replicates and supports the findings of Rosenbaum. Sullivan examines status in the school organization, "how the social networks of the students relate to their statuses in the school organization and ... what processes account for such patterns" (p. 217). Five major inter-related sources of recruitment for the networks were identified: neighborhood, ethnicity, social class, status in the school organization, and activities of special interest. Two additional factors were also suggested, the size and complexity of the school and the stratification of its curriculum. On the one hand, the size of the school and its divergent programs may fragment previously existing interpersonal relationships. On the other hand, the stratified (i.e. tracked) curriculum with its varied programs opposes the process of fragmentation which derives from size and complexity. That is, to some degree the divided curriculum reinforces class and ethnic differentiation. As stated by Sullivan: "Thus, the curriculum tends to fragment neighborhood ties even though it also reinforces class and ethnic divisions" (p. 221).

In part school tracking can reflect the student's internalization of school norms. The more the student learns to acquiesce to the school culture, the greater should be his success (or, minimally, the less trouble he will find himself in). In-school behavior is tied to track placement with school norms and their enforcement varying directly by track location. Regardless of track, however, conformity is highly valued. The school-wise student who learns to avoid conflict and succumb to school rules may be referred to as a "model student", he may even win a "citizenship" award at an end-of-the-year school assembly. Cicourel and Kitsuse (1963) found that such non-cognitive factors as student appearance and demeanor, social and personal "adjustment," social class and "social type" were often as important for students as their own classroom ability and academic performance. As Jackson (1968) so bluntly states it: "(In) schools, as in prisons, *good behavior pays off*" (p. 34; emphasis added).

Although not concerned with tracking as such, Willis' (1977) three year ethnography focused on the transition from school to work among a group of English working class boys. Willis was especially interested in understanding the boys' class culture. "Culture" for him is conceptualized as more than a mental category, more than a set of transferred internal structures. The concept is used to include "experiences, relationships, and ensembles of systematic types of relationships which influence 'choices' and 'decisions.'" Culture sets structure and effects how 'choices' are made and defined. It is, in part, "the product of collective human praxis" (p. 4).

As described by Willis, the school serves to reinforce working class themes and mores. A culture is generated and maintained which prepares some of its members for certain kinds of work, a type of "self-damnation". The working class culture is directly linked to regulative state institutions which "have an important function in the overall reproduction of the social totality and especially in relation to reproducing the social conditions for a certain kind of production" (p. 3). This is apparent in the way that schools "channel" (see Raskin, 1975, on this concept and schools) working class youth into manual labor jobs. The schools are not so much a cause as a conduit in this process. The boys hold certain convictions and insights which finally lead them to an objective work situation which both liberates and entraps them. How does this happen? An unfree condition may be freely entered. That is, there is "a moment in working-class culture when the manual giving of labour power represents both a freedom, election and transcendence, and a precise insertion into a system of exploitation and oppression for working-class people" (p. 120).

Willis' discussion of language is of especial interest for our own ethnography. He suggests that part of the reaction to the school institution by these working class boys is an antagonism to our rejection of language as the expression of mental life (p. 124). In some ways for the working class, their culture is in a battle with the language of the dominant culture. This does not mean that they lack a rich language of their own. What it does mean is that their language cannot express "those mental insights which are ... too much for the received language" (p. 125). What Willis describes is a dialectical process whereby working class boys create meanings (by changing clothes, habits, styles of behavior, personal appearance, etc.) and these meanings turn back onto the group members to shape their stylistic practices and behaviors. Such cultural activity not only "expresses" a notion of the world, but acts to "cast into doubt the workings of the larger ideologies, institutions and structural relationships of the whole society" (p. 125).

This is a clear parallel between what Willis observes among the "lads" and what Bernstein notes about the "net effect" to growing up dependent on a "restricted code" of communication. If one's whole life is lived out amidst a language characterized by its restrictiveness, the ability for higher thinking, for abstraction, for conceptualization, remains unattainable. It is *only* if the leap is made from restricted to elaborated code that greater abstract reasoning is made possible. For Willis' lads, life appears as a deadend street – the end is known at the outset and life is lived within its shadow.

Given that we can statistically estimate the likelihood of how well people will do (educationally, occupationally, economically) over the course of their lifetimes, it is fair to say that lower class children will, by and large, not do as well as middle class children. Just *why* this is so is not yet settled. Some theorists offer (1) biological-genetic explanations. Other suggest that (2) cultural differences exist between social classes and ethnic groups (and propose concepts like the "culture of poverty" along with Bernstein's appealing notion that different symbolic orders are generated by interactional patterns within different social classes). (3) Significant differences in quality of the schools attended by these different groups of children make the difference (Boocock, 1980: 62–63). Different groups, then, begin schooling with different burdens and different resources. Phrased differently, to estimable degrees, people will be differentially handicapped by race, sex, class background, etc. For us, another potentially detrimental attribute is deafness. The end result is unchanged, regardless of handicap: where one starts a race largely determines where he/she will finish it.

The Deaf as an Underclass

Where Bernstein and others discuss the use of restricted codes among the working class; we could just as easily substitute the deaf. When deaf children enter school (whether locally or at a special school), a confrontation may inevitably occur which illustrates the parallel between the members of the working class, particularly working class children. The confrontation is between (a) The school's *universalistic* orders of meaning and the social relationships which generate them, and (b) the *particularistic* orders of meanings and the social relationships which generate them, which the child brings with him to the school (Bernstein, cited in Boocock, 1980: 44).

For the child (whether deaf or working class or possibly both), attending school is much like a clash between two similar but different cultures. The learned, particularistic frame of reference (in which so much can be taken-for-granted) is now situated in a new, universalistically normative frame of reference. One's entire way of viewing the world and operating in it is suddenly suspect.

Caution must be exercised, however, in using this perspective. To say that a child uses a restricted code is not to say that one language is necessarily better than another (as stated earlier) nor that the child has learned language differently. Anastasiow and Haves (1976), Harris (1975) and Labov (1972a) are among those who argue that lower-class children are normal in intellectual functioning, use dialects which are not necessarily inferior and are not raised in linguistically deprived environments. In fact Labov charges that Bernstein's views are "filtered through a strong bias against all forms of working-class behavior" (1972b:229). Implicit is the position that middle-class is "better" than lower-class. Again what we see is the possible reliance on a "blaming the victim" explanation for the child's failure (even though Bernstein recognizes that language is socially rooted) which can and often does lead to an emphasis on changing the child rather than the structure (school) he encounters.

Despite our sympathy for some of what Labov (and others) argues, we are not convinced that it is erroneous to characterize a restricted mode of communication as simply that – restricted. We agree that different groups evolve symbol systems which handle their own peculiar and localized needs, that

> Whenever human beings are thrown together in a common situation and are simultaneously cut off from extensive communication with the outside world, they begin to develop exceptional ways of relating to each other, common rules for behavior, shared definitions of the situation, agreement on the value of certain activities, and many other commonalities (Bowker, 1982:147).

This explains why prisoner groups and deaf school groups develop an argot that "fits" their everyday world. "The more isolated the culture, the greater the number of argot terms" (p. 151). The SSD world is a place where neither sign nor English vocabularies develop sufficiently well in many areas (economic, technological, and even familial terms, for example). In this sense their language system is restricted.

Whenever a child is able to verbally express his desires, experiences and thoughts adequately, he is freed from the necessity of physically acting out his thoughts by mime or gestural processes. As a general proposition, we might say: The greater the use of physical getures, the lower the level of verbal language skills (in the context of the larger society's norms). What remains as a curious thing to investigate, however, is to what degree the bright deaf child can illustrate (or communicate) his brightness via signs. This seems especially interesting in the context of Bernstein's discussion of restricted and elaborated codes because it makes possible the likelihood (as yet to be determined) that those who rely primarily upon a restricted mode of *verbal* communication can still do better – academically and otherwise – than those who must rely on signs. Were we to put signs on a continuum of language ability, it is toward the lowest end where we would place them regardless of how well done. Their excellence may only be normatively understood and appreciated among those who depend upon them for their "talk." If that is true, then those using signs may be doubly restricted: in the sense that they are only used by the deaf *and* secondly, in the sense that even among their most skilled users they must remain as relatively concrete, iconic, situation-specific indicators not capable of rivaling more verbal modes of language. No matter how well done, undeveloped and poorly standardized sign language can only carry one so far – and that distance, in the larger-than-deaf society, may be a very short one.

Chapter III

Those without Language

> Linguists have intensely studied several thousand languages, most of them spoken by isolated peoples who live at the periphery of world events. Yet no language system ever discovered is so primitive that its speakers must rely heavily upon gestures as substitutes for words. Nor does any known language lack a highly organized system of sound selected from the vast array human beings are capable of making, that does not combine these sounds into meaningful words and sentences by means of strict rules, that fails to demand of its speakers the appropriate use of language in different speech situations. All languages possess pronouns, methods of counting, ways to deal with space and time, a vocabulary that includes abstract words, and the capacity for full esthetic and intellectual expression.
>
> Peter Farb

Thinking with Pictures: cogito ergo sum

Society is a world-building enterprise which orders human experience through the use of language (see Berger and Luckmann, 1967). And "... every nomos is an area of meaning carved out of a vast mass of meaninglessness, a small clearing of lucidity in a formless, dark, always ominous jungle" (Berger, 1969). What would happen, though, to an individual if he were linguistically (or spatially) cut off from the social world? Suppose he had little or no language as in the case of a feral child? Or a deaf child? Or someone who wakes up from an operation in a hospital and finds himself unable to speak? Would some type of anomy be experienced? Berger and Luckmann maintain that one's world is constructed and sustained in conversation with others whose definitions and selections of certain aspects of reality are *a priori* posited for him (1967:131). If such a conversation is interrupted, thus making normal words and signs problematic, the individual would be plunged into anomy. The consequence would be separation from society, which amounts to a situation of meaninglessness – the "nightmare par excellence." Presumably, then, language-less children (and other such individuals) would live in a disordered world filled with terror, unable to carve out a meaningful niche for themselves, *until* a language was known to them (Huxley, too, paints a dreadful picture: "...words make us the human beings we actually are. Deprived of language we should be as dogs or monkeys [1962:5]). Given what we know about them, it makes sense to ask, "To *what extent* can one think without language and by what means do they think?" (Again, see Furth, 1966, for a lengthy discussion of this).

At SSD, teachers and administrators believe deaf children think with pictures or images, a possibility allowed by Charon as well (1979:87). We talked to a hearing preschool teacher about the language-thought nexus:

Don: You know about the question on language and thought. How in the world can a little child whose mother lives in Capital City, how can she think about home and Capital City? How can she do that?

Teacher: Well, my guess might be mental images like pictures. She would bring her mother's image to mind and she would probably relive some experiences with her mother – like her mother holding her on her lap. Something like that. Reminisce about the things they have done. I think that way.

Don: You think with images?

Teacher: I have language, too. Do you think this way?

Don: My example is: every night I can't go to sleep because I am talking to people. Maybe a song I heard on the radio just won't go away.

Teacher: Well, I write letters at night. Or I am talking to somebody carrying on a conversation with somebody. No, I can think in pictures too. Maybe I am very low level (laughter; referring to a classification of some deaf children's language skills). I like to fix up my house and things like that. I can visually picture the kinds of things I want to use. But most of the time I think in words. I visually see changes in my home. *Most* of my thought processes are in words. Since they don't have the words I imagine that they just rely on pictures, and they probably have very clear images.

It is difficult to imagine that any degree of sophisticated thinking could actually occur without formal language of some kind. In our minds we are able to think with symbols, to manipulate them, to combine and recombine them but "A picture cannot be manipulated; words [and, we would add, signs] can be" (Charon, 1979:87). Presumably a "movie" of wholistic images can occur inside the head (a right brain phenomenon, perhaps). However, without refined divisions (categories), interpretations of wholistic reality are very limited.

With language a person is able to move from wholistic to more precise modes of cognition. Perhaps it is true that languageless deaf children think with mental pictures or whole images; that such thoughts involve chunks of reality undifferentiated by categories and typifications. Some studies do indicate that normal hearing children "tend to code pictures pictorically up to the age of five; from then on word-based phonological coding predominates" (Klima and Bellugi, 1979:89,93). Language, then, allows them to move on to a higher level of abstraction; eventually an object is mentally retained as a symbol not just as a physical image. And Eastman (1980) even suggests that words (and signs) may be hierarchally organized with superordinate words at the top and concrete words at the bottom. He illustrates: "A speaker lacking the superordinate label *color*, which represents the concept rather than specific instances, would use only labels referring to instances – concrete words with specific referents such as *red* or *blue*" (p. 82). This, he says, relates language to learning in schools since "the type of learning required in schools is context-independent ... . Symbolic rather than iconic representation of thought is required" (p. 83). As Postman and Weingartner (1969) say, "We see through our words." We would add, "We *know* through our words."

Without language the initial cognitive process is made difficult for deaf children. One teacher gasped, "This child has the attention span of a gnat and I think that is an exaggeration." For one thing these children often seem to have a memory problem (remember, their's consists of visual memories without auditory memories). Teachers of young children frequently used the phrase, "Oohh, you remembered!" Implicit was the notion that the expectation was one of failure not success. Again, information is much more efficiently stored with symbols than with images.

One day during a memory-language test in one classroom a teacher hid animal figures around the room. One child later found some ("That's right, you remembered") and failed on others. Again, the expectation is that not everything will be retained. A similar thing happened during an outing to a creek where teachers take young children to feed bread to fish. A teacher told one boy to "Remember Mr. Evans. Try to remember that we saw him today (Friday) so we can write a story about him on Monday." The researcher was told that the children would likely write about the trip to feed fish and not remember that Mr. Evans was there. This is, of course, more grist for the idea that these children are presented with a world which is cognitively captured in a fragmentary yet wholistic way. Thus an overall experience is retained (viz., feeding fish) with little retention of details.

Learning discrete English words and learning to read them is very difficult for these children. According to one teacher:

> Language, reading, dictation (spelling) all of these come very slowly. You and I have talked about the (repeated) exposure to a word that a deaf child has to have. A hearing child is getting it two ways – auditorially and visually. So it takes repetition, repetition. It takes so much longer for a deaf child so I start very, very slowly.

Deaf children, she said, learn "by doing it over and over." And when a child finally performs well he is abundantly rewarded, "When they do something right I praise the stew out of them."

The first days of language consist of wholistic symbols in the form of single signs (go, come, sit), physically acting out ideas (run, jump) and pictures captioned with written words. Soon one learns the picture of one's own name. This is not done by looking at a series of letters like T-i-n-a, but by emphasizing a unitary or wholistic picture of one's name, i. e., a gestalt presentation of the name which is printed with chalk of different colors (see figure 1).

Again, it is the design around the name that is imprinted on the child's mind. The child, at first, is not T-i-n-a but rather a symbol,

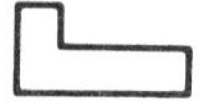

It is a symbolic world of icons, ideograms, pictures and mime – wholistic presentations of reality. But wholistic reality (and cognition) must be dismantled, divided and differentiated. One must move

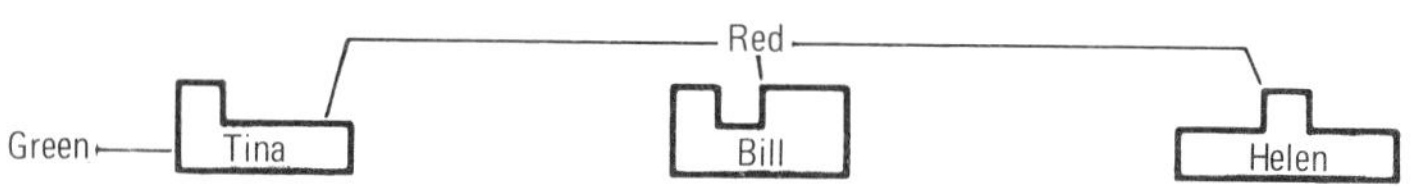

Figure 1. Examples showing how children's names are taught primarily as pictures with shapes and colors as the salient characteristics. The alphabetic name with discrete letters is secondary for the young deaf child.

cognitively from crude gestures and mime to specific linguistic modalities – and within these – from restricted to elaborated codes of communication. In the classroom children must take the whole continuous and unified human body, break it into discrete bits and pieces and name them. This act constitutes a mental world, a world of ideas and meanings, an "inner landscape" (Becker, 1973); it is a carving out of social objects collectively named and defined.

The consciousness of deaf children is largely developed by these ideographic procedures via ASL. As Klima and Bellugi (1979: 194) say about it, "ASL economizes by doing without kinds of grammatical morphenes that English uses; ASL has special ways of compacting linguistic information which are very different from those of a spoken language like English." Facial expressions are used for grammatical purposes and this further compacts information. To us, a relationship between sign language and concrete-mindedness of deaf students (reported by all teachers interviewed) seems apparent. One sign for one object, one meaning for one English word gives rise to the "black-and-white" character of deaf consciousness. One girl marvelled that a car door was signed "door" just as the "door" one closes in a room. Long ago Sapir (1949: 7) claimed that a person who has seen only one elephant "speaks without the slightest hesitation of ten elephants or a million elephants ..." But such facility of generalization is not found among young deaf children using signs.

To carry this further, consider the case of two little girls without language. The words walk, run and jump were written on a black-board. The teacher showed the girls a picture of a child walking and the word walk was written below the walking child. Next, the teacher showed the ideographic sign for walk (two hands move just as one's feet move – one goes up and down again and again). The girls then traced each letter of w-a-l-k on the blackboard with a long pointer. One began to fall asleep but the teacher tapped her desk aggressively and orally said, "Wake up, Tina!" Finally, each girl was taken by the hand and had to actually walk with the teacher to and fro across the front of the classroom. After all this work one thinks of the old adage, "One picture is worth a thousand words." Or in this case, one word may seem worth (and derive from) a thousand hours of work.

Language functions to facilitate not only a "picture" but also an understanding of the social world. A preschool deaf child, with no language, is basically unable to understand what is going on around him. As an administrator in the lower school said,

> We're talking about students who don't understand the world, who don't understand the consequences because of their language. They don't have a real picture of cause and effect. They don't understand the significance of picking up a piece of pipe and hitting someone on the head ... Part of our responsibility is to get across to them a good clear understanding of the world. They just don't have it ... (Why is this the case?) The normally hearing youngster learns right, wrong from watching what happens around home, but more importantly he hears it discussed by hearing people who talk about why he should or should not do this ... Now the deaf kid can see what's happening where he lives but he can't discuss it, doesn't really understand it. He only sees what is apparent from the outside. He doesn't understand motivations nor why people do what they do, or the punishment they may receive. I believe the primary reason is the lack of language.

Language permits one to understand how the physical world is socially divided, labeled and objectivated. In a classroom of thirteen and fourteen-year-olds a teacher explained the difference between cities and states by using a large map, 8 by 6 feet in size. She asked, "What city is largest in the United States?" A student answered, "New York." But when the teacher explained that the state of New York also had a city named "New York" (NY, NY), the students' blank stares indicated a lack of understanding. Afterwards the teacher asked, "What is the capitol of our state?" No one knew the answer and two teenage students signed, "D. C." "No," the teacher replied, "that's the capital of all the United States." Looking at a large map of the United States students wanted to know if there were other deaf people in other states and were surprised to learn that there were. Somehow, the notion existed that their current location housed the entire population of deaf people. Their relationship to a larger world of deaf people mystifies them, indeed for most cannot even be imagined.

In another classroom a teacher taught "the babies" (i. e., the preschoolers) that the human face is divided into parts – "eye," "nose," "eyebrows," "hair." Each child had to attach discrete facial parts (eyes, nose, lips, etc.) onto the outline of a cloth face. A few weeks after observing this, two boys, aged 13, asked the researcher, "What is the name of this (pointing to eyelash) ... is it 'eye-hair'?" They were told that it was "eyelash." Quickly one guessed (by fingerspelling) that the chin was "e-l-b-o-w." He wanted to know if a point on his jaw was his "c-h-e-e-k." This is one more illustration of how a solid, wholistic mass (in this case, a face) is divided into bits and pieces by linguistic means, agreed upon by some group. For young deaf children with little language, such a solid mass can only be roughly divided and understood with didactic pointing gestures. As Cassirer allegedly wrote, "Before the intellectual work of conceiving and understanding of phenomena can set in, the work of *naming* must have preceded it, and have reached a certain point of elaboration" (cited in Postman and Weingartner, 1969:127). The naming process, so painfully absent for young deaf children, "transforms the world of sense impressions, which animals also possess, into a mental world, a world of ideas and meanings" (p. 127). For these children, the whole is truly greater than the sum of its parts! And in a peculiar way their world view is closer to Highwater's primal people who "speak of deer or salmon without any distinction in regard to number. To a member of this tribe a flock or a herd is a singular whole; it is not a collection of individual elements" (1981:73).

Communication, Community and Welt

Language also establishes a community of thought (Hertzler, 1965; Taylor, 1976). With shared meanings – which are human constructs – there is a common reference world whose objects, events, and facts are shared by everyone (bracketed, of course, in space and time; i.e., societally and historically). This is what makes a community. We portray the possibilities of this in Figure 2. There we show an ideal-typical continuum with no language, no community at one pole and full language, much community at the other pole.

Language helps us create a world. As a Don Quixote, one can "dream the impossible dream." He is a small god who can speak things into existence (for example, "I now pronounce you husband and wife"). He can create the "vital lie" which assures him he is not alone in the dark cosmic ocean, that he is in control, that he has meaning (Becker, 1973). From among all possibilities, he uses language to create a fact-like existence. These "facts," are an "artifical representation of reality ... a portrait of one part of it" (Hertzler, 1965:45). Reality, then, is "something intellectual, capable of being apprehended only through symbols" – it is "a language-made affair – which is caught, corralled and encircled by means of words" (or signs; p. 45). As Berger and Luckmann note, in a highly related way, our reality is there whether we want it to be or not. We cannot wish it away.

No Language	Limited Language	Restricted Language	Full Language
Prelingual humans and animals (infants, young deaf children, isolates, all non-human animals)	Deaf children and adults with few words or signs; mental retardates with little language	Extremely isolated or illiterate groups	Multilingual and highly educated people
Limited degrees of community	Simple community	Highly integrated relatively closed community	Diversified, complex and relatively open community
Communication by prelanguage means (calls, gestures), almost totally concrete	Communication by low level human language (words or signs plus calls, gestures); very concrete	Relatively integrated codes of communication based on shared, local experiences. More use of physical gestures and context-tied (particularistic) statements than column four	Elaborated codes of communication based on pluralistic social experiences. More use of abstract universalistic statements
Thought consists of misty mental images	Restricted wholistic and very concrete thought processes	Restricted, wholistic concrete and abstract thought processes	More abstract and diversified thought processes
Virtually no human reality; the animal world	Very elemental forms of human reality; the child's world	Fairly simple (non-technological) reality; an ethnocentric world	Complex reality, the pluralistic world

Figure 2. A diagrammatical representation of the relationship between language and community, language and thought, and language and reality.

The poet speaks of "winged words" because language has a time-bridging function which transmits knowledge (as culture) across space and time. Language allows us to ponder three time frames: what has been, what is, and what might be. But there are some negative and limiting functions of language too. For example, language may canalize perception, it may "acts as blinders – focusing attention only on some aspect of things or events, and not on others" (p. 52). Concepts and expressions of space and time are perceived and interpreted in ways related to one's own particular environment, culture and form of language.

Postman and Weingartner (1969:211) echo the Whorfian view that "The more limited the symbol system in number and kind, the less one is able to 'see.'" Peter Winch (1958:15) is another who believes that one cannot get outside his conceptualization of the world: "The world is for us what is presented through concepts." Where Bertrand Russell (1943:60) sees language as making possible thoughts which could not exist without it, Postman and Weingartner (1969:101) view language as a prison house which "structures what one will see and believe ..." They liken language to a map which may (to some ascertainable degree) establish correspondence to only part of the territory described (Postman and Weingartner, 1969:14; Hertzler, 1965:46).

Although we are not making these issues a cornerstone of our own argument, it is important to state that our interpretation of the above suggests the role to be played by a sociology of knowledge. We do not embrace the narrow side of the Sapir-Whorf hypothesis that language, in a monocausal way, changes culture and thought. Instead, we agree with most anthropologists that environmental changes (and differences), cultural differences, and social changes "are expressed in lexical distinctions ... within semantic domains" (Kottack, 1982:417).

Wittgenstein, Postman and Weingartner, Winch, Russell and Hertzler all seem to be saying that knowledge is bracketed and that the parameters within which it exists will determine how we see the world. From a sociology of knowledge perspective, we may wish to understand (as called for by Merton, [1968], among others) something about the distribution of knowledge. And clearly that cannot be fathomed in any reasonable way without taking into account the role of ideology. In short, knowledge as a socially produced and maintained thing must be understood in an ideological context – and this will hold, equally, we suspect, whether we are talking about

Russia (and Russian language) or England (and English language) or the deaf (and their language). As Highwater (1981:206) says, there are many worlds, many realities, and "We must learn to use our minds to discover meaning rather than truth ... ."

In a very Marxian and structural way, some views of the world (and the words which foster those views) dominate over others and as we have tried to show thus far, language is a key ingredient in this process. Language both liberates man and at the same time, as an ideological phenomenon, constrains him. Language therefore enables one to act upon the world, to think, to mind, to learn, to understand – in short, to make sense of the world as a socially produced and maintained place.

From Umwelt to Welt: The Breakthrough

Aldous Huxley (1962) says, "... where there is no language, behavior is nonhuman ... words make us the human beings we actually are. Deprived of language we should be as dogs or monkeys." In short, if we had no symbols and no language, our existence would be one of physical stimuli and of present-moment concreteness:

> Our actions would be fixed, we would *respond* to stimuli, not to meaning. We would not problem solve, reflect, imagine, recall the past at all, or teach others anything other than simple responses learned through imitation. We would not be able to depend on culture for our action, but would have to rely instead on instinct and/or simple learning. Understanding would cease, worlds outside our immediate physical space would not exist for us ... Certainly communication with each other would not contain anything like concepts, but would be confined to simple 'nonmeaningful gestures' (Charon 1979:53).

It was Anne Sullivan who spelled the word "water" into Helen Keller's hand as cool water simultaneously was pumped over it. The breakthrough refers to Helen's first comprehension that the finger configurations (w-a-t-e-r) referred to the cool nameless liquid she felt flowing onto her hand. For the very first time in her life she actually understood that everything had a name. She had previously developed about sixty homemade signs before the waterpump breakthrough (or, as she called it, her "liberation"). She later thought of herself without language as "the little being governed only by animal impulses, and not often those of a docile beast" (Keller, 1902). Before language came, she was to describe her social and symbolic isolation: "There was no sense of natural bonds with humanity" (p. 37). By her own stirring account the waterpump miracle was the time and place where Helen crossed the bridge from nothingness to the shores of comprehension, from the world of physical objects (*Umwelt*) to the world of *social* objects (*Welt*). Her tutor, Anne Sullivan, wrote: "At the well-house, nothingness vanished, but (she was) not in the real world yet. She did not reflect or try to describe things to herself ... she remembered the words and only used them when appropriate" (p. 42). Immediately Helen wanted to know the names of other things. She had entered the world of symbols and referents, into the universe of mankind, the triadic world. That day at the well-house she "suddenly felt a misty consciousness as of something forgotten, a thrill of returning thought ... the mystery of language was revealed to me ... everything has a name, and each name gave birth to a new thought" (p. 36).

Do similar "breakthroughs" occur at SSD? An administrator believes that one particular teacher continues (after more than 25 years) to teach languageless deaf children for the reward of seeing them "suddenly say, 'Ah-h-h-h-h-h' when they first understand, when they transfer images to symbols." That breakthrough, he said, will "make the hair stand up on your neck."

How does a preschool teacher begin teaching lanuage to a languageless deaf child? First of all, the children receive global gestures and not (signed) English. A preschool teacher showed a little girl her newly created name sign. The teacher signed the initial "M" on the right cheek (an arbitrary sign which could just as easily have other meanings assigned to it; it is local and situated) and said, "Raise your right hand when your name is called." At this stage of language acquisition physicality is the norm. So the TA (teacher's aide) literally lifted the child's hand when the teacher made her name sign (M on the right cheek). This little girl did not understand at all that she is the referent of the symbol, although in time she will spontaneously lift her hand when she sees the sign-signal. Occasionally the teacher or TA actually shaped a child's hand into some sign, or even manipulated her arms when it was time to respond to certain signs.

Many of the first signs learned by these children are negative ones. In one lower school classroom, it was common to hear both teacher and TA frequently telling students, "Mistake!" "Is that the way to spell your name? Mistake!" An eight year old boy without language who had entered SSD late in the year parroted to the teacher,

"Mistake" when he dropped a book. The friendly teacher told the researcher: "That is the first sign they learn, 'mistake.' The second sign they learn is 'bad.'" The TA, a hearing woman, added, "'Mistake' was the first sign I learned myself."

To further illustrate the frequency of this linguistic environment, we present a twenty-five minute segment of classroom observations made by Don in the room with the TA and teacher mentioned above. These field notes included hour and minute markers in the left margins so we are able to see the frequency of the term, "mistake."

> 1:13 pm The teacher says to C---, 'No. C---, that's a mistake' as C--- tries to help T----.
>
> 1:15 The teacher shows A. M--- how to march with a flag in her hand by lifting her foot high. The second new word is 'tipotoe,' which is done by walking (and simultaneously having the index finger on the lip to signify quietness) on the toes. Both of these being iconic and mimetic. A. M--- runs to the blackboard and points to her many stars and the smiling sun face.
>
> 1:18 This time A. M---recognizes the term 'march' and marches without any help. A. M---- taps T---- on the shoulder and signs, 'look at me.'
>
> 1:20 W--- misses one and gets four correct. 1:24 L--- marches. W--- signs, 'Right!' The teacher says, 'Good.'
>
> 1:25 L--- starts crying. The teacher says, 'W---! That is a mistake, whatever you did to L--- (she failed to see what had happened). Tell him you're sorry.' Teacher to Don: 'This next activity is a mental development' (using six large pictures which are placed on the blackboard and six of the pictures will later have to be matched). 'L---! Are you looking? That's a mistake.'
>
> 1:30 W--- tries to match a second set of six pictures. 1:31 'A. M---. Do you think that W---'s work is right? It *is* right. Good! Picture number 2 is right? Good!' W--- and L--- both beat their desk with one hand making the sign for 'right.'
>
> 1:34 A. M--- tries the same sequence of pictures. Teacher: 'I see two mistakes.' Teacher to W---: 'Do you see any mistakes? Do you want to come and fix it?' W---- changes one picture. A. M--- puts her head down on the desk sulking. The teacher says, 'A. M--- is upset.' Teacher to Don: 'She can't stand to make a mistake and they can't stand for another student to correct them.' [A few days earlier the TA told Don, 'Five years ago we had a boy who would puff up from 8:30 in the morning until noon before he would blow up when you made an 'X' mark on his paper which means, 'mistake' on his paper. He would become very sulky].
>
> 1:38 L--- tries the set of pictures. A. M----- puts her head down to the desk. L--- tries to peek behind the picture. The teacher says, 'No! No!' Teacher to Don: 'You will see the difference in the kids now. The difference

> in their abilities.' W--- and A. M--- play as the teacher works with L----. When L--- places the pictures both W--- and A. M--- sign, 'Mistake!' A. M--- signs, 'Hurry!' Teacher to Don: 'They're just dying to tell him about his mistakes.' W--- signs, 'Bad. Me strong.' L--- watches as A. M--- and W--- change four of his pictures which were incorrectly placed. The teacher says to L--- as she stands face to face with him, 'You made four mistakes. A. M--- and W--- fixed it up for you.'

In another classroom a different teacher threatened a sleepy and inattentive child. As she explained: "This is where they learn 'no' and 'mistake' and these are some of the first signs they learn." Two nights later a nurse in the infirmary criticized this negative introduction to language: "These kids learn 'no' or 'wrong' or 'mistake' before they learn anything else."

For a long time, a young student was carefully observed. He was visited in his dorm, observed in the classroom (often from behind a one-way mirror), during recess on the playground and in the dining hall. Of interest was actual observations of some of his first symbols. Would they be positive or negative? Don remained in the dining room until all the kids had gone back to the dorm. The very last ones to leave were the 'babies' and Don was observing Solo Boy. His notes capture this moment well.

> In a little while I saw him make the first sign that I have actually seen him execute (on numerous occasions I have watched him to see when he would start signing). His first sign in the dining room on 11/11/81 was 'mistake.' With one hand he made the sign for 'mistake' while the other hand pointed toward one of his little peers. I sat and watched him for 15 or 20 minutes and saw him make the sign, 'mistake,' four times. Once or twice he made the sign when his peer, another little black boy, was eating a cookie and spilled crumbs and other food on the table. Solo Boy would accusingly point to the table where the mess was and make the sign, 'mistake.' I was sitting twenty feet away and to be sure I had understood correctly (because of the distance) I went and asked the houseparent what sign Solo Boy was making. She said, 'it's the sign for 'mistake.'' This is a significant observation because I have been told by teachers that one of the first signs kids learn is the sign, 'mistake.' [Comment: It may be that social order is so great an imposition upon human beings that it is necessary, to begin teaching the emerging person what *not* to do, to restrict himself, to control himself, to negate and eliminate his/her natural (unenculturated) animal behaviors].

For these late-comers to the symbolic universe, first signs are often one-sign statements and tend to be dichotomous pairs like "yes-no," "good-bad," "right-wrong," and so on. This serves as a way of concretizing the world into polar extremes. Something is one way or another, but there is little room for fine points of distinction. It is a world of single signs for single things.

Much of the emphasis in the preschool program is on "readiness skills," general visual and motor skill development. For example, a child is asked to look at a picture and indicate what is missing. Motor skills include learning to run, hop, bounce a ball and to manipulate a pencil. Moreover, classroom activities include mixing shapes and colors in lieu of "always emphasizing language." Yet these very activities provide an opportunity for introducing language since one can talk about colors, objects and concepts like size: "That's too big," "too little," etc. As one teacher said: "When they get into reading programs they will already have the idea to work left to right ... (and know) well over one hundred signs and will be able to use short phrases."

At SSD we asked a (preschool) teacher about deaf children without language, about the breakthrough of first communication by means of language. No part of our investigation is more intriguing than this. In this particular classroom is a group of children outside the symbolic or the triadic universe with no formal human language system.

> Don: Can you describe what happens prior to that (the breakthrough)?
>
> Teacher: Well, prior to that is mostly imitation; to imitate what you say or if you talk to them they will shake their head like they understand and they really don't. And you can tell that they don't by testing them or asking them to do something and they stand there or they do something else that you did not ask them to do. They really are happy when they are able to respond.
>
> Don: Can you think of any one example? An example of the breakthrough? I keep thinking of Helen Keller when she made the connection. Or is it so gradual that you don't see it?
>
> Teacher: It is so gradual. It is not like a traumatic experience. Its something that maybe I am not aware of at the moment. The first time they learn a new color, the first time you show them a color and this is red and they can tell you everything that is red in the room, they have grabbed the connection that this sign is associated with a certain color. That is a breakthrough right there.
>
> Don: They come in with zero on this (colors). Then you start giving them individual signs. They start learning "water," "bathroom," etc.
>
> Teacher: they learn language much like a hearing child. A hearing child listens for a year and a half, two years before they learn. They are understanding what you say but they can't give you back and they can't talk to you (with) other words ...

Don: By the end of this year will these children be able to do that? Give it back to you?

Teacher: Yes. In short phrases.

Don: Can a child learn language very well after age six?

Teacher: I think they would have much more of an advantage if they came in before.

Don: How about dressing themselves?

Teacher: They know how to do that.

Don: Going to the bathroom?

Teacher: They know that. They do that through imitation.

Don: Are there any types of behavior that they don't know when they come to you?

Teacher: Well, just the fact that they use a lot of gestures and that they don't speak. If they want to tell you something they make up their own signs. If they want to go to the bathroom they will point or grab somebody by the hand or pull them or point to themselves.

At this point, Percy (1983) would argue, these children engage in dyadic events (ego-referent) while those with language experience triadic events (ego-symbol-referent) as illustrated in Figure 3 by Helen Keller's transition via language from dyadic to triadic worlds:

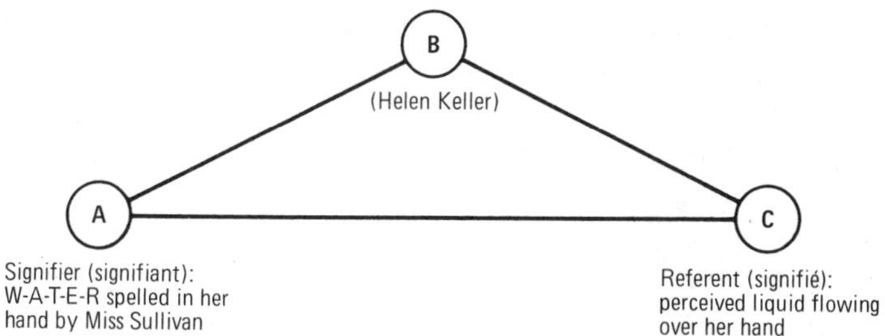

Figure 3. Triadic behaviors: between the symbolling person (B) and the referent (C) is a symbol (A). (From Lost in the Cosmos by Walker Percy. Copyright (©) 1983 by Walker Percy. Reproduced by permission of Farrar, Straus and Giroux, Inc.)

At SSD, "Sachmo" represents another human being who has languished within a dyadic languageless world (Umwelt) most of his life. A young boy of six or seven years, he wipes at a constant drool from his mouth with a rag (hence our naming him "Sachmo"). Unable to hear since birth, he could neither send nor receive ideas, words or signs with any level of sophistication. In his own family unit he was alone. Neither parents, siblings, nor neighbors could reach him since he was unable to meaningfully communicate in any effective way. His head is battered and massive scar tissues spread across his forehead. One person said he had observed the boy actually banging his head against a wall during his first year at the school. "But once we gave him some sign language and some attention and reached him, he became a normal person. In his frustration and desperation Sachmo was crying out, 'Let me out!' as he destroyed his head and eyes."

Certainly not all languageless children respond this way but Sachmo's behavior suggests how unfree, how shackled, bound, limited and stymied an individual is without linguistic competence. Sachmo's case of social and linguistic isolation from society fits Berger's (1975:238) claim that "Separation from society ... inflicts unbearable psychological tensions upon the individual ..." Without language one is relatively powerless, as in the case of Kandy, a teenage girl found in an infirmary bed lying in a pool of her own menstrual blood. Her inability to communicate is itself a lack of power, an inability to reach out and act upon the world, to meaningfully interact with her fellow human beings.

"Solo Boy," age four, is another example of the relationship between language and two forms of isolation: social and ideational (Teilhard's "noosphere" in Capra, 1983). We call him "Solo Boy" because he spent his first week at SSD in the infirmary with a skin disease. In that place he was alone without language, with no understanding of why he resided in the strange building filled with white-coated women. He did not know where his parents were nor why they had left him. Not one face was familiar to him at a school and a town which, for him, had no names. He had no idea he was in an "infirmary" or at a "school" since he possessed no signs or words for those places. He was "solo." He was, as Percy (1983:101) so eloquently puts it, without "co-namer, co-discoverer, co-sustainer" of his world.

Solo Boy lives in an "environment of gaps" where there is no "intersection of nature and culture" (p. 163). He dwells in some sort of Edenic state in which he cannot tell lies nor be ashamed of himself (p. 108). But unlike the first Adam he is unable to name the many creatures around him including his own parents. And while Percy speaks of modern man's self being lost in the cosmos, we say that the self of Solo Boy was never found (nor formed) in the first place – and therefore cannot be lost. At this point he has never enjoyed the "Helen Keller phenomenon;" i.e., the discovery of the cosmos (*Welt*) via symbols. Without language, some argue, Solo Boy even lacks consciousness "that act of attention to something under the auspices of its sign, an act which is social in its origin" (Percy 1983:105; see also Capra, 1983). Certainly he remains outside the group's collective consciousness, its noosphere.

The cases of Sachmo and Solo Boy well illustrate certain costs associated with the absence of language. We wondered about the "nature" of young deaf children who most often are born into homes where no family members can adequately communicate with them. An administrator suggested that these children are virtually *tabulae rasae* when they arrive at SSD; they enter lower school not knowing they have a name and thinking with images not words or formal signs. They seem to have no understanding of what is happening to them when they enter school. One of the deaf teachers, the administrator remembered, tells a story about how his parents took him to a residential school in the Deep South and left him there, unable, of course, to explain to him what was happening. The boy had seen his father exchange watermelons for dollars and when he saw money change hands between his father and school officials, he thought that he had been exchanged (sold) to the school. Again, without language the child was isolated and terrorized.

The manual quality of sign language requires a visual directness and immediacy not necessary for hearing people. One evening in the boy's dormitory a thirteen-year-old put a spider in the hair of a boy who was watching television. When told that he had a spider in his hair, he gave a high, shrill scream which effectively captured a hearing houseparent's attention. This illustrates how the human voice as a sound based medium has a greater range (omnipresence) and is a power more effective than hand flagging (the visual medium) which requires the receiver's more narrow line of vision to convey the call for help. Without hearing (sound input) much of the world is reduced to that which lies within the eyesight; a critical distance sense (hearing) is missing.

In a social world where most adults (teachers and houseparents) are hearing people, the use of the voice is a form of power even when among hard-of-hearing individuals. For example, in one classroom where most students could verbalize, a teacher wrote a sentence on the blackboard for which she wanted the correct tense of a verb. With her back still toward the students Tama, who is hard-of-hearing and can talk, shouted, "I want to do it! I want to do it!" The teacher heard her request without looking and then allowed Tama the rewarding chance to give the correct answer. Tama had won out over the others; she was less limited than her peers because it was not necessary to use the teacher's narrow line of vision in offering her answer.

To further illustrate the imprisonment which results from a lack of language, we report the following exchange (note the parallel between what the researcher is told and the play, *Johnny Belinda*):

> Don: I get the impression that many children here have been rejected or abused.
>
> Administrator: That's for sure. I guess ... not just mild abuse, but the real stuff ... at *least* one-third, at least one-third.
>
> Don: Why so many?
>
> Administrator: The usual inclination to reject the handicapped. Other factors come into play with the deaf that may not be true for other handicapped people. The young deaf child will not have the language to tell someone that something's happened to him, and he's pretty much defenseless. As you come into high school a very high percentage of girls have been molested. Sometimes the child is not even able to tell the mother when someone outside the family does it. Talk with some of the high school girls and they will tell some amazing stories.

Clearly, man acts upon the world more effectively with language (either sign or verbal) than without: But can a languageless person think with any degree of sophistication? Charon (1979) says no because thinking is talking to oneself (p. 57). Is mind really to be regarded as a "process of symbol-use" (Ashworth, 1979:78)? How do languageless children make any sense out of their experience? In the absence of language are events and physical things simply met and acted upon in a stimulus-response manner with little or no symbolic processes involved? That is, how can they participate in the *social* process whereby members effectuate/carve out (social) objects by consensually endowing them with meaning? After all, says Tucker (1978:234), "The world man experiences is the world he symbolically or linguistically designates; there is no other world." In a word, *Homo loquens* possesses an awesome capability and potency. It is an unparalleled cosmic marvel that he linguistically fabricates, nomizes and catalogues linguistic worlds.

Language Acquisition

A young preschool teacher discussed the deficit that deaf children begin life with:

> Most children learn (language) between the ages of one-and-a-half and two. We (at SSD) are at a disadvantage. Children come in knowing nothing. Can you imagine? A two-year-old hearing child may have a vocabulary of 250 words. Our children come not knowing that they have a label, that they are called by a name, that they are Ronny or Donny. They don't know that their primary caretaker is called Mama. They just don't know the labels for things. They don't know that the red thing they just ate is an apple. They know that liquid is to drink and food is to eat from past experience but they don't know the names for things like that.

But nearly all of them have learned to cope, albeit in sometimes crude ways. They are able to dress themselves, feed themselves, use a restroom, and so on. How do they communicate such things without a language? As one teacher says, "They use a lot of gestures. If they want to tell you something they make up their own signs. If they want to go to the bathroom they will point or grab somebody by the hand, or pull them, or point to themselves (genitals)." This highlights a significant point: the lower the level of competence of formal language (speech or signs), the greater the utility of (1) physical communication and (2) local, situated neologisms (more accurately, "neosigns") whose meanings are inherent in the present context. Additionally, deaf children represent the incredible proclivity of man to communicate with symbols. Even deafness cannot stifle that most human of all characteristics.

Artificial Processes and Experiential Deprivation

A common complaint in the lower and preschools is that a classroom constitutes an "artificially structured situation." Teachers believe that a more natural way is needed to teach language to deaf students. This opinion first surfaced when teachers were asked, "What is your most recurring problem as a teacher?" One teacher promptly replied:

> Sometimes I get frustrated because I am not able to teach them naturally ... I have thought if I could just take this child home with me and talk to him all the time. There are so many daily exercises you live through like the feeding and the dressing and going to the store ... that would

> provide such a better basis for learning language than it is to be in a classroom eight hours a day and try and create (natural experiences).

When pressed to elucidate the "artificial" character of this late language acquisition situation, it was clear she meant mundane, everyday experiences of home and family life were absent. To put it another way objects at school are named (signed) and labels are taught to children in a non-utilitarian context: "This is a ..." and "This is a ...", etc. The classroom is viewed as a place of contrived events and experiences:

> Well, I mean you always have to invent activities. You just don't sit down and teach them colors and words. I mean I try to avoid that and it is very hard to sit down and teach them the word *apple* because you are not giving them a way to use it. It's better if you can teach them in some other way like cutting up an apple and eating an apple.

The best and most natural thing for these students, she argued, is "their parents" because they could teach language in natural, everyday interactions. This teacher's notion of language acquisition stands in sharp contrast to students learning a long list of words in a classroom which has few uncontrived objects to aid vocabulary acquisition.

The already amorphous symbolic world remains difficult for the deaf child to grasp in a classroom. As a case in point, Solo Boy was confronted by a large number of differently colored wooden blocks. He was directed to place a yellow block beside a second one of the same color. When he chose the wrong color, the teacher signed, "Where is the yellow one?" But his attention span was so short that he quickly lost interest in the activity. Here is a boy with no labels for colors and a teacher trying to captivate his mind long enough to convey a collage of various color concepts. Again, this illustrates the difficulty of working with a young deaf child versus a hearing child who long ago has learned about the yellow ball, the yellow canary, the yellow car, and perhaps, the yellow brick road. As one teacher lamented, "The deaf are sadly lacking in language experience."

The term 'experience' often occurred in discussions at SSD. To us, the much abused concept of "experiential deprivation" seems applicable since deaf children are literally deprived of significant symbolic experiences (i. e., where mutual understanding occurs). They are deprived of language experience *and* normal interaction with family members, playmates, neighbors, etc. Everyday experiences like going to a store offer an opportunity for a deaf child to learn the names of many objects but unless accompanied by a deaf person or someone else capable of transmitting their knowledge, the trip to a store is just one more collage of things largely enmeshed one with the other.

An older teacher poignantly told how young deaf children are out of touch with the world of symbols. In that condition she sees how they are deprived of the massive flow of human knowledge which, in effect, leaves them outside the substantive world of *Homo sapiens* ("wise man").

> I can't talk to these children like you would the average six year old child about the man on the moon when all that happened (i. e., the Apollo flight). These children can't relate to it. You have to start language at a level they can build from. I can't tell them about the astronauts, something about mother and daddy talking about the Lybians and how the Americans shot down an airplane ... *A deaf child has to experience something (emphasis added).*

On Friday mornings the youngest children are taken to a restaurant in Doubletown to experience their off-campus surroundings. Once inside, lined up and excited, two little girls in their second week of school (and language) used a single sign to denote their choices of ice cream – "brown" or "white." Ice cream (a concept) was not seen as flavors, but instead as colors (colors being "specific instances" and more concrete than flavors). On this happy day of the school week teachers eat sandwiches, potato chips, drink cokes and smoke cigarettes. Nearby, four-to-the-booth, excited students lick and slurp "brown" and "white." A little girl rested her "brown" cone on the table. Quickly her teacher signs, "Mistake!" Just outside the restaurant window flows clear, cold mountain water down a creek whose banks are coated with thick green grass. One little girl giggles and licks her "white." Suddenly she signs "Duck!" (thumb and index-plus-middle finger at lips closing, opening). Soon six or so ducks come into view and Tina's mouth gapes wider and wider – "ahhh!" – eyes popping while pointing and gesturing. This is the real world, a learning laboratory where objects and events can be associated with signs in a "natural" (unrehearsed) way.

A houseparent, when asked to define and discuss the frequently used concept "deaf world," replied in terms of the relationship between hearing and knowing; in terms of deafness and deprivation:

> Houseparent: The 'deaf world' is different in that primarily they can't hear and the things that we take for granted we hear all the time and all

of these things like – we sit down to watch a television program, we *hear* what's going on. They *guess*. They never hear music, they never hear beautiful poems read. They can't hear anything.

Don: What is the effect of missing all that?

Houseparent: Well, first of all it slows their learning ability. Because we learn so much from what we hear from the time we come into the world on. That's the way we learn. So, if they can't hear all that goes on in the world then they are just behind in so many ways the hearing people. So the very fact that it's not a hearing world makes it different.

In the following exchange a postlingually deafened sixteen-year-old expresses disgust with some "dumb" peers who lack knowledge:

Don: Can you tell me what you like best of all about the school?

Student: To learn better ways and not stupid behavior (actions) like other people. People think I am deaf and dumb. I don't like that. I try to influence other students better ways. I want to learn more than other deaf people did before.

Don: Who thinks you are dumb?

Student: Some of my relatives. Some people from Doubletown who think I am dumb. I must be cool and show that I must become smart like hearing people. But I am not handicapped. I want them to think that I can do things. Anything! There are lousy teachers with lousy sign language. My friend _____ from grade 9–1, there is a lousy math teacher, Kathy has problems. Asks me what math means and I teach her and it frustrates me.

Don: Is there anything else that bothers you or makes you mad?

Student: The houseparents ignore the dormitory student. Do not help him ... I heard [this student is a day student] many houseparents don't show their girls and boys. They just ignore them. They are talking while the other boys and girls are having their problems. They need help with their homework and the houseparent says, 'Do it yourself.' I don't like that.

This day student lives at home with a mother who is very skilled with sign language. Again, she portrays dormitory students as people lacking knowledge (or "nit-wits") due to lack of experience and parental teaching:

Don: Are you a happy person?

Student: That I am happy, that I am deaf, yes. But other things about my mother and school bother me ... Like on vacation ... mother always makes me stay home. There is nothing to do at home. I can't drive. I have a license but I do not have a car. Mother says, no. She does not trust me. She is afraid I will have a wreck. Mother truly loves me but she protects me too much.

Don: You are sixteen now?

Student: Yes. My friends tell me that you must learn to be independent. Last year I stayed home and never went out. This year it is pretty good independence. Most dormitory students they don't go anywhere and they are as old as I am. And they act stupid because their parents don't teach. Parents are far away. The children don't see – like brothers and sisters, they don't see it. They are always fighting and they don't understand things. _____ (my friend) told me that students tell lies and they steal and I have noticed it that the parents are far away and not helping them with their problems. The houseparents don't listen to them. They say, 'Go away. I don't care.' I don't like that. I try to advise _____ (friend) and help her to understand.

Don: What do you mean that the dormitory kids act dumb and stupid? What do they do?

Student: The kids from the high school don't act like adults, they act immature. One boy was fighting and picking and the girl said, 'Stop!' And the teacher notices and says, 'Stop'. But the boy does not listen. He is stubborn. They force girls to be sweethearts. If the girl does not want it, it does not matter. You have to be sweetheart anyway.

Don: Can a boy really force a girl to be a sweetheart?

Student: Yes.

Don: How do they do that? How do they force girls to be a sweetheart?

Student: For example, he might say, 'Do you want to be my sweetheart and the people (are) looking at the girl (who) says, 'Okay. I accept that.' I am afraid that the other boys might force the girl until the girl accepts.

Don: The girls are afraid of boys? Is that true?

Student: Sometimes. Sometimes a boy will tell a girl, 'I want you to be a sweetheart with me and sometimes the girl will be afraid and she will accept that and say, 'Okay. Okay.' And she will accept that. Sometimes it will mean that they will have sex and it especially means that for the dormitory kids over here.

Don: Is it true that the boy might hurt her?

Student: If the girl does not accept what he says he will pick on her until the girl gives up.

Don: How does he pick on her?

Student: He keeps on loving on her again and again and again and the girl says, 'Stop it!' And he keeps on picking on her and touching her. The girl should tell the teacher but she doesn't because she was afraid that the boy would beat her harder.

Don: Does that happen often?

Student: Yes. It is common. It does not bother me. I will put karate on them. I wish all the girls would learn karate to defend themselves.

Don: Do boys bother _____ (your friend)?

Student: Yes, they do. When I see boys bothering her I get angry with that boy. I tell him, 'Don't you bother her. That is my friend.' They don't stand there. They take their hands off. I have to explain to them so they will understand clear. If I don't explain to them, maybe they will not understand.

Don: Can you think of another example of boys and girls over in the dormitory (doing) immature behavior?

Student: They are always playing around. They do not work in the classroom. Last year I noticed the girl in the classroom that she doesn't like and she went to the infirmary to sleep and missed one class. Then she goes and fools around all day.

Don: You notice that many of them do that? Just meander around?

Student: They do not work. They are bored. They want to have fun with the girls. They want to have sex and have fun and fool around.

Don: I wonder whey they are like that?

Student: Because it is habit. They grew up that way. Their parents did not fuss at them and correct them and teach them. People, the dormitory students are nitwits. Low minds. They don't learn much. Most of what they know is sex.

Don: Do they talk about that all the time?

Student: Always.

Don: Does that bother you?

Student: Yes, because I have many friends in the dormitory. My (best) friend is _____, a girl like me. Smart. And she is very good at English as I am. She went to a public school when she was young.

Don: Is she better than you with English?

Student: She is more skilled. She could hear before, but I am still happy with her but the problem is trying to help her to understand the deaf [her friend, hard-of-hearing, has come from a public school about one year ago]. She asks, 'Why' so and so and I have to explain to her.

Don: Tell me what she does not understand about the deaf.

Student: Boys are always picking on the girl, like I told you a while ago. I explained that to her.

Don: Does that surprise her?

Student: Yes. She is little bit flabbergasted. One other thing. The boys try to tease her about sign language, that she is (signing) wrong. I say, 'That is not nice!' And my friend says, 'What does it mean?' It means f-u-c-k. That word. And that is not nice so she is embarassed and so they fooled her and I have to teach her all the time. I have to teach her to understand. She is learning fast.

Don: Do the boys and girls have dates on campus here at this school?

Student: But it is silly. Remember I told you about immature? One boy asks a girl ... I told a boy to go out to Mountain City or some place but the boy does not understand what date means. He thinks date means (she stops and trys to find an English word) ... He thought date meant talking. I told him people go out to Mountain City (that) date must be alone. That they should not have a date in school just talking. They quickly become sweethearts!

Don: How does a boy ask a girl for a date?

Student: It is the same problem with a sweetheart: picking, picking, picking. That's what a date is. It is the same. They think that date means big sweetheart, but it is different.

Don: Do they go someplace on a date?

Student: No, but I think all their life no one permits them to have a date. Two years ago, Mr _____ the principal let boys and girls learn how to date and go to Pizza Hut (in Mountain City). Me and some others went and learned.

Earlier the mother of the student above was interviewed. Here she comments on the wide range of experiences she has provided her child and notice how she associates them with greater knowledge acquisition:

Mother: My daughter is as different from the other kids as night from day or as different from them as a deaf person is from a hearing person.

Don: In what way is she different?

Mother: She is self-confident. She studied karate. This karate also helped her to improve her studies since it teaches concentration. Next, she is more socially aware than other kids. By that I mean she goes ... travels more than other kids. These kids in the dorm do not go anywhere and they exhaust Doubletown by going to the grocery store and to the Dairy King. They go in their little huddle in groups. _____ (My daughter), for example, went to the karate tournaments and she was the only deaf kid there! ... When _____ (daughter) was younger other kids made fun of her good clothes because they were jealous. But as they got older they accepted her and the way she dressed. In middle school and the early eigth grade the kids were surprised that _____ (daughter) went home everyday. They respect her because they see my and her relationship with each other. You know they place lots of emphasis on awards and _____ (daughter) got many awards in the past year. The kids tell me how lucky she is. They say, 'I wish I could do that,' referring to the awards and the intelligence.

We have two themes here. One says that deaf students lack certain kinds of knowledge (proper male-female interaction norms) due in part to lack of teaching and lack of experience. A second theme points to a culture of horseplay summarized repeatedly by different interviewes in the term, "pick on." We asked the senior homecoming queen about it:

Don: I want to ask about sex now and if sometimes a boy will try to force a girl.

Queen: Yes.

Don: Is sex a big problem for the people here? Can you explain that to me?

Queen: A boy is a little bit rough on the girl. The girl told me, 'rough.' He hit her and hurt her. He hurt because the boy is hard on the girl. He should be easy and not hard.

Don: What's the biggest problem you have everyday in your life?

Queen: Boys bother me.

Don: They bother you? How?

Queen: They want me to be their sweetheart. I say, 'No.'

Don: How can a boy get a girlfriend? What's he got to do? How to be successful to get a girl?

Queen: If a boy acts nice to a girl, talks nice to the girl, maybe they will accept them.

[Earlier we had discussed her duties as homecoming queen]:

Queen: Many boys and girls come to see me for advice. I explain to the boys not to pick on the girls. Not to make fun of the girls. Not to hurt the girls. And they would ask different ways to be nice to girls. They say, 'Should I respect a girl?' And I say, 'Yes, and be nice to the girl.'

Don: Sometimes the girls come to see you also? Do they need the same advice?

Queen: Sometimes if a girl says, 'No' to a boy he would get angry and maybe pick on her.

Don: And hurt her? You mean hit?

Queen: Hit them or anything.

Honey, an upper middle class girl who just arrived this year at SSD initially faced much hostility and rejection from her new school peers. SSD students, she said, were jealous of her fancy car, her expensive and attractive clothes and her good speech. She, too mentions how some boys are physically rough with her:

One day I thought and thought and thought (that) the people here should not know my life. My other life (the hearing world) is not the same as here. One day I put on my jewelry and I dressed up like a hearing person and I came and they looked at me and they were surprised and they changed a little, more and more. I try to be patient. I try to hold my temper and not to show them that I was hurt. If they pinched me I just would not let them know that I was hurt. I would not let the boys bother me. One boy today, he pinched me and I was just quiet. He said, 'It hurt you!' But I was quiet. I held myself. So they did not bother me any more.

More discussion is given to this topic (horseplay) in Chapter Six.

Chapter IV

Signing as "Language"

> The detailed standardization found in oral languages is lacking in sign language and clearly limits the power of sign language.
>
> Aaron Cicourel

English and Sign Language: Words versus Ideograms

In this chapter we discuss differences between sign language and English, an issue introduced in the previous section. It seems axiomatic that some languages are more limited than others in terms of scope and breadth. For example, the language of one culture may include terms with no clear referents in the language of another culture. Too, the lexical terms of some languages allow more abstraction than others, thus their users have different worlds open to them (for example, where physics is and is not known). And within any given example, the greater the ability to use the language, the greater is one's ability to use abstractions. This is of importance at SSD since sign language may work very well *in that particular social world* with its parameters clearly defined, with its "life world" (Schutz's term) well known. But in stepping off the SSD campus into a more technological, complex world, the students' own language may no longer work well.

Sign language's uniqueness stems in part from its visual-physical quality – it must be seen. It is not English "in the air." It is an independent language which has its own rules. As one teacher said of SSD students, "They have a language of their own, a pattern, it seems to me from my observation. I don't know. I can't describe it ... their sentence structure is not what you would call standard English." ASL's conversational quality is generally understandable in the conversational context. It is literally a form of situated meaning. Unlike words, iconic signs do have a relationship to their referents (signs often resemble the things to which they refer). One observes deaf children who pucker, distort, exaggerate, stretch and shake their faces, heads and bodies; movements of face, eyes, eyebrows, lips, arms, shoulders, and knees give meaning not in *words* but in *ideas*. This necessity of physical dexterity makes ASL a whole style of communication which is only understandable by being observed.

Hand-to-Eye "Talk": A Public Language

Sight and hearing are the "distance-senses" for human beings. With peripheral vision, man can see half of his frontal surroundings. Hearing, however, is 360 degrees (omni-directional); you can hear what you cannot see. Deaf persons do not have this access to the world. As we said earlier, their tube-like, visual-gestural communication is restricted in its field of communication. Moreover, the visual-gestural side to sign language makes it a highly public form of communicating.

At SSD a girl attempted to "call" a boy who sat in front of her by fanning his back with a book. Banging on a desk is another technique for calling someone. In high school one student showed off his newly acquired driver's license but not all interested students could *see* what was going on. Three students were all making signs at the same time trying to get the attention of the licensee. For hearing people the analog would be a shouting match. In another situation two young boys, 11 and 12, sat in a crowded bus carrying students home for a weekend. With hands gesturing this way and that, many of the students necessarily sat backwards in their seats in order to converse with those behind them. In order to see what was going on, in order to participate in this larger community, the two boys sat on their legs in the seat but an ever-present houseparent told them to "sit down," thereby cutting them off from the flow of social language. For them and other deaf people, language must be seen to be understood.

One deaf teacher told of working in an office with hearing people and recalled how they would talk all day while they worked. At the same time, when she talked to someone by writing on a pad, her supervisor warned her about "wasting time." She felt it was unfair that others could chat during work but that she would be punished for briefly joining their symbolic community via pencil and paper. It is this pubic, necessarily visual quality of sign language that is especially problematic.

Privacy of language can be obtained, however, For example, two girls were observed "whispering" to each other on a school bus. They did this by fingerspelling at the bottom of each other's sweaters; in that way only the two of them could easily read the "whispered" message. (After dark this can be done by fingerspelling inside of one another's hands, as deaf husbands and wives do.)

Putting some physical distance between people is another technique to gain privacy. In a dorm one night, a teenage boy led Don away from another boy and with their backs to him, he pretended to "whisper" some gossip about him. This led to a series of exchanges as rebuttals, always having one's back to the person to be offended. Or, one boy would stand between one group and the other. It was always done in jest but it illustrates how deaf students "break" communication by blocking the view of the signers and how they "whisper" with a language that is otherwise public. Young students often dismiss frustrated teachers by simply closing their eyes.

This highly public quality to sign language permeates life at SSD. This, in part, explains why the sign "nosey" is used so often. It also explains the strong negative reaction of deaf students to those who speak English verbally without signing at the same time. If a hard-of-hearing student or a new student from an oral school uses vocal English, students will sometimes deride, stigmatize and reject the person. Why? Because the talking student is using an esoteric language which leaves out of the symbolic exchange those students unable to speechread. While all students do need and want some privacy, they are most often public or group minded (having a tribal consciousness as some anthropologists would say), and thus resent secret exchanges of information – particularly when it is done in English. They will only accept a deaf peer speaking English if he/she signs at the same time.

Sign Language of the Deaf is Stigmatized

While it is true that it is popular today for hearing people to learn sign language and that television stars can be seen "doing" a phrase of two in signs, the language remains different and "different" is often stigmatized. Minority groups have long fought and suffered attacks against their native languages because English-speaking schools have attempted to supplant their languages with English. Even at SSD there was a time when children were forced to sit on their hands to enforce verbalization and to stifle signs. Deaf adults have common stories of paper bags being tied over hands, of hands being spanked, etc.

In the public world there is stigma too with painful consequences for the signer. A deaf teacher (prelingual and profoundly deafened) tells how, in a restaurant, he was 'passing' as non-deaf until it came time to hear (i. e., his expressive communication was sufficient, but not his receptive [hearing, lipreading] skills). He is being served by a young man and things are proceeding smoothly; he has ordered food and then

> I tried to speak nice to the boy. The boy said, 'Uh huh.' He did exactly as I wanted. Everything I ordered he got and brought it to me. I said, 'Hey wait!' He was talking to me, but I said, 'Hey, I can't hear!' He was stunned! I tried to talk but he couldn't catch anything I said then. In the first place I should not have told him that I was deaf. As long as he thought I wasn't deaf, it was all right. He wouldn't notice that I had the incorrect voice. He thought I was deaf and he was shocked and he couldn't understand what I said. Before that, I didn't have any problems. After I told him I was deaf he was shocked.
>
> Don: Do you refuse to tell others now that you are deaf?
>
> Teacher: Right. If I go into a store I refuse to tell them unless I have to. I never want to depend on hearing people to help me. I rather do it myself. Depend, depend, depend. No way. Like a blind boy that came in one day, people said, 'Let me help you.' He said, 'No. let me do it myself.' I have the same feeling.

One mother of a deaf son tells how the public first reacted to their visual language (and the son's response):

> We've learned to adjust to many situations because of his deafness. Like going out in public and being stared at because you're signing to a child. Which never bothered me that much but it used to bother Gerry. And I told him, 'No problem.' I said, 'They're just interested. They're not staring because they think there's something wrong with you. They're just interested in what we're saying. And he accepted that. Then after that for a while he didn't want to talk anymore in public. He didn't want to be different. I told him it's all right to be different. It doesn't matter, no one's to blame. I said, we'll sign and talk. We'll talk with our hands but that's fine. Don't be ashamed. Never be ashamed that you're deaf. Always accept it and be proud of what you are. And he'll say, 'Why am I deaf and Bill (his brother) can hear?'

A high school student who resides at home discussed problems he had with parents and with deafness.

> Don: What else bothers you about being deaf? You told me it was a hard life. What is hard?

> Student: I have a hard time communicating with hearing people. I am afraid of hearing people. I am embarrassed. I can't communicate because I try to use my voice. My voice stops and I can't. I am just frustrated and I just leave.

Another deaf teacher at SSD told how she and her brother, who was also deaf, came to SSD at age 13. They had attended public schools before and could speak but did not know ASL when they arrived at SSD. "My parents made me promise not to use ASL, but to continue using my speech. I promised them that I would" (she made the sign of the cross over her heart then raised her right hand as if to take an oath). Her parents valued speech and devalued ASL which, nevertheless, eventually became her master language.

During an interview, one deaf adult who works at the school was asked, "What is the most important thing in your life right now?" At first, she thought it would have to be "independence," but then she added, "Education. I didn't learn enough language development (before) and I want to continue learning here ... I mean English language." Both hearing and deaf youth and adults tend to speak of the English language in a generic sense as "language." To be certain requires the researcher to ask which language one means, ASL or English (again illustrating the lack of taken-for-grantedness so common to a hearing person's everyday speech).

One night in the infirmary where Don lived, a 19 year-old senior sat in the lobby in her pajamas watching television and talking with staff members. When she saw him, she was talking to a deaf maid and, with him looking directly at them, she said, "Who is that man? I don't know him." She had seen Don sign to others and knew he had read her question but, presumably, it is normative to bluntly ask such questions even in the presence of visitors or strangers. Afterwards, Don sat and chatted with her. She told how she plans to go to college and study English. He asked, "Which is the better language, English or ASL?" "English," she said. Why? Her response was not expected. "Because they said so at a meeting." For many students and adults alike, sign language is a lowly second to English. Consequently, for others, there also exists language loyalty (something Fishman [1982] said needs to be researched).

Another example of this "English emphasis" was found in the lower school. The assistant principal, the only male in the lower school, called out two students from their classrooms so that he and Don could ask about their "inner selves." He had been told that students were unable to answer the question, "Tell me five things about yourself." He sent for his best student (who, it should be noted, was postlingually deafened). While sitting behind a large screen, in a private place, the boy was asked about himself and he began to list his school experiences: "Number 1, science; number 2, social studies; number 3, language ..." "What do you mean, 'language'?" "Verbs, nouns, period." In a generic sense, "language" meant English to him and school (group) life information was given in response to a query about his self.

Cultural Imperialism: Many Sign Systems

Although SSD is a "school for the deaf," those students who possess even limited hearing are at an advantage. Hard-of-hearing students often appear stupid in the hearing world because they frequently fail to respond appropriately to what was said to them; but at SSD these people have found a home. Indeed, with some speech and some hearing they are usually superior to the truly deaf in reading and writing and enjoy the added advantage of manual language (ASL) to fill in what their ears miss. As one hard-of-hearing girl said, "I feel good with myself. I understand with my fingers of signing." These students are more bilingual and bicultural than totally deaf students. When asked who learned English best at SSD (and consequently have better life chances after leaving SSD), an administrator quickly responded, "Those with hearing." In sum, we can state a simple and helpful proposition: The greater one's residual hearing the less one's cultural and symbolic deprivation. Again, *most* of our knowledge comes by learning language.

Like other languages, sign language is a symbolling system which is influenced by the social structure. In many ways the language is controlled and modified by hearing people. For example, the conventional sign for "coke" (Coca Cola) is to jab the index finger of one hand into the other arm just above the elbow. We usually mnemonically describe that sign as representing "a boost," "a pickup," or "a shot in the arm." (Don's father [born in 1901] would use a similar expression by saying "Let's stop and get a cold dope [coke]"). At SSD, nondeaf people (moral entrepreneurs) have decided that the sign conveys a bad connotation and they are trying to change it to a new sign which depicts and represents "pop." The old sign, they argue, looks too much like shooting drugs into the veins and might cause immorality among among deaf youth. They, too, believe that language influences behavior.

Nondeaf people not only dominate the school, its curriculum (there is only one deaf administrator at SSD and his power is small), and the moral value system, but also how the "native language" (as Cicourel and Boese, 1972, would have it) of its native speakers (signers) is to be used or changed. Nondeaf people at SSD invent new sign systems and modify the existing ASL for the deaf. Many of these efforts are intended to "improve" sign language which usually means to make it more like English. Consequently, many hearing "experts" now work to improve or develop basic ASL. Small wonder that detailed standardization is a constant problem.

Even Alexander Graham Bell, whose mother and wife were deaf, insisted that speech is the way to restore deaf people to society, that the use of both speech and sign language simultaneously (which is essentially what is used at SSD) has the disadvantage of injuring the precision of ideas (Moores, 1978:62). Bell is said to have believed that sign language is "ideographic, imprecise, inflexible, and lacking in subtlety and power of abstraction; it is a narrow prison intellectually and socially" (p. 79). The irony is that the language (signing) of otherwise languageless people is not seen as liberating but rather as imprisoning!

One deaf adult at SSD clearly stated a pervasive linguistic problem at the school:

> The worst thing in America today is that the deaf children are multilingual because one teacher will use ASL, another teacher will use SEE (Seeing Essential English), another teacher will use PSL (pidgin sign language), and so forth. Therefore, the children go from classroom to classroom and from school to school where they must be multi-language people – even with manual languages! Compare that to hearing children who hear Russian one hour, German the next, Spanish the next.

Most teachers and houseparents did not appear to be skilled with any sign system, and almost none of them are able to use ASL, the languages of the students. At least twenty percent of the teachers volunteered, "I am not very good at sign language." There are exceptions of course, including deaf teachers and deaf houseparents and some (but few) of the hearing people.

A top administrator is one of the skilled ASL users who can hear. During one of several interviews, he said that he feels we mistakenly "try to quantify things that are qualitative," which means that it is impossible to compare English to ASL. That, he says, is analogous to comparing oranges to apples. He, too, argues the belief that nondeaf people are trying to change sign language.

> Administrator: ASL is an art form and not a science.
> Don: What do you mean?
>
> Administrator: It is an art in its form and it is individualistic ... The attempts that we see going on today ... trying to make ASL have grammar and syntax ... we try to make ASL into our own English mold. We try to make ASL a delivery system which will fit into the English mold and I think that is why deaf people holler about ASL. They say the new grammatical and syntactical and initialized forms of sign language like SEE (are) not ASL and they tend to wish that hearing people who are developing ASL would leave it alone.

The real issue for us is not that deaf people should discard their ASL. The real issue is whether or not they will be bilingual, i. e., have the ability to use English as well as ASL. Yet deaf leaders and deaf teachers at SSD adamantly insist that TC (total communication) be used in academic situations. Again, TC at SSD does not include any speech training worthy of mention; it basically transmits ideas, not English words and children will not learn English with this system. This is the dilemma: deaf adults prefer TC but it will not effectively teach English.

While the majority of deaf teachers and staff eagerly provided assistance during the research, one of them suggested that deaf people keep *some* things to themselves (i. e., they do not tell hearing people all that they are thinking). Some ideas and practices are theirs in an exclusive way. This may be a reaction to the many hearing people's efforts to "improve" their language. As this person said, "Deaf people keep their secrets. For example, how do you spell moon?" When this had been fingerspelled, he responded, "A deaf person spells it 'm-o-n.'" He does not mean that moon is misspelled, but rather that native signers blur double letters whereas hearing signers (using their second language) are careful to include each of the double letters. Then he showed how a deaf person would spell the word "walking." As the letters were rapidly changing on the fingers, the entire hand was twisting and rolling. In this context, the deaf man said,

> We cannot tell black people to follow white English and it is the same for deaf people. We cannot tell deaf people that they must follow white English ... signed English. In fact, the old deaf people refuse to use the new signs. They continue the freedom to use comfortable language, ASL,

> and to communicate with ease. What will happen ten years from now with all these new signs and these new sign systems? I predict that ASL will be king.

Some deaf students hate English but simultaneously fear failure and rejection in the hearing world if they do not learn it. The researcher was somewhat surprised when the most popular senior boy, who is perceived by both teachers and students alike as very bright, told him his hatred and fear of that language and its users. Note how his self is threatened:

> Don: What bothers you most at SSD?
>
> Student: Well, (he blinked his eyes and pensively looked up) English is hard for me. I try to learn but never did put it down (get it down) and (it) made me bored. I tried, tried, made me angry. Study, study at home. Got me tired, but I have to learn. I must learn for when I finish school and try to talk to the outside people. They don't know what I say.

Sign Language Quality at SSD

We next turn to the quality and styles of manual language systems used by teachers, houseparents and staff. Manual languages are referred to generically as "sign language" because there are several types of sign language on campus. Officially, all teachers are supposed to use TC (total communication) but they do not. Most use a system of signs closer to signed English. Those students and adults who were prelingually deafened and/or who are profoundly deaf (and this is the majority) use ASL. In contrast to this, the postlingually deafened individuals are more likely to use something closer to signed English. As we shall see, this diversity of sign language codes is definitely problematic for the majority of students whose primary means of expression is ASL. Any judgement of "quality" of skill of any given signer is based on Don's own evaluation. In the following pages, different individuals' signs are assessed as either "good," "fair," or "poor," an admittedly subjective evaluation but one that is necessary to more adequately describe language use at SSD[5].

A number of empirical studies show that "the quality of adult-child interaction is related to children's intellectual development and academic success" (Boocock, 1980:76) but the overwhelming majority (over ninety percent) of parents do not know the language of their deaf children and do not teach them their own. One of the most unique attributes to ASL is that it is primarily peer learned. As one

SSD administrator said, it is "taught by children to children" not because it is restricted from parents, but because the children are the ones who need it for communicative purposes. They can teach it in a relatively unsophisticated manner of usage not requiring formal training. This is a case of the social structure determining the symbolic order. If ASL is generated and perpetuated informally by youth, then the possibility that the language is relatively undeveloped, unelaborated and unsophisticated is quite real (although it clearly can be sophisticated in its own way by creating context-bound situated signs for specific objects and events).

In light of ASL's preferred use among the children, one of our most striking findings is that most of the teachers, houseparents, administrators and staff are poor at using ASL (when they use it at all). The institutional emphasis at SSD is on the communication of ideas by any and all means (i.e., TC); emphasis is not solely on acquisition of English. This combination of using TC and late language acquisition results in the inability of *most* students to read or write English with any notable degree of competence. Because of this, they have serious problems wherever precise and sophisticated language is required.

At the same time that the students know little English, some teachers know very little sign language of any kind. One example is found in the vocational school where the formal educational level of teachers is far lower than that of teachers in the academic program. A teacher was asked if he taught his students the names of parts of a common office machine (upon which they were trained). He said,

> *Some* names, but not many. Their (English) language is very weak and that is understandable. (Why is their language so weak?) Well, the houseparents do not know how to teach deaf children. *I am not very skilled in ASL myself* (emphasis added).

After observing the teacher's sign language skills on two different occasions, they were indeed limited. Once during the interview he shook his head and spoke of the difficulty of ASL, a foreign language to nondeaf people:

> Our students use ASL and they leave out lots of information when they talk to each other. It is chopped up, and they reverse words. And their sentence structure is different. Rather than saying 'guess who?' they say 'who, guess?' *I have difficulty understanding them when they talk ASL.* On the other hand, if you put in every article and every word the kids get confused and don't understand what you're saying (in signed English) (emphasis added).

Although he had more than ten years experience working with deaf people at another social agency, he remarked again, "I am not very skilled in ASL myself."

For one week an experienced high school teacher was observed. Her sign language (which was not ASL, nor was it always TC, but was perhaps closer to a form of corrupted signed English) skills were no more than "fair." Her signs were small (in a spatial "box" and were relatively unexpressive) and moved in brief spurts, haltingly. As the students worked in their workbooks, the teacher said, in an apologetic manner, "Students have a sense of humor, especially when a teacher does not sign well, like me." During the course of the research at least 8 to 10 teachers made such "apologetic" remarks, i. e., disclaimers, about their lack of sign language skills.

During one interview she discussed how deaf and hearing teachers interact very little on the playground or in the teacher's lounge. She was asked why the two groups were so segregated. She, too, perceived the language problem between hearing teachers and deaf teachers (who use two different codes):

> Well, they're interested in different things. And there's so *few* of them (deaf teachers). But they can sit down and go into great length ... you don't have many hearing teachers that can communicate (with sign language) well because we haven't had total communication that long.

The latter statement refers to the days of strict oralism at SSD which ended in 1973. To illustrate the language barrier she explained that if two deaf teachers and one hearing teacher got together "the deaf have to go so slow." The hearing teacher might be able to sign to the deaf teachers, "but when the deaf persons talk (sign) to them, they don't know" (what was said). To put it bluntly, hearing teachers often have problems with receptive communication.

> They don't even know what these kids are saying! ... And they (deaf adults) won't take the time. Just like the hearing don't want to take the time to explain to them different things. So, rather than waste the time, the hearing go this way and the deaf go this way (left and right gestures which indicated opposite directions). I don't believe one of our deaf teachers has *ever* been in that (staff) lounge!

Do *deaf* teachers notice the lower level sign skills of their hearing colleagues? How would they feel about them? One of the (six) deaf teachers was asked about this. He said that recently "the deaf demanded that hearing people use signs when we are in their presence." Secondly, he said, "the deaf demanded that hearing interpreters be very expert, very skilled," signifying that deaf adults at the school were unhappy with sloppy interpreting. Another deaf teacher told how deaf-hearing relationships often intersect along communication and language lines. He wished the administration would set up a system whereby teachers would be paid and promoted "on the basis of experience and communication skills ... But the administration accepts (academic) degrees ahead of communication abilities." And still another deaf teacher said

> I tell them, you know one thing only! You don't know enough yet. I emphasize communication here. I emphasize that teachers should communicate on the level of the kids. *One thing that bothers hell out of me is that the teachers come in here (SSD) from a hearing school and they cannot sign!* (emphasis added).

While the deaf teachers get angry with the hearing teachers, the relationship is reciprocal. In some conversations with hearing teachers they would get red-faced with anger because they "interpret for free" (i. e., they interpret for hospitals, attorneys or others who have a deaf person there but no one who can sign). In general, however, the hearing teachers seemed well aware of their inability to sign well. Two hearing teachers were asked, "Do you have any idea what percentage of teachers can use sign language well?" Without delay the first teacher estimated, "about ten percent sign well. But *most* teachers in lower school can't (sign well). It would be a very high percentage ... ninety percent (cannot sign well) I would say." The second teacher made an estimate of the high school situation: "I would say forty or fifty percent sign well, really sign well" (the same figure was cited by two high school students, independent of each other). The first teacher chimed in, "But when it comes to reading signs they don't understand it."

During an interview with two other teachers, a deaf teacher expressed a similar view that many teachers at the school do not sign well:

> I think Ameslan (an acronym for American Sign Language) is what we need at SSD. *Most* teachers, *most* teachers do not know how to sign. They use SEE, signed English, and the kids sit in their classes and are bored, bored. I think it's OK to use SEE in an English class but ASL should be used in all other classes. They should be given concepts, the children need concepts.

The other teacher commented that "I don't really think it's (English) teachable."

There are, of course, some teachers who sign very well, and this was true at all grade levels. Too, some age and grade levels of school require less sophisticated language, as in the lower school where many teachers command sufficient signs and skills to communicate with young, near languageless children. However, even where skills are relatively good, the signs are usually closer to signed English than to ASL. Although certainly not true for all SSD teachers, the comment of one staff member seems poignant: "Some teachers here sign sloppy, sloppy, sloppy."

The following narrative told by a nurse illustrates the general poverty of sign language abilities on campus:

> Workers here get eight hours per week of in-service training, of sign language training in the summer. The teacher (giving signs to staff members) in this case was a hearing person whose parents were deaf. To the class he signed and mouthed, 'I not have BM today.' No one understood, so he signed and mouthed, 'I not shit (thumb pulled from other clinched first) today.' Many houseparents did not know what he said!

She definitely believes that considerable numbers of staff members are unskilled signers and it is not unique to the infirmary.

> No one evaluates me to see if I can sign. My supervisor may write *something* about me (for the record). All of us signed a paper that says we must be fluent in sign language within twelve months, but we know it is not enforced at all.

Of all employees at SSD, houseparents and infirmary personnel had the lowest level of sign skills. Most nurses and their aides use sign language very poorly. They have difficulty with both expressive and receptive aspects of sign language. Out of a total of eight nurses and aides observed only two nurses could sign "good," two aides were "fair" and all others were very poor.

The following incident illustrates the barriers and language inadequacies involved in the health care region of SSD. Anyone who has ever fallen ill or suffered some accident in a foreign country can understand the type of problems faced by sick or injured deaf students whose caretakers (in the infirmary) may not know their language. One evening a teenage boy assaulted a teenage girl. Immediately afterwards Don walked into the infirmary where the injured girl had come for treatment. In the meantime, the nurse's aide (no nurse was on duty that night) had fled down a corridor of the adjacent boys' dorm with a silver spoon because the boy (who had beat up the girl) was now having a seizure and was swallowing his own tongue. A second nurse's aide was left behind in the infirmary but she was unable to effectively sign and communicate to others who were waiting until the urgency was over in the boys' dorm. Using awkward signs and gestures the aide tried to tell the others to sit down, and to wait because a boy was having a seizure. Because the aide was unable to transmit that message in sign language, Don explained to the bewildered and curious students just what the commotion (and the delay) was all about.

For resident students, houseparents are a very important group. They spend more time with students than any other set of adults on or off campus. Thus, they have much more time to talk and interact with them. Houseparents could be significant others for these youth who are far removed by space *and* language from their actual family members. This fact has long been recognized by SSD administrators and other similar schools.

In the 19th century residential schools were viewed as custodial places and not as educational ones. Houseparents had little education and thus received very low salaries (N. A., N. P. – from a mimeographed article supplied by SSD)[6]. The superintendent of the Oregon State School for the Deaf allegedly worked to "drastically" upgrade the houseparents position because "Counselors [or houseparents] work with the pupils more hours per week than do the teachers" (p. 136, above article). He assailed the 6 to 8 hours per day in which children are "under the care of untrained people who are only babysitters or policemen" (p. 136).

Unfortunately, the greatest waste of human life and of potential mental development is located in the boring and useless after-school hours at SSD. Houseparents are primarily policeman and babysitters and, in general, mere custodians of inactive baggage during their working hours. The overwhelming majority of houseparents have low, low sign language skills. During a bus trip home for a weekend, it was possible to observe a houseparent who accompanied the bus driver. Along the way he would frequently stand up and angrily shake his index finger and/or shake his head negatively *and* either spell or fumble with a few rough signs in order to fuss at excited students. After almost 5 years at SSD his skills were minimal.

One of the few deaf houseparents was asked about the signing ability of the hearing houseparents. Can they sign well? His terse response was, "No. Many of them don't." Both students and (some) parents were aware of this problem. As one mother said, "Some of the houseparents don't have signs enough to explain things to the kids!" Complaints were common among the students. For example: "Sometimes I help the houseparent understand." (Understand what?) "They are a little weak on signs . . Most of them talk." "Weak" is probably too kind a characterization. The damning aspect of this, especially given the good which could be accomplished by caring, competent people, was dramatically stated by another student.

> [Houseparents] always sitting talking to another houseparent (who) can hear. They never talk with students ... They don't learn sign language so it's best (for them) to talk ... We read their lips ... It makes me angry inside. My stomach goes around and around (churns). I need houseparents (want them) to learn sign language.

The Uses and Misuses of Icons

Part of the reason that many faculty and staff members are weak signers may be that they come to SSD quite by chance. In the words of one staff member, "I fell into it ... I got it basically because I live in a nearby town." He said that he knew no signs at that time. In this rural section of the state the school can hardly expect to have access to a large pool of adults trained in special (or deaf) education. Consequently it often draws upon the local populace whether or not they are acquainted with deaf people and deaf language.

SSD does provide some sign language training for its personnel. For example, a video tape recorder and player were placed in the infirmary with tapes which were lessons of basic signs. A nurse and Don examined portions of the first two or three tapes which were so elemental as to be useful for someone who has never seen a sign. (There were staff members at the school who actually needed that kind of help). Other tapes, presumably more advanced in nature, were available yet only once was anyone seen watching a tape. Since Don's room was near the infirmary, where he would have easily noticed people viewing the tapes, it is certain that the tapes were used very little.

One administrator had recently visited another school for the deaf where success with learning English is said to be the highest in the country. He wanted to find the key to such success.

> There must be consistency of the sign system no matter what system (of signs) it is. If it is ASL or SEE or Manual English or whatever ... We must lay a base and build on it but we have not yet done this at SSD.

> ASL can be a base by modifying it to give syntax, etc. and by initializing many signs and modifying and improving the basic ASL.

He says it is clear to him that SSD uses multiple sign systems, and none of these especially well; that ASL is more of a restricted than elaborated code. It can be a "base" but not the whole language.

A deaf (former) teacher (now working at SSD in another capacity) said, "One problem at SSD is that teachers do not know how to sign properly such sentences as, "My nose is running." Many teachers, he said, use the wrong sign for "run"; they might use an ideographic sign which depicts bipedal running instead of using the ideographic for "dripping," (four fingers flicking in a downward stroke from the nostril). Again, the point is that coherent, consistent instruction is impossible in the face of multiple sign systems, none of which are executed meaningfully for students and teachers alike.

One teacher permitted students to sign, "I spent my vacation in Canada." Students used the sign "spend," which ideographically represents the idea of spending money (the right hand repeatedly removes money from the left hand). Such errors were common among students. One student used the sign for "blind" – two fingers in front of the eyes signifying lack of eyesight – to refer to window blinds.

A communications specialist at SSD helps to standardize and, sometimes, initialize signs (making a gross sign into a more specific – elaborated – sign) as well as disseminating information about the never ending creation of new prefixes and suffixes for sign language. He, as much as anyone, is sensitive to the problems with multiple sign systems at SSD.

> The students should not be multi-lingual people where both deaf and hearing teachers are using different sign languages to the children, such as SEE-1, SEE-2, ASL, Pidgin sign language, and so forth. It makes no sense for a hearing teacher to teach kids French and Spanish at the same time they teach English. Therefore, deaf kids should not be exposed to many sign languages in different classrooms. It is a crime. Many hearing people use signed English because they say ASL is 'bad English.' Who do they satisfy? Themselves! Not deaf people.

This person (and others as well) believes that teachers in classrooms should teach deaf students standard signs, but they do not. And if a child says, "I see five bird," the teacher should tell him "bird" with an "s" (in sign language). As the specialist commented, "I believe in 25 years ASL and SEE will converge ... Some books are adding new affixes, but they are not throwing out ASL." Phrased more analytically, ASL is moving from a restricted code toward an elaborated code of communication, from particularistic to universalistic forms. It is having its range of abstractions (subtlety, nuance, and so on) expanded. The supreme expression of that move is the use of fingerspelling which is probably used more often as one's level of education increases.

A real problem at SSD is the lack of speech training, which makes the use of TC especially troublesome. One person said his "dream" was for deaf students to acquire good language although he despaired somewhat because basic ASL is not now widely used at SSD. Several hearing parents of deaf students especially complained about the paucity of speech training at the school. TC, of course, requires – by definition – the use of speech, signs, gestures, writing, mime and so forth. To learn it requires a kind of Gestalt philosophy of language which students must fully comprehend. Our observation is that sign language (defined here as near signed English), not ASL (the language of the students) and not TC (the ideological philosophy of the school), is the *modus vivandi* inside classrooms at SSD.

On one occasion Don was talking with three teachers. All agreed that speech (which is, of course, English) is underemphasized today in contrast to a decade ago. As one teacher said:

> I don't know that I can explain it but we've had kids come here who had a good bit of hearing and then later on *they're acting more and more deaf* ... and it's not just the fact that *they stop using their speech*, which is a bad thing that does happen, I hate to say ... (about ten years ago) when we had the teacher training and every teacher was a speech teacher, our kids had pretty good speech, most of them. I don't mean *great* speech ...
>
> Another teacher interrupts: They could pronounce the words anyway.
>
> First teacher continues: And now since we don't have that, the kids really don't get speech training. (A former teacher later said it was a "lie" that students could generally talk orally ten years ago, that signed English is not the panacea for SSD).

This supports our contention that (1) TC is not really the principle language system of the school, and (2) English is given lower emphasis than other codes. Who benefits from this approach?

In general, what happens in classrooms at SSD is that ideas are transmitted with condensed, abbreviated and compacted phrases as opposed to elaborated, full, and more explicit phrases or sentences. While ASL is said to be compacted too (see Klima and Bellugi,

1979:87,194) and can give information in single sign units because of its simultaneous organization, nevertheless, there is an important difference when used by incompetent, inexpressive signers. Much information (meaning) of ASL is located in the "grammar" of the body – facial and eye movements, intensity of motion, etc. These meanings are absent whenever a hearing person provides compact phrases without using the extra body information. It seems inconceivable that students could spend 16 years with diverse types of sign language and then graduate with any degree of competence with the English language. The quantity of English acquired in the English classrooms is microscopic compared to the ocean of non-English within which students maneuver throughout the years at the school. To argue, as one administrator did, that English is reinforced in every classroom (teachers correcting students' poorly signed English) is a myth. Students are literally environed by multiple manual codes, the least one being a standardized system of signed English (SEE).

Compacted Language: "I'm a man of few words"

At SSD deaf students punctuate the completion of a sentence or an idea with the signs "finished" (which also means, "completed") and "that's all" (two signs). This pattern of language and thought is seen in the quotation below. These are interesting since they derive from interviews with hard-of-hearing students who signed and verbalized simultaneously. Their speech was not clear enough to tape record although, while watching their signs, it was possible to hear and understand most of their statements. Often their speech was "choppy" and condensed like the ASL they use (Klima and Bellugi, 1979, say ASL is "compacted" and "economizes").

One middle school boy was asked to tell a "story" about the events (schedule) of his life during a typical day at SSD. These excerpts of "deaf language" are not more than 70 or 80 percent of what he literally said since it was necessary to "interpret" his messages into nearly correct English, while trying to retain a sense of his overall form of expression.

> In my class my teacher ask me to go to town and buy some clothes in town. Bought some shoes and toothpaste (first interpreted as "brush my teeth") and then we finished and go to the Burger King and eat a big, big sandwich. Eat, eat, eat. *Finished.*

It is noteworthy and perhaps significant that personal pronouns are often omitted, especially "I." But, after all, "ASL uses no pronouns" (Benderly, 1980:1975) and, says ASL expert Louie Fant, it relies heavily on context to clarify [imaginary persons, objects] pronouns ..." i. e., objects pointed to (1972:24). Sometimes a deaf person simply points to an imaginary second (or third, or fourth) person instead of signing or spelling "he" or "she". It is hardly a surprise, then, that a high school teacher said her students often do not know the English pronouns! The boy was asked to explain what he did early each morning:

> Houseparents come in little late and we have to get up and take bath, put on our clothes, brush teeth, sit ... TV, at 7:00 o'clock it's time to go eat ... all of us. *Finished.* Talk, talk, talk. Come back to the dorm about 8:00 o'clock [most pronouns added].

In another part of the narrative he said "we go to P. E., play volleyball, finished at 11 o'clock ... then we go back to class and have math until 12:50 and go eat, *finished.*"

A hard-of-hearing high school boy also punctuates or "summarizes" his sayings (or perhaps it is a sign which functions like a period at the end of a sentence or like the lowering of one's voice at the end of an utterance).

> Don: What's the most important thing in your life right now ... today?
>
> Student: Grow up in my life. Become an adult, a man. I can't wait to graduate from high school. I want to go to college to be an actor and then I'll be playing on the TV. Work to be an actor. *Finished.* But I want to have good food and health in my life. *That's all.*
>
> Interviewer: What problems do you have at SSD?
>
> Student: Yesterday I had an argument with my friend. Then we got mad with each other again. Then we forgot about it and become good friends again. *That's all.*

He was asked to tell about events that transpire during the course of any given day of his life.

> Sunday morning, same (as other days). Get ready to go to church at 9:45. At 12:15 come back to the dining room and eat and then go back to the dorm. *Finished,* I rest ... Last time (last weekend) boys and girls go home. School close and *that's all.*

A third and final example of this abbreviated closure to conversations and streams of thought comes from a hard-of-hearing boy from the lower school. He was asked what he liked best at SSD. "The best thing I like about the school is reading and I like the teacher, Mrs. Mayday. (I) like the gym, play basketball and track. *That's all.*"

The compact syndrome and the "finished" summary statements are salient in this boy's sign and verbal communications. His responses, using signs and voice, were extremly condensed and very dependent upon contextual factors to help fill in the gaps. What do you do when you go home?

> I went home and I met some boys and girls and I said, 'Hi.' Some boys and girls ... for me ... happy ... come here! . . play, play ... dog run with me ... walk to fishing . . many, many fish. Bass, catfish ... *Finished.* Go home ... walk, walk. Eat, eat. *Finished.* Travel with grandmother. Clothes, shoes, toothbrush and visit grandfather ... loves me.

It seems fair to say that the students cannot be more competent at signing (in whatever form, including signed English) than those around them. The world they experience is a fragmented one in which most of their own "scripts" appear as a pastiche – bits and pieces of some larger text. While English is the language of the dominant culture, English is something that SSD students are generally poor at. And this skill deficiency is exacerbated by an instructional staff which – by its own admission – is often not on the same (sign) wave length as the students. As one teacher despairingly said: "We don't teach our kids any language patterns ... Our kids don't learn to read and write. Why?" Indeed.

Behind Closed Doors: Student Ignorance in English

At SSD the world is primarily a concept-world much more like that of primal/tribal peoples than of Western (scientific, linear, rational) peoples (Highwater, 1981). It is the one in which students are comfortable; it is the one they generally prefer. But after leaving SSD, their entire lives will be surrounded by the "word-world," for it is in that world they must earn a living and act out their daily lives. Many students (and deaf teachers) seem to have little realization of that reality as they push and fight for ASL or TC as their first language at SSD. They seem unconcerned about the future world where reading and writing (literacy) are needed. Many students said sign language was the "best" language. While the ethnocentric side of this is understandable, a widespread attitude at SSD naively says, "take your stinking English and shove it. I have a language of my own"[8].

The overwhelming majority of students at SSD displayed an incredible poverty of English abilities. For them it was the "other symbolic world," to be ignored whenever possible. A veteran high school teacher painfully contrasted her present students with an outstanding former student who could recount details of things observed. She is frustrated at the lack of students' observations of written English "markers" out there in the world:

> I tried to get the other kids to notice things and come tell me ... when they're with mom and daddy going to the store to notice signs like, 'so and so river' or 'so and so street' and learn the word *river*, learn the word *street*, learn the name of the store. They won't do it. And I'll think, how many rivers have they gone over (and) seen that sign? Why don't they know that that is what a river is? And how many street signs have they seen? Why don't they get that in there?

Whenever she asks students to spell "river" or "street," students reply, "never seen that word before."

Even the brightest students do not know many common English words. The homecoming queen, described by one teacher as *the* student who best understands English and English idioms, did not know the word "abstractions." Another example is seen in the attempt of a high school teacher to discuss with two students the use of frequent negative signs (terms) on campus. The teacher, competent with ASL, first tried to ask the question in terms of "positive and negative attitudes." Afterwards, he intended to ask specifically about the common usage of many negative signs (stupid, dumb, MR – mentally retarded, NG – no good, etc.) The boys, however, had no understanding of the concept "positive and negative attitudes." One boy said he had never heard of it. Then, as the usual approach is, the teacher embarked upon a long story which illustrated hypothetical situations involving positive and negative responses in social encounters. The point here is that two normal high school boys had no understanding of "positive and negative attitudes," whether presented by fingerspelling (English on the hands) or in sign language.

One day a staff member, while discussing ASL and its syntax, mentioned the extent of the problem:

> We don't teach our kids any language patterns. some use ASL, some use signed English, some TC (total communication). ------- (a deaf female colleague), a college graduate can't write a one-paragraph memo. She gets me to rewrite all her memos. She said if there was a workshop of her choice it would be on writing memos. A college graduate who can't write! Our kids don't learn to read and write.

These examples are neither unusual nor atypical. Whether rivers, streets, abstractions, attitudes, etc., for many SSD students, English is a conceptual wasteland and stories often of some length are required to illustrate meaning at practically any level.

The poverty of *word knowledge* is accompanied by the general inability to use English syntax. TC and ASL are not English. Mindful of that, one teacher declared, "I can't say to the kids, 'Write a sentence the way you sign it.' They could do that maybe if they had the (English) vocabulary." Don suggested that "The sign is an ideogram and if one doesn't know a *word* for an ideogram, then one doesn't have (English) vocabulary." The teacher agreed, "Right. Like the sign (shaking the right hand, fingers spread). How are you going to write that?"

In ASL there are many signs whose mimetic qualities are situated to a given moment and/or place. Consequently a teacher would have difficulty telling a signer, "Now, write in English what you just signed." The difficulty would involve changing an ideographic spatial message into a set of sequential discrete words (as mentioned earlier, many signs represent and resemble referents whereas words do not, i.e., many signs contain much iconicity while words are purely arbitrary symbols of objects). From classroom to classroom, very few teachers actually train students to write *complete* English sentences. Most of the time students fill in blank spaces with words or a single letter (e.g., _ able = table). This occurred commonly at most grade levels. Can students learn English well when some other language (ASL, TC) system is more often used? Can students learn English syntax and vocabulary by filling in tiny blanks?

It is necessary to emphasize and to illustrate how deaf students at SSD occupy a visual-gestural-iconic-ideographic-global-conceptual (non-English) world. The following is a classic example. It is provided by a high school teacher who was told by one of her students that he had found a job.

> Teacher: What is the name of the place where you're working?
>
> Student: I don't know.
>
> Teacher: You work there and you don't know the name of it? Tonight when you go to work, you look and see what's the name of it (the store).
>
> Student: I clean up and I fix Coca-Colas.
>
> Teacher: You don't work at the Coca-Cola company. I *know* that. Where do you work?

Student: I work in the mall.

Teacher: That's fine. What's the name of the place? Tonight you look.

The following day the conversation resumed as follows:

Student: The name's up there (points upward meaning over the entrance of the store).

Teacher: What?

Student: It's colored orange.

Teacher: What's the name (of the store)?

Student: Orange (teacher: That's all he could remember).

Again he was told to look for the name of the store where he worked. The teacher recounted, "Well, he came back (the next day) and he had learned, 'The Orange Bowl.' And I said, 'That's the place you work when somebody asks you.'" With a look of incredulity and with head shaking to and fro, she added, "And he was a senior." A second teacher sitting nearby added, "It amazes me that they don't notice things like that. It amazes me."

Another example derives from an interview with a girl who was labeled "slow" by several teachers. "Do you want a car in the future?" She said, yes, and when asked "what kind?" She said, "Green car and brown. I forgot the name." Like the male student above she lives in a world of global symbols where objects are often signified by their intrinsic properties, large/small, pretty/ugly, green/brown, as opposed to English symbols which differentiate objects by name/labels and/or properties. One student said he would "go to college" after he graduates. Which college? "I forgot its name," he replied. This was repeated by a girl who said she wanted to be a nurse. Where would she study? "Forgot name of a college." These examples further illustrate a major point: the students do not know much English. *Ipso facto,* little English gets used in their thought processes. One wonders how much of their world is unnamed? Could they sit in a room with 100 objects (and/or events) and know what only 25 or 50 of them "are?" This is what we mean when we suggest that some of them live in a world of "gaps."

If one thinks of a place but has neither signs nor words to label the referent then what sense of the place exists for the individual? Is it only a kind of ideographic, mental picture? How sophisticated and complex can thought be under those conditions? In fact, more fundamentally, what is "thought" under those conditions? (Again, see Furth on this general point). Is reality holistic, undifferentiated and more blurred than, say, sharply divided regions of the hearing or word-cut world? We believe the holistic concept-world dominates the word-world at SSD. It is a more simplistic, less abstract view. This notion is supported somewhat by a teacher's comments below. She explains some preferred qualities for anyone who might want to teach deaf children. She calls for even more pictures:

> I've always thought that if you were going to teach deaf that first off you ought to be able to draw ... There are so many things that you need to explain to deaf children and you start trying to explain it and draw it. I wish so much that I could draw. If you could draw you could show them.

A child with language ordinarily moves from a focus on the physical world to the social to the ideational; from unreflective activity to abstract conceptualization (Boocock, 1980). But this movement towards the abstract is less complete for many deaf children. The teacher above listed other traits a teacher should possess: patience, good working use of TC, some skill with ASL and "it helps a lot if you can pantomime." There was no mention of skills for teaching English words. Another teacher says her (middle school) students are 'concrete minded,' because "if I write 'Uncle Joe, is coming to see me Saturday' the kids say. 'Who is that?' I say I just imagined an 'Uncle Joe.' But they feel that I *must* know him if I write about him." During an interview ten years earlier at SSD Don had a similar problem. Don would ask students, "If you take a date to the movies, who pays for the tickets?" Student after student replied, "Never have a date! Never a date to movies!" The "if," the hypothetical, is beyond them.

The concept-world of deaf students is global, restricted, and often presented in polar types. It lacks fine, precise pictures/signs/ideograms with which to partition reality, especially as such realities are experienced in industrialized, urbanized, pluralistic, technological society. In the vocational school at SSD, where one finds much technology, there is a world of objects (tools, machines) which have few or no signs to represent them. In twentieth century advanced industrial society, technological knowledge is a must and the technology which exists grows ever more complex. The inability of deaf students to comprehend even a simpler technology (such as auto mechanics) illustrates the problems they have. As a vocational teacher stated:

> Our language has verbs, adverbs and we have to change our (English) language for them. For example, I'll tell them to go measure a micrometer but they don't know what that is. They don't know what a lathe is. And they have trouble putting a new word (labeling) on a machine. For example, they don't say, 'alternator is broke,' they say 'motor broke.' A boy told me last year about his girl friend. He made her sign, but he could not spell her name ... You are either ugly or pretty. You are bad or good. The hardest thing for me to tell them when they are working on a machine is 'a little bit more' (pressure, or twist). They know just enough to get by.

Images, Ideas, and Language: Features of the Group

Social structures and symbolic orders exist in a type of dialectical relationship, each helping to give rise to and maintain the other (see Berger and Luckmann). In this way, language at SSD evolves; it is largely shaped, nurtured, and maintained by children for children. While such a system may have its own sophistication, the degree of sophistication (no matter how ingenius it may seem) is not likely to rival languages whose very foundation is dependent on adults. It is not likely that children will teach other children a language that is terribly abstract, subtle, and so on.

Of course in small, closed societies characterized by mechanical solidarity (such as those discussed by Bernstein in his comments on Durkheim), members may take-for-granted that other members understand the *full* implications to all symbols utilized. In fact, the language used may be a code of implicit meanings peculiar to and functional for the local group. SSD is such a community. It represents what Shibutani (1978) has conceptualized as a "social world" which is "a cultural area, the boundaries of which are set neither by territory nor by formal group membership but by the limits of effective communication" (p. 113). It is a social world of common communication styles and common perspectives (i.e., shared world views). As Shibutani (and virtually all authors cited thus far on the deaf) notes, such worlds can develop from segregation. As examples he cites, "the academic world, the world of children, the world of fashion." We would add "the world of the deaf."

Not only does every social world have a communication system but as Shibutani states, there also "develops a special universe of discourse, sometimes an argot. Special meanings and symbols further accentuate differences and increase social distance from outsiders"

(p. 113). Of course these same points have been made (and cited by us earlier) by Cicourel and Boese, Bernstein and Goffman. At SSD, the "special meanings and symbols" are given very localized referents, the isolation of which is exacerbated by the normal, everyday peer group surroundings. Thus, virtually all of one's time is spent with other deaf peers. This leads to a kind of homogeneity to not only things experienced *but*, importantly, to what can be experienced. As one teacher said in describing the students going to McDonald's and saying little about it later: "(T)hey all do it together. Maybe that's the reason. They do it together and everyone knows it (the experience of the trip) so why tell them?" Marx, in an initial formulation of the sociology of knowledge, posited that what was known (i. e., existing knowledge) was equatable to what could be known. Homogeneous groupings, not unlike the Dark Ages, give rise to limited views of the world *and* it is the language in conjunction with the prevailing ideology which determines the degree to which this will be found.

Like Goffman's "inmate," SSD students do things together – always in groups. Their social world is truly a restricted one. It is a "we group" characterized by a kind of mechnical solidarity. Whenever they travel to the outside world (e. g., McDonald's), their unique network of communication remains unbroken. They are virtually untouched by the English speakers of that other universe of discourse. They rarely return to campus describing and/or embellishing upon what some hearing stranger said or tried to say to them at McDonald's or elsewhere. The hearing and deaf worlds seldom meet and ideas between them are seldom exchanged. For these deaf children, for whom English is truly minimal, the future in a hearing world is grim. In a painfully candid confession, a high school teacher said:

> I'm saying this on a tape recorder, but our deaf people are going to have a terrible time. The ones that graduated 10 years ago are in the lower strata of society by and large. They're mopping hospital floors and working on assembly lines and still reading on a fifth grade level – very isolated, lots of them.

Chapter V

The Institutional Side of Life: The Official Culture

> Deaf adolescents do not have access to the means of communication that other young people use to learn about things like sex. They do not spend time talking with friends on the telephone. They do not hear radio or records or go to the movies. They do not read novels, because most of them do not read well enough to plow through an edition of say, *Catcher in the Rye*. Even Rapunzel, in an impossibly high tower, could not have led a more narrowly circumscribed existence than do the deaf.
>
> Jayne Greenstein[9]

Philip Jackson (1968) is among those who have argued that educational researchers may need to move "up close" to adequately study and understand in-school processes. This is a position we support. Although not antagonistic toward surveys and other quantitative research procedures, we agree with Lofland (1971) that face-to-face interaction is "the fullest condition of participating in the mind of another human being."

In the tradition of the Chicago school of sociology we, too, have chosen a qualitative, ethnographic approach to our subject matter. We believe that to understand how language is acquired, one must observe first-hand the social processes which occur in a language-learning context. At the same time, the context itself (i.e., social relationships and their situatedness) must be investigated – its dynamics must be charted. Bossert (1979:ix) has criticized the typical school study because of the "simplistic, input-output and 'black-box' designs" which are so often utilized. This approach, he contends, fails to relate structural properties of schools and classrooms to what students and teachers actually do. For Bossert, the social organization of the classroom is the important object for inquiry; recurrent instructional tasks, the structure of activities are the factors which shape both teacher and pupil behavior. It is this institutionalized quality of life that we explore in the next two chapters.

The Total Institution

The total institution is conceptualized by Goffman (1961) as "a place of residence and work where large numbers of like-situated individuals, cut off from the wider society for an appreciable period of time, together lead an enclosed, formally administered round of life" (p. xiii). In such places, all activities are controlled by the same authority; everyday life is highly regimented. The typical normative process is one of mortification – a deadening or denying of what had previously been accepted as "normal" behavior. At SSD, however, total enculturation is the common and typical normative process since there is insistence on learning the norms of the society at large. This includes a school policy of students acquiring skill in spoken and written English. As a total institution, then, SSD transmits not only its values, beliefs and sentiments but also language which will enable the individual to adapt him/herself to the general society.

Our analysis focuses upon the official and unofficial cultures of SSD. This entails a brief analysis of the school as published in the *Student Handbook* – a graphic example of school norms constituting the official culture. Too, in examining the official culture, it is necessary to present world views of administration, teachers and staff. This also allows for discussion of different types of sanctions utilized at SSD. Next, we consider the student culture including the underlife, student world views (with special mention of sexual beliefs) and the student stratification system. This allows us to analyze the unofficial school culture as acted out by its main participants.

The Official Culture

In its fifteen pages, the *Student Handbook* provides a succinct statement of the school's official culture. Similar to most school handbooks, the one at SSD begins on a positive note, emphasizing attainment of the "best." Thus, it states on the cover sheet, "Our goal is to help every student to do the best that he or she can ..." On page one it states, "[Students are expected to behave] in such a way as to make their education the best." Thereafter, there exists a fairly common school practice of providing a litany of things which "are not permitted." These run the gamut from very serious (e. g., drugs, sex, abuse of staff) to less serious (tardy for class, horseplay on a school bus, etc.). Throughout, the message is crystal clear – in helping every student to do his/her "best," those in control must have a firm grip on running the school. The prevailing axiom is the greater control, the less trouble hence the "best" education.

Unlike a regular school, however, at SSD most students board; students are technically wards of the state since the school legally serves as *en loco parentis*. Thus, the tenacles of school control and authority reach further than they otherwise would; consequently school may be a "far more important later life determinant (as an independent variable) – than for hearing children ..." (Fishman, 1982:15). As Goffman (1961:6) notes about total institutions more generally, they are bureaucratically organized to handle "blocks of people" with their diverse needs. These needs are met not through individuation but rather, regimentation whereby one must adhere to prescribed norms in nearly every situation: "minute segments of a person's line of activity may be subjected to regulations and judgments by staff; the inmate's life is penetrated by constant sanctioning interaction from above" (p. 38).

Above all, life at SSD is group life. Sunrise finds one moving sleepily to a crowded lounge where crowds eventually lead one to a breakfast with yet a larger group. It's to class in groups, to lunch, to movies, to play, to town and bus trips in groups. A popular thirteen-year-old boy, M. _____, who is hard-of-hearing (and whose speech is quite good) and very skilled with sign language, describes his daily routine.

> Don: Tell me what you do every day, starting early in the morning.
>
> M. _____: Houseparent comes on a little late and we have to get up and take a bath, put on our clothes, brush teeth, sit TV. At 7:00 o' clock its time to go eat, all of us. Finished. Talk, talk, talk [i. e., we talked a while] at the high school. Come back to the dorm about 8:00 o'clock. You can go back to the school.
>
> Mrs. C. _____ at 9:20, the bell rings and we go to science class. At 9:50 the bell rings and we go to recess and play basketball. Talk, talk, talk (we talk a while), [then] basketball. And the assistant woman who helps watch us takes us all go back into school to the teacher ... after basketball finished.
>
> We go Monday ... to P.E. at 10:10, we go to P.E. Play volleyball. Finish at 10:00 o'clock, I forgot ... at 11:30. Then we go back to Mrs G. ___ s' class and have math 'til 12:50 and go eat. Finished [we] come back to recess [and] play, play, play [His voice literally repeats the word] a little in the afternoon.

> The bell rings at 1:05 … 1:00. Come back to black woman's classroom (for) reading, reading, writing, pay attention, writing something. Bell has rung at 1:50 or 2.00. Go back to Mrs. C_____'s class for language and write verbs and nouns, adverbs, adjectives, write like book, pay attention, look up, understand, write, write, write, finished. Talk, talk, talk. Time for bell 2:40. Bell rings. We go to Cagle's room and play, play, play. Three ten its time to go to the dorm so we all flock/migrate to the dorm, finished.
>
> Go to the dorm at 4:00. Play, play. 5:00 come wash hands, line up, go down to the dining room. Eat. About 5:50 we go … we're free 'til 7:00. Six til 7:00 we have to study work 'til 7:00. Free now. Go over to rec (recreation) room to play. Gym or outside. Any (thing). Watch tv, football. Any. 9:00 anything. 10:00 we clean up the building. Ten-thirty all go to bed and that's the end.

Tipton remembers his days in a Missouri school (written under the heading "Embarrassment as an Older Student"):

> Though I was at the advanced dorm, I still had to stay with a group to go downtown for movies, but by then we were allowed to wear casual clothes. I felt embarrassed having to go with the group accompanied by the dormitory supervisors because most hearing kids of my age were not accompanied by their parents. Why could I not be like them?[7]

This regimentation is well illustrated by passages from a prison newspaper. It describes the way life in prison was organized by an old fashioned dinner bell on a tall pole:

> In the humdrum of everyday existence, only one thing stands out – the ringing of all these damn bells … the bells represent the unemotional authority governing a prisoner's life …
>
> The bells first ring at 5:30 a.m. every weekday morning. They ring seven days a week, 30 days a month, 12 months a year …
>
> The bells tell us to get up, and again in a short period of time, that we have to line up for breakfast. Next these same hellish bells tell us its time to got to work. Towards noon, they ring again so that you may be aware that you are going to be counted and then fed again. Later, they ring again, return to work. At the end of the day they signal that work is over … in a short time the bells ring again, you must stand up and be counted. Then you can relax, do what you want … the bells have stopped ringing until 5:30 tomorrow morning. Then it will start all over again (Le Premier, 1972:8).

This same kind of daily monotony is found at SSD. There, too, whole "blocks of people" must be moved from one place to another. To accomplish this, daily life is scheduled and regimented. The Handbook's statement about home life policies (p. 10) dictates for preadolescent students the daily rhythm of life:

Wake-up time Monday through Friday is 6:00 a.m. Leave for dining room at 7:00 a.m.

Return to dorm and perform duties before leaving for school.

Wake-up time Saturday and Sunday is 7:30 a.m.

Breakfast at 8:10 a.m.

The bells of prison are replaced by various omnipresent authority figures. The regimented student does not stop when classes conclude. Instead, students are told by the handbook that they should sign in with their houseparent no later than 3:30 p.m. Study hall is to be conducted for younger students from 3:30 till 4:00 p.m. and then supervised play extends from 4:00 p.m. until 4:45 p.m. Supper time is 5:00 p.m. and then free time will be given after supper until 7:00 or 7:30 p.m., which is a total of 1 to 1½ hours of free time per day. Lights are out within the dormitory at 9:00 p.m. Sunday through Thursday. The weekends, however, are considerably freer.

The daily schedule of life for high school students is more flexible, although they, too, have after-school schedules. Like their younger counterparts, on school days they must sign in with the houseparent no later than 3:30 p.m. and weekday evenings specify time for study hall. Because older students occupy a campus which is close to Doubletown, they are permitted off-campus privileges by the following schedule:

1. Monday, Tuesday, Thursday and Friday for one hour.
2. Saturday and Sunday after 2:00 p.m.
3. Wednesday [a day when town businesses are closed all day] not at all; do not even cross the bridge [between the school and the town].
4. No students will be permitted in town after 6:45 p.m. on town days.

The regimentation of time is but one way of maximizing surveillance (Goffman, 1961:6–7), or direct observation by those in authority. In the total institution there is off-limits space, surveillance space, and space ruled by less than usual staff authority (Goffman, 1961:227–238). These refer to the setting of the institution, regions where the underlife may occur. In off-limits space mere presence is prohibited unless one is accompanied by an official agent. At SSD, dormitories are out of bounds during school hours and one must not leave campus (except during the one-hour allotted time). Too, wooded areas near the school are off-limits. SSD differs somewhat from Goffman's mental institution (or a prison) in that students must be protected from exploitation (boys from nearby towns often attempt to pick up deaf girls) and other potential problems: runaways, accidents, etc.

Surveillance space is "an area a patient needs no special excuse for being in, but where he would be subject to the usual authority and restrictions of the establishment" (p. 228). Finally, spaces ruled by less than usual authority are places where inmates or students use concealment devices to hide activities for their forbidden behaviors. That is, they may devise means of "maneuvering freely within the structure of ward politics" (p. 228–229). For example, one might openly read a forbidden book after it has been placed into a dust jacket which bears some acceptable book title. In short, members of total institutions find *free places*. For example, restrooms at SSD were used as a cover for smoking. Empty buildings, wooded areas and stairwells were places for sexual encounters. Students and staff may tacitly cooperate in the emergence of these places where surveillance and restrictions are reduced. As Goffman says, "Free places are backstage to the usual performance of staff-inmate relationship" (p. 230).

As noted above, SSD students are allowed one hour per day to visit Doubletown. It could be assumed that this is a period and a place where one is outside the surveillance space, relatively free of authority. However, this is not always the case. One administrator was frequently observed watching students walk the streets of the little village as he sat inside one of the two small restaurants. On one occasion a young deaf adult male came in and told him that there had been a theft at the school; the administrator then used his two-way radio to have school authorities investigate the story. Thus, even in town school authorities are able to monitor student behavior.

On the campus itself, the rule to be followed is "let your houseparent know where you are at all times." School supervision is meant to include virtually every on-campus act by the individual. Food brought from home on the weekends is to be checked in with the houseparent. The Handbook directs students to "accept correction at all times from any supervisor or houseparent (do not say, 'you are not my houseparent')." Older students are told how to use dormitory washing machines as well as the school laundry. They must not visit people on other floors of the dorm. The only transportation to church is on the bus; they must not walk to or from church. Visitors must be cleared through the home life director's office. Visitors are not permitted inside the dormitories but they may enter the recreation center. Finally, to use the telephone or the TTY (teletype communication system) requires the houseparent's approval and "all long distance calls must be made collect and conversations must not be over five minutes in length."

The 1981–82 *SSD Handbbok for Home Life Department* employees indicates the orientation staff members are to take in their work with deaf students. The prevailing adage seems to be, "Trust not thy students." Indeed, the need for a close rein is aptly stated in the following passage: "Wherever your children are, that's where you should be." Surveillance is paramount. One key area to watch is dormitory rooms.

> Frequent visits into rooms are vital. Room checks are like taking your dorm's pulse. It gives you indications of your students' conditions. It will not only keep down mischief, but will also help you learn who studies and who does not, who associates with whom, etc. It will allow time to make closer friends with your students. Keeping a close and frequent eye on each room will solve problems before they happen.

Our extra field notes of observations and impressions recall such heavy supervision:

> I returned Kenny to the dorm at 9:45 p.m and chatted with _____ a while female houseparent for a few minutes. One problem, she said, about her work as a houseparent is checking on the boys so frequently and trying to 'stay on top of the situation.' And checking [them] constantly makes you tired.
>
> Comment; the checking of boys in the dorm is a constant procedure in which they are under steady surveillance ... Constant supervision and watchfulness and students (are) being corrected endlessly. After a whole day at school then the evening and the afternoons are filled with supervision and authority over one's every moment of behavior.

During an interview we asked this houseparent how she entered work with the deaf and then to give us an account of a typical day's work. First, she tells how she resisted the "call" but was compelled into the work:

> I did not want to do it. I was fighting it. But everytime I turned around there it was. I believe God wanted me to go to SSD because again and again it was 'Go to SSD.' 'Go to SSD.'
>
> *A typical days work*
>
> I come to work at 3:15. Boys come in at 3:30. First thing is to check if all boys are here then I help them if they need me. I am constantly checking where they are because that is the duty of a houseparent. If they

get into something and you don't know where they are, you are accountable and you have to stay on top of the situation for their protection as well as my own.

We go to the dining room at 5:00 p.m. The boys sit with the girls if they want but I sit where I can see them.

Don: Why do you have to watch them during dinner?

Houseparent: They might fight, pester the girls too much and slip out of the dining room. He might tell a girl to meet him outside or he might smoke a cigarette, or go outside to settle an argument or to steal something, or go to town.

Changes in Lattitudes, Changes in Attitudes

The Handbook, of course, is only the tip of the proverbial iceberg. It is an easily obtainable expression of how SSD, like most public schools, is a bureaucratic organization replete with rules upon rules. And rules, in their statement of normative parameters, almost always give emphasis to what the individual cannot or must not do. As Freud would describe it, civilization is attained at a cost – the chief cost being some loss of individual freedom. Likewise at SSD, and in other total institutions, regimented behavior provides for little "official" expression of individuality.

Much time at SSD was spent querying staff members (including administrators) about what, if any, changes had occurred during the past five to ten years in the way children are treated at the school. This was done for two reasons. First, it was clear in many interviews that the general orientation at the school altered each time a new superintendent was hired. Second, given the national press for "mainstreaming" and allowing handicapped individuals greater access to the society-at-large (especially through hiring programs and other such reforms), we wondered how school personnel felt about the school in 1981.

Without using any specific historical date as a point of reference, vivid impressions of the "caretaker's" view that things are too lax were gained. This offers further support for Goffman's regimentation thesis. Students and staff exist in a kind of dynamic tension – each wanting to gain and/or maintain some advantage over the other. For teachers and other staff this most often takes the form of maximizing control and resenting any infringement on existing arrangements which strengthen students' positions.

Many teachers in the middle and senior high schools felt that SSD was too permissive and offered too much freedom. One teacher cites the widespread student use of vulgar language and the reluctance of teachers to punish its use.

> I say to them that you're talking ugly and I don't want to see it. But this used to be something that we didn't see because the kids knew that if they did it they'd be punished. The kids used to know that if they had sex, man, they were going to get it! Or, they'd get sent home and never get to come back. Or if they stole anything they'd go to jail. But then it came in with 'do your own thing' and there's no punishment involved.

Many teachers believed that the current administration (in place for several years) changed things for the sake of change when it took over. Some thought the administration was now coming back to some of the older ways, i. e., back to more discipline on campus. In the old days a houseparent would know where the children were but this administration came in and said, "Don't watch them so close. Let them be free." As another teacher put it:

> His expression was 'Don't eyeball them.' The thing that bothers me is that students may need to have some freedom but it should have been maybe a gradual [thing]. I'm not saying I know how it should have been done, but it was almost too much ... you're free to do your own thing no matter what! Even if it's immoral, if it's illegal, no matter what – do your own thing. That's alright. And so things went haywire.

In the early 1970's the school was caught up in student unrest with a school strike which resulted in some of the school's best students being expelled. At that time the school would not tolerate any challenges to its authority. Long hair was equated with being rebellious and could result in expulsion. Too, the school was forced to desegregate. One deaf staff member believed that racial integration (and too much freedom) had caused the school to degenerate. In the past SSD was more like a jail but that aspect of it has been improved, he said. But then came racial integration.

> Staff member: In the past black and white were separated and then they mixed them up and it got worse. White girls went with black boys and white boys went with black girls. Before that it was limited. They were separated ... now they're mixed together.
>
> Don: Is that worse?
>
> Staff member: That's worse. Yes.
>
> Don: Why?

> Staff member: Sign language is all mixed up, dirty minds, dirty communications. Now they (are) free, independent, sneak around. In the past there were many heroes who played football and pretty girls would go after them. Now its different. More independent. The kids don't understand right from wrong. They see the hearing people and imitate them. Now they are free to go, to sneak around, and do this and do that and go places. In the past it was more strict. Now they go to town and travel around everywhere. We need to spank them. The older kids, you cannot control them.

What techniques and tactics are used by those with authority at SSD to achieve more social control? Those with authority can maintain surveillance and use informants as well as search squads which check out dormitories during evening hours. One nurse's aid feels that "The kids are under supervision all the time. Whenever they walk to town a houseparent is supposed to ... check up on them." Another social control tactic is unannounced searches of student dormitory rooms. A houseparent from a dorm that had just been searched by the director of home life and a security guard during the second or third week of the new school year explained, "We heard a little something suspicious and we ourselves asked for the search. The director says that it will help the boys to know that we *will* search the place from time to time." Later some of the teenage boys said they were neither surprised nor offended by the search. One boy remarked that the authorities were just doing their job. Another boy added, "They are doing this to help us."

There is, of course, an informational network among staff members. Teachers learn about students' problems from houseparents and teachers tell houseparents about in-school problems. After the teacher learns from a houseparent that a given student was in trouble the night before then the teacher passes that information to administrators who eventually ask the student himself about the problem. But, as one administrator pointed out, "There are many voices in the wilderness;" that is, there are many informants. An administrator was asked if he always talked to the students involved in dormitory problems.

> Yes. Eventually. But I try to find out indirectly first. I talk with the people in the dorms. Talk to other students. Always some student wants to tell you what is up. I lost my best one last year in high school. There was one young man who would tell you how it was, and what was up, and he understood. He was real helpful.

His answer was revealing in terms of the conspiratorial ambience which can exist in a total institution.

Views of the Students

Officials at SSD frequently mentioned that many students have poor relationships with their own parents. Many parents, they say, reject, ignore, and abuse deaf children. School officials believe that many parents have "dumped" their unwanted children on the school. There they are received by surrogate (house) parents, most of whom are poor at sign language. Moreover, these houseparents are often transient and temporary people who walk in and out of the daily lives of these somewhat parentless children. Parental neglect at home, then, is not necessarily rectified at the school although, for many, school is a better place than home because there is community and common language.

A top administrator estimates that one-third of all students were "abused and molested" children because without language they are vulnerable and defenseless. He tended to downplay the role of social class in this abusive behavior. Instead he emphasized a deaf child's vulnerability, his/her lack of language and his/her naivete. He seemed to summarize the situation at SSD by saying, "We have an awful lot of hard-luck stories at this place."

One city official in Doubletown stated, during an informal interview at the popular town restaurant, "What makes me feel bad is that some kids are just dumped at the school by their parents." He explained that his observation derived from his own experience as an employee at the school. The top administrator cited above also provided a specific example of such dumping or rejecting of deaf children:

> This little emotionally disturbed boy that I was telling you about ... his parents have always rejected him. They have lots of money. They brought him up here and then they picked him up from a hospital where they kept him all summer. They brought him up to SSD for registration and dropped him and they were driving a new car. Obviously they have a lot of money and the child has never lived with them. He's been in and out of state hospitals and places all his life.

This little boy, the administrator said, had recently spent one year in special studies (for slow students) but was now attempting to function in regular academic middle school. School personnel describe this child as having "A big dose of emotional disturbance because of parental rejection."

Interestingly, one prime reason given for rejection at home is that these students are handicapped. They cannot easily communicate with their parents. As one administrator said: "Some students want to stay here at SSD because their home is a place of isolation, a place without communication." Parents, he said, seek the cause of their child's deafness, many feel guilty and consequently reject them. Several people volunteered that when students first enroll at SSD they want to go home. But when they get into high school, most of them do not want to go home any more because "they cannot talk to their parents."[10]

One secretary, like many of the teachers, felt that too many SSD employees are transitional and they drift in and out of the lives of these deaf children. "They have so many people to relate to. They go to bed with one houseparent and wake up with another one, and then numerous adults engage them all day long. they must deal with various administrators and different security officers throughout their lives here at SSD." This compounds the problem of poor sign language skills. It compounds the problem of the children being adrift in a kind of no man's land.

Some staff members, secretaries, and several teachers expressed the feeling that houseparents no longer had strong commitments and dedication to the work of being a houseparent. As one former staff member opined, "Sixty percent of the staff is over there to get the paycheck." Teachers and secretaries expressed dismay over the idea that houseparents are merely paid hands now as opposed to strongly devoted, caring and concerned surrogate parents which, they said, was typical of houseparents a few years ago. One former houseparent also indicated that some houseparents abused the students. She explained how two teenage students were found trespassing in a house in Doubeltown and were whipped with a large leather belt by a houseparent who believed "you have to break deaf kids when they're young."

In recent years the student body has changed in significant ways. Not only are there more blacks and more poor, but there are more multihandicapped. Thus, among administrators and teachers at SSD it is common to hear conversations about "normal deaf." So many students are multihandicapped or have some mental disability that the phrase 'normal deaf' had evolved to refer to students whose only physical handicap consists of deafness. SSD operates a diagnostic and evaluation center where psychological tests are administered in order to determine which persons are "normal" and which ones have other mental or physical disabilities. Few, however, seem to fit the 'normal' definition. Those who are "normal deaf" may serve as role models for the other children, something mentioned by staff members.

Goffman emphasizes one important dimension along which total institutions differ from each other, this is "permeability," the degree to which the external world can enter the institution. This refers not merely to visitors having access to the place but "includes the receipt of printed materials, having access to television and radio, phone calls, and having mail privileges to write and receive letters to [*sic*] friends and relatives" (Bowker, 1982:145). Deafness and its usual barrier to hearing and reading severs one from TVs, telephones and printed linkages to the larger world. Therefore, the isolated quality of the institution cannot be ignored, even for the normal deaf children, something which leads to a kind of paradox: being normal inside the institution does not necessarily equal being normal outside.

One staff member emphasized the effects of institutional life upon deaf students rather than a more psychological explanation. He was asked in what ways he would change the school if he had the power to do so. His answer is interesting and echoes some Goffmanian ideas regarding total institutions.

> I would have older kids live in cottages and learn survival skills. As long as they live together in a group they'll not learn how to sew on a button or even to cook. Not long ago a teacher asked one group of sixteen and seventeen-year-old boys and girls to sew on a button. They did not know how, and during that experience they probably learned three new words, needle, button, sew. These students are just not exposed.

Staff members consistently criticized the cloistered, restricted, and relatively deprived form of life at the institution. When a counselor was asked what the greatest effect of deafness is, he replied that

> Isolation is the main effect. Isolation from the hearing world. The hearing world itself does not understand deafness at all. It makes me mad. I wish I could get them to understand. Hearing kids in Mountain City, for example, are scared to death to play football or any other game with these deaf students. They think that if they touch them they will become deaf or something.

Again, normativeness is situated and stigma is literally some observable and reacted to difference. One staff member of the infirmary, whose signs were quite good, described the world of deaf children as "a newspaper. It is a sea of unfamiliar things."

The protective, almost womblike quality of SSD, especially manifests itself for high school students. They grow restive and are anxious to have greater involvement in the social world beyond that at SSD. Their preparation for this, however, is not always very good. One staff member, who has a deaf child at SSD, told about taking her child to a restaurant where she could observe young boys and girls dating and dining out. Her daughter often remarked, "I wish I could do that." But, her mother explained, "The problem is that there are no boys at SSD with cars and secondly most of the boys don't know how to ask a girl for a date ... All the kids know is to take a girl to the woods. That's all they know about dating." This is but one more example of their lacking general knowledge about everyday life, thus requiring more than normal supervision. Two staff members strongly insisted that day students (who commute from home daily) are very superior to residential students on academic and social affairs. Why? (1) At home there is more normal (and frequent) parent-child interaction; (2) at home they live within an English (not ASL) environment; and (3) there is more freedom and more personal responsibility.

As we have argued throughout, language is *the* pivotal issue for the deaf. In the most Kantian fashion, reality lies somewhere behind the eyes. As Postman and Weingartner note, we see the world through our words. Of course Postman and Weingartner are assuming the capacity to hear and verbalize. For deaf people, the world is experienced through signs more broadly, words being but one form of experience. In the absence of words (or signs), of course, there is little about the world which one can in any way make sense. More sociologically, the symbolic nature of the world is lost on most young deaf children since they have no linguistic, culturally defined frame of reference. Thus the roots for their general societal ignorance are sown early on. An administrator described deaf children as "amoral" (at the same time, really implying *im*moral as well), and explained that this was because deaf children are outside conversations at home: they cannot hear and understand. "It is a lack of language."

Above all, to be deaf as a young child is to be isolated. If the child does not have supportive, understanding parents, then the sense of isolation is amplified. One solution for parents is to place the child in a residential school such as SSD. Ironically, though, in doing this one form of isolation is replaced by another. As the mother of a deaf child commented, many normal behaviors are unknown to deaf children. Would she place her child in an SSD dormitory? Her answer reflects the conflicting pros and cons to such a move.

> Well, the dormitory kids don't have a mother and father here to tell them right from wrong. They have someone who is paid to keep them and these people come on by shifts and then they leave. They don't stay with them. Thus, the kids have many bosses. There is no way one houseparent can teach 20 kids right and wrong things. There is no family foundation. [But] SSD is the only family they have. The majority of these kids are glad to be back here from home after summer vacation because they have such loneliness and poor communication at home.

So, while basic principles of the primary family are missing at SSD, for many children it may be the best alternative available. They prefer and enjoy SSD life over nuclear family life at home where they may be largely excluded from things.

Two Worlds: Languages Apart

Some administrators, teachers, staff members and townspeople perceive deaf students as occupying an entirely different social world, a subculture, *in* but not completely *of* the larger culture. In a local restaurant, a resident of Doubletown gave his impressions of the deaf people at SSD. He stated,

> The kids live in a different world. But I learned one thing! They are not dumb. For deaf students there is no race to them other than deaf and hearing categories. It seems to me like the community of Doubletown is split into two groups, deaf and hearing. And the only way to help that is for hearing people to learn sign language, because the kids cannot learn to hear.

This man is one of the few people who see the deaf-hearing schism as requiring greater reciprocity. At present, the larger culture and its presentation at SSD necessitates that deaf children adapt to the larger culture. The burden is totally on them. Their success is always guaged against the larger culture's norms. At a minimum, it is necessary to understand the world of the deaf as a subculture – something recognized by this man. But that need not be in a pejorative context. One staff member described the discoveries she had made by working with deaf students at SSD. Her answer could not have been more sociological.

> One of the big discoveries was the language limitation. What it does to you not only in terms of being able to process things auditorially but how it can change your entire living structure, your internal living structure and the way that it is a subculture kind of existence. You are isolated and

> even though most minority groups are isolated in one way or another, to me this is the one that is most isolated because without the communication [skills] most people simply cannot communicate with the deaf. That is just a restricted way of living! You tend to seek out those who can communicate with you, those who know what your world is about, and that automatically limits you.

The current homecoming queen at SSD provides an example of this "seeking out those who can communicate with you":

> Don: Do you want to marry a deaf or hearing person?
>
> Queen: Deaf or hard-of-hearing.
>
> Don: What is wrong with a hearing person? What happens?
>
> Queen: My fear is he might leave me out of his group of friends and he might not know how to sign.
>
> Don: He wouldn't understand about the feelings of the deaf. Can you somehow explain what you mean by 'the feelings of the deaf'? How do deaf feel?
>
> Queen: Hearing people may not understand me, and they say, 'I don't understand that.' I'm afraid. Talking [people] should know that deaf hard to understand because they can't hear. Hearing can't understand the deaf [do] try.
>
> Don: Do you think that deaf people are different from hearing people? Their feelings, their ideas?
>
> Queen: I don't know. I don't know.
>
> Don: Have you in the past had a date with a hearing boy?
>
> Queen: Never a date. No. A few talking boys asked for a date and I was shy.
>
> Don: You were afraid to date them?
>
> Queen: At that time I was afraid that maybe they might not understand the deaf. Maybe leave me out.

The staff member (above) further described ASL as a "black and white restricted language" and implied that it has a smaller vocabulary bank than other languages (the limited vocabulary has also been noted by McCay Vernon, [1974] prolific writer on deafness).

> I think ASL is restricted. The thing we were talking about before, about being able to express those feelings. I can feel a thousand different ways. And there are times that I grope for the words to put what I'm feeling right this minute into the right words. Sometimes words are not adequate but I still know that if I try harder I can hunt around for the right word that will get close to what I'm feeling. I may never hit right on it, but it'll come close. I know that. I know that bank is there within me.

Because students use a "black and white" language they tend to view the world in simplistic black and white divisions. "Some say they are 'good' either because they never have sex or because they make good grades. It's either black and white. There are no shades of gray. It's so clear-cut and dramatic here."

The extent of the communication problem was *the* discovery for this staff member in her years of work at SSD. Until one is emersed in this 'deaf world,' one can neither understand what the communication gap is like nor the importance of the spoken word. Students know they are isolated, "there's a feeling of that," she said. Especially the blacks, and the "lower average people," who make remarks like "hearing people are against me," or, "if you were deaf you would know ..."

Deaf students are perceived as different from others because of structural arrangements at the school such as constant group life, low degree of permeability (defined above), and relative isolation from the larger world (themes we explored in the previous chapter). A staff member stated the problem this way

> Spend a lot of time together in the dorms – they spend much more time with nonsiblings in a much closer relationship than do normally hearing children because of the residential environment. I think that having to protect yourself and to assert yourself with other students more than a normal hearing student does – I think that leads to some shorter fuses and you have more blowups.

One is reminded here of Zimbardo's (1982) study of a simulated prison. That important sociological experiment recognized that the negative behavior of guards and prisoners was largely a consequence of structured social arrangements and not merely personality or character traits (deficient individuals) of the persons involved. As Shover says of institutional life, we can understand the individual only by looking to the collective as well (1979:112).

At SSD there was a general tendency for officials to explain deviant or undesirable patterns of behavior in terms of individualistic and psychological variables. For most officials the cause of student bc-havior and misbehavior lies "under the skin" of each individual. The top administrator cited above believed that students fight because, "They lack emotional controls. I don't think they mature as quickly as normally hearing. And I think they stay in that young stage longer." Two veteran teachers agreed that deaf students are immature. Therefore, they criticized the administration's past attempts to run SSD "like a college."

Teacher #1: And these kids were not ready. They are not as old as college kids and not ready for that responsibility mentally. Physically, maybe, some of them are as old, but mentally and emotionally they are not as mature as hearing college kids and that was the way it was going to be. And we would have an honor dormitory with no houseparents and all that sort of thing. And the kids weren't prepared for that.

Don: When you say they are immature, do you mean high school as well as the young students?

Teacher #1: Physically, they are mature. Mentally they cannot handle it. They can't control their own feelings.

Teacher #2: They don't realize the consequences of some of the things they do.

Don: I want you to define immaturity by giving an example.

Teacher #1: They know they have feelings and I guess it's your abstract [i.e., problems with abstractions]. They have this feeling, this desire, everybody has. Deaf people have it. But they don't know how to control it, to react to it, to channel it right.

Here, again, language deficiency is thought to be related to immaturity, feelings and emotions. But causal variables are many and complex. Is language the major variable? Or is it institutional arrangements? Or are the sex and fighting behaviors class-based? Is this a case of lower class behavior imported into the school? (see Shover, 1979) Or a combination of these?

Chapter VI

The Institutional Side of Life: The Student Culture

> The greatest distance between people is not space but culture.
>
> Jamake Highwater

> If we are justified in asserting that deaf children lack normal environmental stimulation toward an intellectual attitude, we can parsimoniously associate their observed intellectual retardation to this environmental handicap.
>
> Hans G. Furth

For residents of a total institution, the ebb and flow of daily events is largely determined by others. Residents have little say or control in establishing and enforcing rules, the formalized norms of the institution. In sociological parlance, they must be "other-directed," and act as others want them to. As Peter Berger (1969) has eloquently phrased it, these people are saddled with the "yoke of society." But in society at large, as well as the total institution, not all life is regimented and acted out in accordance with the official, institutionalized view. Short of behaving as an automaton, all of us innovate to some degree. We may usually act in predictable, hence normative ways but, importantly, we ad lib in some small way. Phrased differently, in a society of Americans, each individual subscribes to certain societal norms yet each is also a unique, existential person – a self.

According to Goffman, in the total institution with its extreme conditions of regimentation, individuals who are confined develop an "underlife." The underlife is a type of culture within a culture (sociologically, it is a subculture). It, in a collective way (viz., as a cultural aggregate), has its own norms, its own rules. For residents of a total institution, the underlife offers inmates and residents a form of self preserving behavior. It is a way of expressing one's individuality. This may take the form of engaging in insubordinate behavior or other acts which are interpreted as antagonistic toward authority. As Goffman says, the underlife is a way of "reserving something of one's self from the clutch of institution," a way to express that one is one's own man (1961:319). Lacking the willingness to completely identify with the official, institutional world view, the underlife allows the individual to maintain at least a modicum of attachment to a group *and* to have his/her self predicated on such attachment. In Goffman's terms the underlife consists of "secondary adjustments."

It was theorized at the outset of this study that an underlife such as Goffman describes would be found at SSD. To the degree that this exists, this study would document ways in which individuals resist the pull of official, institutional life. In the following pages we present ingenious, subtle and sometimes explicit ways in which residents of SSD engage in secondary adjustments. We describe how residential students resist the constant presence of school authorities as represented by teachers, houseparents, administrators and other SSD adults. The underlife of SSD is a place where students can occupy free places and free time away from the rules, regulations and official definitions of the system at large. We will see that students find places in school buildings, dormitories and secret places on the school grounds as well as off-campus sites where they can engage in forbidden sexual behavior. There are niches, crannies, crevices and cracks where individuals escape in order to smoke cigarettes or marijuana, both on campus and off-campus. We will see that free places and free time regions provide escape and possibilities for self-expression.

If freedom is a "primal thrust" as some psychologists argue, then students at SSD and other members of total institutions will press hard and long against the walls of authority, rules, and coercion. They will find free time, free territory and zones for expression of self. One teacher in the vocational school put it this way. "Our kids at this school have a routine. They are told when to get up, when to go eat, and when to go to school. So, whenever they slip off to secret places they have some little freedom." One top administrator gave some examples of how students circumvent the rules.

> Well, they do it hourly. They lapse into esoteric sign language, you know. I've watched kids sit in classrooms and very rapidly use esoteric sign language with enough basic signs that the teacher will recognize and ask for permission to go next door to have intercourse with their girl friends. The teacher will say, "Yeah." And everybody will just burst out laughing and they can tell the teacher to "go stuff it" or "bullshit" and the teacher never knows it.

One is reminded of how prison inmates are said to use insolence or remarks made under the breath as well as muttering, sneering, and glaring in order to express anger and frustation (Goffman, 1961). Inmates are said to express contempt for authority in numerous ways such as groups of prison inmates marching in a goose-step or seating themselves simultaneously at a dining table or laughing hilariously at some feeble joke made by an individual who had authority over them (p. 316). Sometimes, the administrator said,

> They'll pretend – passive aggressive – and hide behind deafness. They'll say, 'Don't understand.' They're dumb. And sometimes they'll just flat refuse to look at you. You know that's the easiest way to frustrate a system. If the teacher's chewing you out just close your eyes. If I close my eyes you'll go away – to a deaf person that literally happens.

Free Places and Free Time: On Campus

One of the best illustrations of the underlife at SSD is sexual behavior which includes all forms of sex play, not just intercourse. On campus, SSD residents have found places and time for sexual behavior which is outside the grasp of school authorities. One staff member, who was himself a former student at this school, told about the secret places of the underlife:

> We used to have secret places. Right now they usually do it [have sex] in the school when the teacher is gone talking somewhere. And then they do it in the closet or do it downstairs somewhere or they meet after going from the dining room or somebody going to the dining room they'll stay in a room. You really have to watch out for that kind of thing.

Sometimes, when students are supposed to be cleaning up, he said, they might slip into a closet "just a few seconds and that's it, you know." I asked if the two students made a plan the day before?

> Staff member: No. Just do it. Just like that. Just meet and do it.
>
> Don: You didn't tell the girl yesterday to meet you tomorrow?
>
> Staff member: No. Just do it [He snapped his fingers]. Just like that! Just a moment.
>
> Don: You just asked her?
>
> Staff member: No. Just happened to be blank [empty], nobody around or we just knew that was the time you could do it and you did it. Only one time I did plan, but all the other times there was no plan – it just happens.

A teacher explained how students will have sexual relationships in empty rooms on campus. Students are said to use empty rooms above the superintendent's office as well as secret places inside the gym. One boy told her how he entered the girl's locker room in the gymnasium "and the girls didn't hide. They showed me themselves. I didn't want to see them, I just wanted to see one girl but the one I wanted to see had finished dressing already." The teacher, who had been a student at SSD, remembered that female students used to enter into different rooms and especially the boys' locker room in the gym.

> When we had halloween parties couples would be kissing and kissing. There was the fishing pond where students would get behind a curtain and kiss a little bit and we'd watch them and that thrilled us. Sometimes if we had all women teachers we knew they'd never go into the men's restroom, so girls would go to the boy's restroom and kiss the boys in there.

Both middle and high school teachers referred to stairwells and dark rooms in the administration building where students would go for sexual encounters, places also cited by high school students. One middle school student said that students would leave the dining room after eating and run to an empty building and "do it quickly." When the weather is cold, school security guards tend not to drive around very much which provides opportune times for such encounters.

A top administrator at SSD agreed that students were indeed "quick to discover holes in cupboards." His account provides insight into human ingenuity regarding the posturing against official authority.

> They've discovered that if you really want to get together and neck a little bit or whatever, you arrange with your girl friend – and you go to the gym and pretend that you are coming to the snackbar, but instead you cross the yard nonchalantly and go down into the basement of the art room. I'll [a student] come in from the other end and we'll have a good 15 minutes before people even know we're anywhere around.

He noted that students would often get "one of those retarded ones" to act as watchman or guard while the couple is in the basement. Afterwards when the bell rings the couple meanders out, one of them leaving one side of the building while the other emerges from the other side. As a student described this: "We put the mentally retarded ones to watch – 'you do that or I'll beat you up,' and he believes us so he doesn't say anything." Another high school student explained how his peers arranged to find free areas and free time:

> Most of the houseparents go to the recreation room. Sometimes the boys tell the girls what time, what place, don't let the houseparent see you. Try to fool the houseparent. The boy explains the place where to go. She goes and the boy waits until the girl goes there and then he goes. Most of the time they go to the recreation room and then leave for the next building, to its basement. The girl goes down into the basement and the boy goes up into the dorm and then he goes down inside the dorm, down the stairs to the basement and they have sex and various things.

The houseparent is unable to notice where everybody is, he explained, and adds that a second boy will go to the basement and give his friend a signal that there is no houseparent around, to come on out. Students and teachers also said the dormitory rooms were used for sexual liaisons.

Not only do students discover free places in school buildings and dormitories but they use hiding places on or around the school campus proper. Some of these hiding places have been used for generations and are passed along from one cohort of students to another. One administrator, for example, told about free places that existed in the Arkansas School for the Deaf in the following story.

> They were tearing down an old building and a deaf teacher who had been in that school remembered that there had been a tunnel, an underground maintenance service tunnel between the boys' and girl's dormitories. They used to go down into the tunnel and meet and do whatever came naturally. So they passed it on from one class to another and he [the teacher] had forgotten it. But when they started tearing it down, it reminded him of the tunnel and he went to check it out and sure enough it was still going on. For 75, 50 years maybe the kids had been frustrating the system in that regard.

A staff member, who is also an SSD alumnus said,

> There are places like the coal pit. It's cold in the winter time but we still did it there or up in the washateria. (When I was a student) I'd go to wash clothes and somebody would meet me there or in the back of the bus. The girl didn't wear panties, she just sat on top of you while you were riding in the back of the bus.

There is a quaint old barn located on one of the two campuses at SSD. A teacher remembers that a girl in her class last year had gone to the barn with a boy.

> The student said, 'We kissed' and she explained everything to me and I said, 'shame on you!' I found out it was a man who worked here and that girl thought that I went to the barn with the same man. She thinks because both of us are deaf we do the same things, that we have these things in common.

This illustrates two points: First, deaf students (in general – not just slow ones) are especially curious about sex. Second, they treat it very much as a "natural" not "social" drive. Freud, in a very sociological way, discussed how civilization curtails our natural drives. It takes a drive like sex or hunger and directs it in socially prescribed ways to make it normatively acceptable. For many students, the general norm of sexual behavior being *verboten* (forbidden) except under certain circumstances is poorly understood. The confusion over this (especially for slow students) is well illustrated by the teacher's account since the student involved assumed that her behavior was normal, in fact that the teacher would have done the same thing.

A high school teacher explained that boys take advantage of some of the "slow" (intellectually not well developed) girls in the nearby wooded area, the basement, or a boiler room somewhere. He believes that these girls are easily exploitable. "They can't tattletale because they do not have enough language to tell someone." Another teacher told how students would out-maneuver and manipulate the authorities in the following way:

> I used to have an art club and the kids would want to join the art club and come down here at night to work. And I would write them passes to come down here, and then for one reason or another they wouldn't show up. They were meeting their boyfriends in the woods someplace. The houseparents thought they were here and I thought they had for some reason decided not to come and then by the time the houseparents and I got straightened out – it may take weeks. And so that's what was going on last night. Some kids were supposed to have met one of the coaches for some tennis practice in the gym and they didn't meet him.

Not only do students use tunnels, coal pits, washaterias, wooded areas, but they have also use the shelter of a bridge which is very near campus. One teacher explained how a couple might be under the bridge with a student-guard sitting on the top of the bridge. The guard's role is to throw rocks into the water if some adult is coming near the bridge. This teacher also told about a bank of dirt near the gymnasium which is covered with kudzu vine. He described an encounter which had occurred during a basketball game.

> One of the security guards came up to me and said, 'Did you see anybody go into that kudzu right then?' I said, 'No,' and he said, 'well tell me if you do.' I said, 'Oh, why?' He said, 'Oh, they got sheets and blankets and pillows and everything up under that kudzu where they have their parties.'

Free Places and Free Time: Off-Campus

Both teachers and students mentioned that a local city park which adjoins the property of the school is used as a place for sexual intercourse. One girl described how this is arranged.

> Some kids have cars and they go down to the park and have intercourse. They hide. They take the car down there. They turn in a key at the office, but they keep an extra key in the pocket and nobody knows it. So they sneak out at night – the girl just fools the houseparent and tells them I'm going to eat and they go over there and have IC (intercourse) in the park where the trees are.

One teacher said that students have been caught in an old Negro church which is located very near campus. "I don't know how many times they used it before they were caught." We told earlier about a houseparent's account that students have been found using a crowded school bus for sexual activities. A nurse in the infirmary stated that "when you see a bus with students sitting up high in their seats, go check it because they are hiding some couple." This was confirmed by the top administrator.

> Oh yes. Occasionally we have houseparents who are not quite as sharp as they should be. The kids will get in the back of the bus and some of them will get in the seat in front of them and they get a big bunch gathered around, you know. Shoot the breeze while the two in the backseat are doing what comes naturally.

Students also go to ballgames where few of them actually watch the game. For example, at the homecoming football game it seemed that most members of the audience were conversing and not paying attention to the game itself. As confirmation for this observation, the following day a teacher asked Don if he had noticed how deaf people talked to each other and ignored the ballgame? Another teacher commented, "Hearing kids go to a game because they want to see the game. Of course, they do some other things too but mainly they go to see the game. But our kid's don't go to see the game. They go for every other reason in the world but they don't go to see the game." At a ballgame there are many new faces and many new people to talk with. There is a great deal more freedom as one slips and slides in and out of different groups within the large crowd. In short, there is less close supervision and more freedom.

Getting Free by Getting Sick

Many sociologists talk of a "hidden curriculum" in classrooms. We, similarily, note that many activities at SSD have a "hidden" purpose to them – something of a behavioral double entendre. It is hidden in that it is not stated but it may, in fact, be why one group of participants, usually the students, participates at all. In short, these activities offer an outlet for student camaraderie free of adult supervision even though adults are usually present. The infirmary at SSD, with its plush sofas and whiteclad nurses and large color TV, was such a place. Two nurses told how three students came to the infirmary for eight consecutive days claiming to have stomach aches, fingernail problems, and headaches. When asked why the students so frequently came to the infirmary, one of the nurses replied, "Just to hang around a new place. They don't talk to us, but to each other." Again, it is a place for private conversation; a place where there seems to be less authority and relatively more freedom; a place which is different from the dormitory and the classroom. In Goffman's terms, this is a way of "working the system."

One nurse asserted that students exploit houseparents and teachers by frequently claiming to be sick. As she said, "They can play the medicine game for a long time." Why do students do this? "Maybe they come here because they are tired of eating, sleeping, studying, and playing with the same people all the time," she said. Again, here we see an explanation which suggests that the activity is a form of escape.

This same theme was repeatedly stated by infirmary nurses. Two nurses laughingly told how "it is funny to see two girls come in all dressed up with flowers in their hair in order to see some boys or just to walk out near the boys' dorm. We told them they seemed to be sick because they came here so often. We told them 'you must go to bed until seven o'clock this evening and stay in your pajamas.' Both girls started crying and said, 'I not sick.'" Clearly dressing in pajamas and staying in bed until 7 p.m. is an authoritative response to those who too obviously are 'working the system.'

Visits to the school counselor are another form of escape. One staff member put it this way:

> Last year one of the children was coming over for counseling sessions. She really had some bad problems and really hated one of the classes she was in, and really came over here a lot during that time. And being an astute

> obvserver it took me only a month to figure out what was going on. 'You have this problem and it just happens to surface every 10 o'clock English class period. It's just that it really gets bad at 10 o'clock every Tuesday morning, it's just one of those things you can hardly handle on Tuesday at 10, so you just have to be here (with a counselor). And so you come to see me and you talk to me for a while, and you talk to me for 30 minutes and 'I'm feeling better now I can handle the rest of the day. Pass me back to class.' Pass them back to class; it sounds easy enough.

The counselor explained how students would also come to see an audiologist maintaining that their hearing aid had broken. Whenever a student arrives in the office of the audiologist, if there are others being tested, students will wait for an entire class period. "This is a good place for messing around," the counselor stated.

Understanding by Not Understanding

Always in the underlife, students learn how to cope from within the system by "conning" it. While they are "in" the institutional system, they are not necessarily "of" it. The old adage that "rules are made to be broken" is a lesson well learned by many SSD students. Students learn just how rigid the official culture's parameters are. These are learned in an enterprising, ethnomethodological way. In a style which would make Harold Garfinkel proud, they daily engage in ethnomethodological "experiments." That is, they push the norms to their extremes to document for themselves just what they are. As one staff member said,

> We have some kids who know just how many times you can break this one rule before they really come down on your head or they'll be retricted to the dorm. 'I can live with that so I'm going to do the following things,' and so on. You do what you want to do and you get restricted and next week you can do it again ... You can do it again in three weeks and say 'Oh, I forgot!'

Of course they have not forgotten, quite the contrary. They have remembered very well that you can push so far but no further. But you do push to the extreme because the axiom that holds is: The closer I get to the extreme, the more my freedom has been maximized. Even a trivial daily activity like riding the bus offers a chance to test the normative boundaries. As a teacher explained:

> They used to be able to make the bus wait on them a few minutes but now the bus will just go on without them. Now you walk, but that is a

> choice, that is manipulation of the system. 'Miss the bus. Sorry, sorry, pass me to class.' Pass them to class and they have a nice leisurely walk. I have had some of these kids walking through the fields picking flowers, you know. But they learn, they learn to manipulate the system.

Life at SSD is a kind of tug-of-war with the advantage accruing to one side one time and another side another time and the reality of this is not lost on school staff members. They understand that students at SSD (like students elsewhere) will "rebel." And in rebelling they effectively assert their own sense of self and worth. A top administrator describes the struggle between individual selfhood and the social system in the following way:

> We have a lot of kids who tell me [by their actions] 'I'll beat them with my mind. I'll be so stubborn and so passive-aggressive – that your patience will wear out!' And you'll say, 'To hell with it.' And you have kids coming in from P. E. and the teacher's got 8 kids there and ready to teach history. You're late to class and you come wandering in 10 minutes late and 'Where've you been?' 'Can't hear you.' 'Why are you late?' 'Lost my shoes. Somebody stole my shoes.' That's a favorite, 'Somebody stole my shoes,' or something.

The administrator understands that this is the student's way of inverting the power relationship between student and teacher. The student has the power to disrupt, and to do so in a naive way, as though he/she is unaware of the net effect. As the administrator rhetorically asks, "What can a teacher do?" but proceed with the class lesson. Bright students learn that if they want to they can be manipulative and possess a certain kind of power. As the administrator says of this kind of student,

> He can pull his passive/aggressive bit and he knows that nine out of ten times, if he just perseveres, folks are going to give up and not pursue it because he pretends – 'I don't understand.' Most often, 'I don't remember.'

The World View of Students at SSD

The major social division of the world made by deaf students is deaf and hearing, however, this is not easily accomplished. Students define "deaf" in various ways. For example, some younger and/or slower students will say that one is "a little bit deaf" if one is able to use sign language. They do not understand that one could use sign language and not be deaf. A teacher in the Special Studies

Department (for slower students) tells that a student will say, "'My Mom is deaf,' and I will say 'No, she is not.' The student will say, 'Yes, she is a little bit deaf because she can sign a little.'" Other teachers also commented about this confusion among deaf students and being able to tell who is and who is not one of their own.

Deafness is such an important attribute to deaf students that it, alone, transcends the importance of other common determinants of social groupings (recall the city official who said there is no "race" for the students other than 'deaf' and 'hearing'). A hard-of-hearing high school girl who attended public schools also finds a more racially integrated world:

> [Off campus, in my hometown nearby] if I am a white girl, okay? I'm white and some other people see me with a black boy, they call me 'Nigger-lover.' It's a title, 'Nigger-lover.' I remember when I was in public school in the ninth grade, my freshman year, there was one girl, she was a new girl from Oak Town. She was always with Blacks and she had a black boyfriend. They went and they rolled her yard. They messed her yard up and they burned it. Come here and it is totally different! They have got black boys going with white girls and white girls going with black boys and its just different. Before I used to think it was weird but now I am just used to it.

One teacher tells that a black boy and a white boy insisted they were cousins because they were from the same hometown. These students could not understand that race might preclude their being cousins. To them, cousins was a bond of geography and deafness with race being given no consideration.

Not only do some deaf students at SSD divide the social world into deaf and hearing people, not only do they identify the use of sign language with the status of "deaf," not only do they sometimes equate kinship with similar locale but they also view certain school symbols as indicative of deaf and hearing. For example, certain school colors are "deaf" while another color is "hearing" (something discussed in the next chapter).

Newcomers' Views of Life at SSD

As we have shown elsewhere in this report, there is much concern at SSD about schooling students who can exist in the "real world," the world outside of the walls at SSD. As one approach to the students' views on this, it was decided to interview students who were relative newcomers at SSD. It seemed wise to talk with hard-of-hearing students because they had had greater audio participation in the hearing world. In particular they had had experience in hearing schools but they had come to SSD because their experience was not a good one. Thus, they come to SSD as "converts," as marginal people who experienced the radical change of moving from one world to another world.

One of the most interesting cases of a student fitting the "marginal peron" category is Honey, a day student from an upper middle-class family in a nearby town. After nearly four months at SSD she had numerous insights into the student subculture at the school. She was able to do this because she herself had come into the school as an outsider, as a person reared and schooled in the hearing world, and as a person who knew no sign language nor any of the subcultural ways of life prior to attending SSD. During a second interview with her (two months after the first interview), she was asked, "What is the deaf world?" She immediately replied that

> Honey: Communication is very different. I tried for a long time to understand their communication. I changed a little to try to belong to their group, acting the same as them.
>
> Don: How do they act? How do you mean, 'act like them?'
>
> Honey: They use their hands, they move their body, they move so much! They do silly things in their movements. They show action. They act out a story, show you actions. In a restaurant hearing people don't show their actions much, but the deaf move a lot in a restaurant, inside or outside, doesn't matter. Any place. In Hill City, at a movie – they move a lot. Sometimes it embarrasses me because I don't want others to know I'm deaf. But I understand their feelings too. I understand I am deaf too and I am changing my actions like them.
>
> Don: Are you imitating them? (Becoming) same as them?
>
> Honey: No, not the same, but move around, talk around in the movies. My boyfriend got a little embarrassed in the car [the boyfriend is a hearing person; another couple, a hearing boy and a deaf girl are with them at the time]. And I talk with Judy ... We were talking in the restaurant and my boyfriend was sitting across the table and Judy's date was on the other side also. Our boyfriends wanted to know if we enjoyed the food and we said, yes, and we just kept moving a lot, very much, good action. Judy's boyfriend was looking. He didn't know what was going on.

It is a common story. A young deaf person, reared in schools where speech and speech-reading are emphasized, realizes at some later point in life the need for sign language. Eventually the person becomes aware of the numerous difficulties of performing and functioning smoothly in the hearing world. Often, it is a very slow and gradual migration from the world of words to the world of signs, from the world of traumatic communication experiences to the sign-world of community, comfort and identity. Honey offers an excellent example of someone learning to be deaf. From her own account, she is "acting the same as them." For her, and other comparable newcomers to residential settings (be they schools, prisons, asylums, whatever), the institutional world becomes, in Berger's term, the paramount reality against which all other worlds are judged.

There is evidence that hard-of-hearing students, relatively skilled with English, also enjoy higher status than others. This was observed by the school's new audiologist, who said, "I think that hard-of-hearing has a status here because the kids will tell you fast, 'I am not deaf. I am HH'" (in signs: hard-of-hearing). More than a year later, however, he had second thoughts about this. It's possible, he said, that deaf students consider the hard-of-hearing as outsiders, that the deaf often "use" them. Some of these newcomers have been at SSD as long as five years or as little as two years. Since they had spent much of their life in the hearing world and then joined the deaf world, we assumed that their comparative insights would be useful in discovering significant differences between the two worlds. As we shall see, these students point out ways in which the deaf subculture differs from the hearing world from which they migrated. They will discuss different linguistic expressions and modalities, different interpersonal relationships as well as differential knowledge of the outside world.

Several newcomers said they made good grades at SSD. They claimed that the school was not very hard. One girl's picture of deaf students is telling:

> There are only a few deaf people who can really understand what you say. Like if you try to explain things to them they don't understand it. They ask me to help them with English and I try to explain it – over and over again! But they don't understand.

Some of these hard-of-hearing students have become true believers, converts who have been integrated into their newfound deaf world to they extent that they now denigrate the hearing world from which they come. For example, one young girl, a cheerleader, said that she wanted her children to be either deaf or hard-of-hearing: "I want a deaf child because a hearing child is spoiled.

My favorite is deaf and hard-of-hearing. I hate talking people because they are spoiled."

Another newcomer who is hard-of-hearing told how uncomfortable she felt upon first arriving at SSD, having spent nine years in public schools. She dreaded to walk in front of other people because she felt everybody was looking at her. "I had never been around so many deaf people at one time. I was so different. I was nervous and scared at the same time."

One unique linguistic quality of the school is the meaning of certain colloquial phrases, something which newcomers are quick to learn. Sometimes these words sound oddly juxtaposed against each other. One newcomer mentioned the difference between the expressions "fired home" and "suspended." "I think 'fired home' means no more coming back. But suspension is one week or two weeks – something like that. I say something like, 'Jim got fired home.' and they would say no, he got suspended." This expression, "fired home," is interesting in that it is an abbreviated form of saying: "This person was fired and sent home." Of course being "fired" is an American euphemism for being dismissed from one's job (in Britain the expression is "made redundant"). On numerous occasions students remarked that someone had been "fired home." Obviously fired home is used to refer to more serious offenses than is the term suspended.

The same newcomer who explained "fired home" also described how her spoken as well as her sign language had expanded since attending SSD. She gave this example: "They [SSD students] say, 'late touch,' when they mean 'have you ever been there before?' I say it myself like it's a slang word. It's just a habit because I say them and memorize it." Students would not say, "I have never been to that city." This is similar to another expression in ASL which is signed, "I think touch you" which means "I will keep you in mind." In each of these expressions the sign "touch" makes an idea more physical or concrete. Touch is the most fundamental means of communication. For the deaf students it takes on special significance since so much of their language is, of necessity, physical. Thus "late touch" conveys an act not yet done while "think touch" becomes the cognitive shorthand for bringing to mind someone not physically present. The physical connotation of touch also has importance for hearing people who wish to "think touch you." For them, however, it gets expressed to a departing friend or loved one when they say "Keep in touch."

Subtle? What's That?

It has been shown throughout this report that a real problem for deaf students is dealing with abstractions. One outcome of this is to be incredibly direct – blunt to the point of rudeness. As one senior girl who had attended public schools put its, "... in public school nobody goes up to your face and says, 'You are a whore!' They do that. Here they do." Too, despite some ingenius ways of duping the authorities, students at SSD often tell authorities about the misdeeds of their classmates. For example, one morning in high school a student raised her hand to inform the teacher that another student had smoked a cigarette the previous night in the dorm. Such behavior at SSD was common. The same senior girl (above) again compares SSD culture with public school student culture:

> Girl: Here ... well, like in public school you tell a friend something and she keeps it a secret. But here they don't keep secrets. Like I tell one of my friends something and I say, 'Keep it a secret, don't tell!' And she goes around and tells somebody and it gets around fast. I noticed that. That was the first thing I noticed. Hearing school you can tell somebody something and they won't say anything. Another thing I noticed was hearing people, they smoke pot at school and nobody goes and tells on them because they know you would get in trouble if you do. Here, the kids would be smoking or something and the other kid goes and tells on him. That was something I noticed too.

A houseparent related that one student might tell a police officer who is searching a dormitory room that some marijuana was hidden in the ceiling by the student's roommate. She explained another type incident:

> Houseparent: Someone went in and stole my cigarette lighter and some cigarettes out of my pack. We found two of the cigarettes lying outside the door. We later found out who got the lighter.
>
> Don: How did you find out who got the lighter?
>
> Houseparent: Some of the boys told. You have boys who are really good boys and they'll tell you what's going on. If they ... When they learn that they can trust you, they'll come to you and they'll tell you what's happening.

Two nurses in the infirmary gave this example: "A boy might come in here without a pass and later on five or six students will rush in here to tell us that he did wrong! That he had no pass to come in here!" Each of these incidents suggests that loyalty to one's peers may get subordinated for loyalty/deference to the authorities. It is not, however, that honesty is some well adhered to virtue. In a type of exchange, they engage in certain behaviors (e.g., informing) that may enhance their own situations at least for the moment (one houseparent told of rewarding certain people with spending money which had been given to her by outside charitable donors).

A good example of student bluntness is in considering the informal student dress code and how one's appearance has attributes associated with it. In her desperate attempt to achieve acceptance at the school a new girl decided to dress plainly and without jewelry. What would happen if she wore a dress to school? "The kids would ask me, 'Why are you wearing a pretty dress? Why did you change? Are you trying to show-off?' A popular hard-of-hearing high school girl now in her second year with the new culture of SSD remembers:

Girl: They've got this thing up here right before when I first came here like in the public school all the girls wear make-up, and they carry a pocketbook with them and everything. When I come here I brought my pocket book with me everyday because it was a habit, and I always wore a little bit of makeup. I come here and they call you a whore or different things (looking embarassed).

Don: Go ahead. Name them. I don't care.

Girl: Whores, or ... Let's see.

Don: Fast!

Girl: Fast! They call you fast. They just spell out f-a-s-t. It means like you can get any boy you want to. You know like get him, break up with him and then you can go right on to another boy.

Don: How do you get him?

Girl: Okay. It would be like I break up with this guy on Monday and I go with another boy on Tuesday. Then I stay with him for about three days, and break up with him on Thursday or Friday. The next day go with another boy. They would call me 'fast.'

Girl: They think you are out of place if you wear makeup or something like that. I don't know why. It's something I never did find out. Like, for pictures, all they wear is makeup. You can look in the yearbook and you find out every girl had on makeup. Then after the picture they won't wear makeup anymore.

Don: Everyday (they don't wear it)?

Girl: Sometimes, but then when I wear makeup – when I feel like it – they say 'Whore.' I can't help it. Makeup is something I have always done since I have been fifteen.

Don: So not many girls wear makeup here?

Girl: --------, my best friend ... . A few others do like ----- and -----. If they have enough time to put it on they will wear it.

> Don: I wonder if you noticed anything else since you first came in, you know, that was different by the way they dressed, or acted, or thought ... their thoughts that were different here that surprised you a little bit?
>
> Girl: They get mad easy ... But when I first came here they would put their arm around me, but after a while they would say 'Go on back to public school.' They were sweet to me and would say things like 'your hair is pretty' or they would go on and they would be nice to me. After a while, there are a few of them like ----- and the boys that can't get enough of the girls and will put their arm around you and pat you and they are always doing that. They are just like a family.
>
> Don: You think they are flirting a little when they do that?
>
> Girl: Especially -----, he flirts with any girl. Any girl he feels like he will flirt with. *When I first came here they are just totally different from hearing* [emphasis added].
>
> Don: Explain that to me.
>
> Girl: Wearing tight jeans, tennis shoes, tee shirts or a good shirt. I always had my hair fixed up but I came here and they have on dress pants all the time. Sweaters, real flowery shirts. It was just different.
>
> Don: You mean you dress better here than at home?
>
> Girl: Both of them dress good, but it was just totally opposite. Like you never hardly saw hearing [students] wear dress pants. Hardly ever. Come here and almost every one of them had on dress pants. If you wear tight jeans ... I got this last year ... I wore tight jeans, its something I wore in public school. I wore them to school one day and they came up to me and said, 'Are you a whore? Go get them off!'
>
> Don: Is that boys or girls saying that?
>
> Girl: Both of them. They said, 'That's not right. You are not supposed to wear tight jeans.'
>
> Don: Does the school permit you to wear them if you want to?
>
> Girl: It's not a rule or nothing. It's just that they were jealous or they didn't like it or something. But after a while now I am wearing them. The pants. It was just the opposite [in public school]. I never saw them wearing dress pants. Come here and everyone of them has on dress pants.

Don asked Macer about the practice of calling girls with makeup 'whores.'

> Don: I notice here that girls want to wear makeup and the boys call her 'whore,' 'prostitute.'
>
> Macer: So I notice talking people (but) I don't notice talking boys call (girls) 'whore,' 'prostitute.' Talking boys don't do that. The boys look at the girls and the girls make up their faces and the boys see their faces are beautiful and say, 'Wow!' And make a girl proud of herself, makes the boy go after her. Makes a girl happy, proud of herself, not like here. Deaf people think that the makeup, the deaf people most of the time in town

> and in country they see a pretty girl, woman, its like a whore or prostitute. They are afraid that they will copy/imitate or will spread their reputation of a whore.

The homecoming queen, obviously a person who comes from the inside student culture, discussed the popular campus term "show off."

> Don: What about the way people dress sometimes. Do they show off that way?
>
> Queen: Yes. If somebody dresses up fancy, that's show off. If a person says about himself, 'I play basketball well' without people asking you, yes.
>
> Don: Do a lot of people show off everyday?
>
> Queen. Sometimes.
>
> Don: I notice that not many girls use makeup.
>
> Queen: The reason is that girls would like to use it, but they may make fun of the girl.
>
> Don: Call them names? What?
>
> Queen: 'Clown.' 'Show-off', Boy.
>
> Don: You mean the boys themselves are teasing the girls, or (is it) girls *and* boys?
>
> Queen: They say 'You're showing off for the boys. You're a clown.'
>
> Don: Do you, yourself, prefer to use some makeup?
>
> Queen: I never use makeup. Just a little on the eyelash.

At SSD students experience considerable student-based pressure to conform. And subtlety, as noted above with the use of the term "whore," is the exception not the rule. Those who deviate are quick to be pointed out by their peers. The term "show-off" is often used for this purpose. It is a leveling device by which one is ridiculed for displaying some higher status behavior or appearance. It is used derisively by SSD students when wanting to isolate the deviant (student stratification will be discussed in more detail shortly). In the use of all descriptive terms for enforcing conformist norms, subtlety is ignored. Honey, a new high school student, was asked about this. Why are SSD students so severe on each other?

> Honey: When I came here I realized that the deaf are very, very different.
>
> Don: How are they different?
>
> Honey: Communication is very different. I try to communicate in the same way as in the hearing world. I am used to the hearing world. I thought it would be the same but the deaf don't like the way I communi-

cate. They make fun of me in front of me (my face). They think that I am stuck-up and I want them to understand that I live different [from them]. I have parents who want to take care of me. The houseparents here care for their children, but I grew up different. They (the students) don't have responsibilities and their personality is mean. I look at their personality and I think, Wow! I hate to tell people that I have a car and I say, 'Yes,' and I hate to say that but I like to be honest that I do have a car. When I first came here I didn't want to wear my rings to show them that I had a lot of jewelry, that I have a lot of clothes. I wear the same clothes again and again and again. I want to be the same as they are. Many times the deaf are surprised that I can drive at night time. Go to [three different states], they are surprised that I can drive. I want to show them a picture of my house but I hate to show them. One day I brought a small picture and showed them the picture, and they looked at it and said, 'Rich! Rich!' I said, 'No, no. Not rich, not rich!' So they complained. Then they said nothing to me. If they say, 'You're rich,' I never answer them ....

I try to be very friendly with _____, the pretty girl ... Inside she wants to be friends with me, but outside she doesn't show me. Sheena's not around, so [the pretty girl] is quiet and fun and teases me and we just have fun, but when Sheena comes up ... maybe she says I'm stupid and she takes off.

[Sheena is an aggressive leader who seems very threatened by this very attractive upper middle class girl. A teacher who befriended her comments]:

Teacher: Honey came into my class and Sheena (also in that class) is my best art student. She is a very powerful young lady in many ways. She immediately took a dislike to Honey for the obvious reasons.

Don: Was she threatened by Honey?

Teacher: Oh, yes! Severely threatened. Her power was severely threatened. And so Sheena immediately set out to cirumscribe the possibility of her being a part of the situation. You can set out rumors and all types of vicious rumors that the kids here, because she was an outsider and because she is not really deaf and she does communicate orally and because she is wealthy. All these things were very bad against her (and) they accepted these rumors pretty quick.

[But others also reject her in painful ways. Here, a black girl with good speech meets Honey the evening after being introduced to her by a teacher]:

I helped a teacher and I saw the black girl coming so I said, 'Hi.' I met her and I showed her and she was nice, and then last night she said dirty words to me. She just did double talk. [Later]: I was talking to an adult and this black girl comes around and watches me, eyes me. She said, 'She talks funny. She's ugly. Not good talk.' And it would hurt me. And I never saw anybody who would say that in front of me. She said that in front of me. When I went home, I asked my parents, 'Do I talk funny?'

[The following day, more of the same]

(A girl) grabbed me by the arm [and said in the presence of a teacher] 'Not your favorite man.' And I said nothing ... The thin girl says, 'Always flirting. You always flirting.' I said, 'No!' I said, 'No. That's a lie.' The big girl says, 'Not lie. Always new girls come in here and they flirt.' The teacher says, 'Not true.'

.. Many times the boys put their arms around me and try to hug me. And I just sort of push them away.

Don: The boys?

Honey: The boys put their face next to my face in front [of others]. Maybe if I will hug them they probably push me away. So I'm nice and I just kind of push them a little bit. I don't want them hugging me ... Joe is a big, big, big basketball player ... He's always hugging me, telling the other boys that I am his girlfriend. I tell them, 'No. He is lying. He's not my boyfriend.' But I never used that word 'lie.' Never before. Here I am using it, 'lie.' My parents don't like me to use that word lie. They say, 'Don't do that.' .. They hate the word 'lie.' But here (they use) 'lie.' My peers understand me if I use the world, 'lie.' ... I'd like to explain more than that [more than the condensed one word], but a shorter way they understand better. If you say, 'lie,' they understand. I'd like to explain more than that, but they don't understand, so I just say 'lie,' that's all.

Dolly, another hard-of-hearing student, also perceived that her school peers have a problem with manners: "In public schools students go home every day and their mothers and fathers can teach them manners. But here we have to stay in the dormitory and they (the parents) can't [teach their children manners]." Neither teachers nor houseparents can hope to have as much influence on a student's behavior as the student's own parents who would have only a relatively few children to deal with at one time.

Honey arrived at SSD driving a sleek automobile, wearing pretty clothes and jewelry, and using speech and speechreading as her primary means of communication. Having come from a world of expensive private schools and skiing trips in foreign lands this deaf teenager met with some strong opposition at SSD. During the second month of her tenure at SSD she explained, "Hearing people do not hurt other people's feelings. Here they hurt your feelings, they don't care about your feelings." She gave an example. "Many people do not think I should be in school here. Sheena says many, many times to the boys and girls, 'Honey is trying to show off, she thinks she is on top.'" Although she had made considerable progress toward adjusting to her new world, even claiming Sheena as her best friend, in a follow-up interview (two months later), Honey repeated her first observation about the bluntness of the deaf student subculture.

> I like hearing people. They are always careful what they say to another person, but deaf – they don't care. They say anything they feel inside. They just gush/pour it out, just say it, and spew it out. But hearing (people) are patient and keep it inside. Maybe one (hearing) person feels sorry for me the way I talk, my voice is funny. But they don't tell me 'Your voice is funny.' But here, they'll tell you your voice is funny, your actions are funny. They'll say anything, but hearing [people] think about other persons but here they don't care.

Karen, another relative newcomer, offered some similar observation:

Why are students so painfully blunt and direct to each other? Did they fail to learn subtle manners, respect for others, and diplomatic techniques during the socialization process? Why do they exhibit so little loyalty to one another? Why will students tell the authorities on each other? Is this behavior something like that found in tribal societies like the Yoruba where the basic need of the individual is "attachment to other human beings?" Where the "Self is completely identified in an undifferentiated way, with the group ..." (Kearney, 1984:74–75). Or is this just the opposite, i.e., is this an example of an "isolated self" which is the only kind of self that "can act selfishly and egoistically vis-a-vis other selves" (p. 78)? Are they merely unusually honest?

The socialization process at SSD is viewed by one staff member as truncated because intonation of language is absent. This has the consequence of creating individuals whose behavior is "blunt"[11]. For example, students typically say to staff members, teachers and others, "You're fat" or "You're old," or "You're sloppy today." This abrasive and blunt linguistic assault was explained as follows:

> Staff: They do it within the community themselves. They do that everyday.
>
> Don: You mean it is their norm?
>
> Staff: Yes. Just to be more blunt. Well, they can't pick up on the social niceties. When I am being sarcastic hearing people *know* I am being sarcastic, my facial expression changes. While deaf people can pick up on facial expressions they don't get the intonation of the voice, and so what they get is a direct message, the blunt message. So sarcasm can be wounding to them sometimes where it is not to other people. And I think that is basically what they do all the time. Instead of saying to others 'I think you are gaining a little bit of weight' what they would say is 'Gain weight.' They are not going to say, 'You put on a little bit of weight maybe.' They will just ask, 'Fat? Fat now?'

Students frequently say to her, "You stupid!" whenever she fails to respond as they expect. On one occasion a student told a teacher, "Crazy, you." Another day while crossing campus a high school boy joined Don, sized up the way he was dressed and signed, "Sloppy, you." A staff member thought deaf students in general were direct and blunt because it is simply their way of life (i. e., normative for them).

> When they are angry, they say they are angry. They don't tone it down and sweeten it down and all those things. They just tell you that it makes them mad. I like that. That is one of the things that I like most about the deaf. Once I got over the fact that would tell me I was fat or my hair looked ugly or I should wash my hair and all these things – they would just tell me. Once you get over that I really like their blunt way. I wish a lot of times hearing people had that going for them. I would like to be able to do that more than I can. I enjoy that generally about the deaf, although there are times when it has made me a little upset and frustrated but then I look back and realize that I could be dealing with people who were trying to lay hidden traps instead of dealing with me honestly and I really like the fact that they want to deal with me bluntly.

What is called good clean honesty here is described by Goffman (1961) as a failure to support another's act, which is essentially the way interacting people sustain social order (harmony) and/or impression management. Goffman argues, in fact, that we must *not* speak in a brutally honest and frank way. Instead, we must display a form of politeness, "a veneer of consensus," by supporting each other's act – the exact opposite of what we found at SSD. But Goffman's theory has been criticized and his "con man" is said to be a product of Western capitalistic culture. That is, impression management, game playing, and facade presentation might typify behavior within very competitive and individualistic cultures but not tribal ones. Clearly interaction and social order exist at SSD without much artificial 'supporting the act of the other.'

During the entire time spent at SSD, the extremely heavy usage of negative terms, much of it name-calling, was noted again and again. One needs only to spend some time in almost any prison to observe a similar phenomenon. Cindy (popular senior homecoming queen) was asked about negative signs:

> Don: Cindy, can you tell me some of the signs the kids use all the time? Like m.r. (mentally retarded)?
>
> Cindy: (signs the letter "i" over her right shoulder)
>
> Don: What does that mean?

> Cindy: 'I don't believe you.' They say, 'Yes, yes, yes.'
>
> Don: What else?
>
> Cindy: M.R., You stupid, you lousy, n.g. [no good]. Everyday (it's) 'n.g., n.g., You know nothing!' That's all I can think of.

As we have stated at other points, no matter how good the school environment, it still may not equal a proper home living situation. Students at SSD live in a constant group situation without personal and individualized parental guidance and teaching. The students at SSD give some credence to the adage "familiarity breeds contempt." One must always be mindful that SSD is its own little world. As in other institutional settings, a world is created which acts back upon those who created it and in the process denying them their individuality. Taken to an extreme, everyone would behave alike. Tact would be unnecessary in the face of a constant, naked candor with no pretence of civility in any form. One very articulate and popular young high school teacher, whose sign language skill is outstanding, talked about the "uninhibited" and blunt ways of deaf students:

> Teacher: Freud would be very happy to come here because this is a microcosm of what he said. Because the language is blatant. These people have been together for 14 years day and night. The subtlety, all the Freudian things that we have been taught to suppress as members of the hearing middle-class society, all the thoughts that we are supposed to never articulate, these kids take as everyday communications.
>
> Don: Blow it out.
>
> Teacher: They just blow it right out. They walk in and they are liable to say anything. Now there are some staff people who intimidate them, very few, but the kids are just about willing to say anything concerning sex. And they are convinced that sex makes the world go round.

While sex is almost a preoccupation of many SSD students, it is something about which they are very confused. Wearing make-up is quickly equated with being a whore. Too much time with individuals of the same sex may lead to being called homosexual.

One teacher told how students would often see a male and female teacher talking together and would ask them, "Are you sweethearts?" A high school boy saw Don walking with an attractive high school girl (headed for an interview). "Flirt," he signed (and this is a common reaction at the school). Many students seem to have no conception of a casual relationship between a male and a female hence, they tend to suspect some deeper sexual involvement between individuals. This same teacher also said that if students see her talking with another female teacher, they might say "lesbians." They might see you (the male interviewer) talking to another man, she said, and call you all homosexuals.

> Can you imagine saying something like that to one of your teachers when you were in school? Now we had (someone) who teaches science, a very respected teacher, a good teacher, a very respected person and Mrs. ____ who was principal ... One day they were standing outside the library talking. One of the girls walked by and said, 'lesbians .' Can you imagine a hearing child saying that to a principal and a teacher?

These quotes well illustrate both sexual confusion and the bluntness with which things are expressed. Too, they show a certain naivete in dealing with authorities which precludes deference as it is usually found among school children and their immediate supervisors.

Deaf children were also seen making fun of handicapped deaf children on campus. Several informants mentioned such behavior. According to one very bright, articulate student, Macer, one student might call another "mentally retarded" (MR) in order to make him mad. As he said,

> Sometimes I see the handicapped teased, teased ... make him feel it cause he can't help it. Sometimes a deaf kid will laugh at somebody in a wheelchair. They say he's crippled, 'You can't run, you can't walk. I beat you. You can't beat me running, you can't run. You're crippled. You can't go fast. I think I can beat you.'

Karen, the hard-of-hearing newcomer, had observed a similar pattern of behavior and seemed puzzled by it:

> If she is really mentally retarded they will go up and say, 'Gosh! She is handicapped! She is ugly!' It is normal. I mean if she was born that way, she can't help it. And that's what they do and they have a handicap themselves. They are deaf! I don't understand.

This kind of derision illustrates an important sociological point. Much like Gordon Allport (1958) found in *The Nature of Prejudice*, nearly everyone seems to have someone that they can feel superior to. With deaf children we find a group of already handicapped individuals who are even further constrained by living almost exclusively among other handicapped children. So what do they do? They find a target for their own hostilities, in this case focusing on those less fortunate than themselves.

This same thesis was expressed by a high school teacher, who had worked at SSD for many years. The deaf children fail to learn the appropriate reactions to different behaviors, and importantly, they must feel superior to some other deaf group.

> I've been talking to a lot of the coaches around ... We have a problem with teammates criticizing teammates. We have problems with a JV (junior varsity) team making fun of a varsity team or vice versa. Girls (team players) making fun of the boys ... This is unheard of in public schools. You would be obstracized in a minute.

Just Teasing: Horseplay as a Norm

The school culture at SSD (like many other schools, perhaps most) is one where classroom activities are constantly referred to as "boring." And many social events outside the classroom are termed "fun." It would be accurate to speak of SSD high school culture as a "fun culture." There is considerable horseplay and clowning around in all places: dorms, classrooms, cafeteria, on the bus, etc. An interview with Macer (a popular high school senior) captures this sense of 'fun.'

> Don: Macer, tell me the story of one day of your life beginning early in the morning. What happens?
>
> Macer: Before I go to bed, I sign my name that I want to wake up about 6:00 a.m. And I sign my name and let the houseparent know that I want to get up at six. So I go to sleep. In the morning the houseparent comes in and shakes me. 'Wake up! Makes me ... Oh! Makes me so mad. I don't want to eat and the houseparent says okay. And so I lay there lazy and sleep. Again, the houseparent shakes me. It's 7:00 or 7:30 and I'm still asleep. Really, I need more sleep and I suffer, suffer, suffer.
>
> I get up and I talk to my friend, Dan. And we just talking. 'Did you finish eating breakfast?' He says, 'No. Not yet. I haven't eaten breakfast yet.' And he says, 'I want to sleep' And he says 'I can't help it.' So we take a bath and brush my teeth and I put on my clothes and fix up my hair with a comb, put on my shirt with some deodorant. Put on my clothes and I call my friends – ready to go to school!
>
> The boys say, 'Okay. You ready? Everything ready?' So we get our books and we go in. Before we start class we talk, talk, talk. I see a pretty girl. My friend says, "Yes-s-s.' And we pick, pick, pick all the time on the girl.
>
> Don: Who's the girl?
>
> Macer: Many of them. Many of them. Different girls. And we just tease them. We tease them. When its time to start class we go in. All the ugly girls. Cindy. 'Hi. Good morning, ugly girl.' And we talk, talk, talk. 'What you doing? Why don't you see me? I want to talk to you.' And the girl says, "I can't help. I can't help it if I forgot. So I say, 'Okay. Don't worry. That's fine.' Then I call (wave to) Dan and I say, 'Did you see Cindy's funny behavior (actions, doings)? She's pretty. Yes-s-s. And I wish to go with her.' I'm talking to Dan. I'm teasing and make Honey smile at me.

I always tell stories, joke, tease, tease, tease Honey to make her laugh at me. Mrs. _____ says, "Stop, silly. Our class time. You must work.' Macer: 'It's boring. I hate school [head swings negatively back and forth]. I want to have a good time. Good time, favorite time. Enjoy myself. 'No,' she (teacher) says, 'You must pay attention and work. Don't bother the girls. Pay attention.' And I say, 'Oh, no! The law permits me to bother them.' Teacher says, 'Stop that, silly,' Macer: 'So, I'm not silly. I'm honest story [I'm telling the truth].' 'Ha!' she says. 'Ha, ha, ha. So you think its funny.'

So I'm working, working, talking, talking and Dan he's picking on Cindy. Making Cindy [mad]. Macer: 'Let me bother her.' Dan: 'I don't care. Go ahead and pick on her.' She wants to talk to Tiny and I say, 'Go ahead, I don't care! That's fine. No problem with me.' Tiny calls me, 'Ha! Ha! Ha!' The bell rings. Go to another class walking, 'Hi, girl. Are you fine?' 'Good,' Locker, open door, put in science books. Science class, talk, talk, talk and see Cindy. 'Stupid girl!' Cindy is making mad at me going 'Ha! Ha! Ha.' My teacher says, 'Start lab.' Fine. I make coal. Macer: 'How can you make it work?' 'Take test tubes and a jar and mix some fire to make it very hot and make a fire and it can work.' The fire, because oxygen, it can work. That's the reason. Coal makes oxygen, makes burn and end [of] jar below smell horrible. Makes coal tar for surface of the road. I think its better to ask Dan. Its better to try to give the odor to Cindy's nose. Better to tease than ordor(ize) her. Okay, so he puts it all under her and she makes mad and [he] goes, 'Ha! Ha! Ha!' And teasing her. 'Don't be mad with me. I want to play with you. Cindy says, 'Okay.' Macer: 'I don't mean to be mean to you. No, I just like fun with you before graduating.'

The bell rings for recess time, break time. I run into the snackbar. I want to buy because a great crowd will flock in, just crowded and wiggling [pantomimed] and fighting to get in and interrupt and steal and break in line. I don't want to be late time going to class so I'm hurrying, hurrying and I'm pushing the girls. Make them mad with me and I'm just laughing and I called Dan, 'Come on Dan! Let's pick on the girls.' 'Okay, Okay! Pick, pick, pick.' And he [Dan] sees we're talking, talking, talking and says, 'Oh! Look at the ugly woman.' And the girls says, 'Ha, ha, ha! I am ugly?' And I say, 'Yes. You are ugly!' Then I say, 'No. I'm just teasing you. You're a pretty girl.' And [this] makes the girl happy. They say, 'Thank you.' Okay [I] love, hug [them] and this satisfies [them]. 'See you later.'

I start class time. Go back. Mrs. _____ says, 'Good Morning. How are you doing?' I say, 'Fine. One hundred percent fine. No problems.' I ask, 'Any homework?' Mrs. _____ says, 'Yes.' 'I have work.' [Teacher]: 'It doesn't matter. Do your homework because now it's okay. Write your homework. I want to read the paper.' Macer: Can you read?' Teacher: 'That's fine, okay.' So she reads.

Macer: 'Dan, did you see the picture [of] Herschel Walker? Wow! Did you see the picture? That running?' Dan: 'Two hundred eight yards, wow! That's wonderful.' Macer: 'I think maybe Georgia [university of] can go national tournament if Georgia can do better, if they win.' Dan: 'They can get the tournament, I hope so.'

Bell rings. Another class ends. Math time. Mrs. _____, the teacher [sees me] fooling around, playing and she says, 'Stop playing. You need to do your homework.' And I say, 'I don't have enough time at dorm.' Teacher: 'No. You must work at the end of the first quarter.' Macer: 'I can keep up. Don't worry, please. Okay, I will work.' So I'm writing, writing, writing. When it's leaving time I have to hurry and run, get in the bus because many people are running, crowding to get in and seize the front seat. I want to sit in the front seat. When we leave and arrive and stop and park, I run from the bus to the line to eat. Then we eat. Don: who do you sit with? Macer: One table: Cindy, Tiny, Dan and Max and sixth is Henry. And we eat. 'Do you like to eat that?' I say. 'No? Can you give it to me?' So I take if from his plate. I love to eat it very much and I eat, eat, eat and I ask Tiny, 'Why do you [act] so snobbish? Why do you snob me?'

Tiny: 'I didn't mean to. Oh! Stop being silly.' Macer: 'True? Really? I doubt [it]. I don't believe it. You trying to fool me. I'm not stupid, you can't fool me. I'm teasing! I'm teasing!' Oh, Tiny. Oh, then she's satisfied. She thinks I'm a true story [thinks I'm serious] and I'm just teasing her. When I finish eating time and I go vocational building. I say, 'Hi,' to Mr. _____, welding teacher. 'What you doing?' Teacher: 'Working. I want you to make wood stove. Okay, so I'm working and making and welding and he calls, 'What you need?' Macer: 'I'm working here.' Teacher says, 'You need to fix it a little differently here. Weld it, work on it.' And its break time.

It's been so hot, so hot! So hot! The welding. The sweat is pouring and we're going to rest for a few minutes, relax for a few minutes. So we just talk. I ask teacher: 'I want to [go] your home to help work with you because the dorm's nothing. Just sit, sit, sit. I want to do something and go help you.' Teacher says, 'Okay. Anytime you want to help.'

When the bell rings again time come in the bus and get in and everything's finished. Everybody's in the bus. Go (to) other school, back to other school, the main campus and we get out, get lesson books, go to dorm and let houseparent know where I'm going.

[There is a brief description of a football practice session, then we continue the long interview in a private booth of a small restaurant in nearby Doubletown]

Don: Go ahead (continue) about your eating in the rec (recreation) room with your friends.

Macer: They throw potato chips to Cindy's face and it hits her. (They) throw, throw, throw, play, play, play. Steal her food. Steal, steal, eat, eat and throw it and shove and shove. Teasing and talking. She calls Dan. Dan: 'What's that woman mean.' Macer: 'I don't know? Who is that? New girl? Dan says, 'I think so.' Cindy says, 'Stop, silly.' Macer: 'Who is that?' So we talk. And we tease her and we make fun and we go to the

> pinball (machine) and we enjoy (it) and we finish that and (it) makes me mad. Low score. I want a high score, but anyway I can't get it so I'm just talking, visiting and talking and go outside and talk and run around playing. Touching Tammy on the shoulder, playing. When closing time the Rec room we go to the dorm, go in and study today and get our homework. And get our pencils and we write. 'I really am bored with the homework.' And Dan says, 'I know that you don't want your homework. Fine! There's football on TV.' Macer: 'Yes! Let's go up and see.'
>
> Houseparent in the dorm says, 'Okay. Clean up.' So we clean up and we finish and we dry and we take a bath, wash our hair and then Dan – it's his time. He takes a bath and we talk and go down to first floor and we talk. See what's happening on football. What's the story (talk) about. And we talk and then go to bed. 'See you tomorrow morning.' And then we go to sleep and that's it.

The preceding is from a lengthy (3 hour) interview. The initial goal of the interview was to query Macer about regimentation at SSD. The irony was that this goal was soon replaced by virtue of the conversation which evolved. As is often true in field research, one must go with the flow of the conversation – not always certain what one's destination may eventually be. In this case, it provided a good opportunity to see how one of the brighter students described a "typical" day. At least for him, the 'typical' day contains a good deal of time spent on activities which are really by-products of school. They are part of school only because it is in that context that they occur. For Macer and many students like him, school provides the occasion to "have fun." Indeed, Willis' (1977) "lads" were repeatedly described as "using" school; that is, for them, too, school gave them a stage to perform on and the ideal was to not only use the occasions as they naturally occurred *but* to actually create them whenever possible. Of course, this is exactly the kind of thing we find in Macer's statements – the everyday drama of school is played out with a script which the actors help to write as they go along.

Although one might assume that a school for the deaf is a quiet place, that sign language entails only silent "dramas," just the opposite is what one finds. A school for the deaf is a very noisy place. And deaf people are *not* at all "mute" (a term despised by them). One can stroll down the halls of academia and hear waves of sound, voices, cries, laughter and even some verbal conversations (remember deaf children also call each other by hand flagging plus shouts-cries; too, they have fun by screaming unexpectedly into the hearing aids of some poor souls). The gymnasium is another place filled with flashing hands and loud voices, even cheerleaders signing and shouting simultaneously. Shouts, calls, laughter, normal voices, etc. make the place electric with sound.

The dining hall at SSD is yet another setting where loud sound and horseplay prevail (especially at evening meals). Here is the scene of an evening meal described in our field notes:

> A girl and boy are sitting next to me (the older boys and girls are in fact integrated, mixed). The boy spells to me, 'S-h-i-t,' then made the sign (for shit) and pointed at the girl. As I looked toward the girl she fingerspelled the word back to me. Apparently each one was squealing/ratting on the other for saying dirty words (a practice not tolerated in many other total institutions). [I had recently discussed with a junior administrator the concept, 'deaf behavior,' which is sometimes used by hearing people at SSD. I was attempting to observe such behavior tonight].
>
> The older kids are so extremely active. There is much play, clowning around and boy-girl flirtations, kidding, etc. For example, one older boy (about 15 years of age) across the table from me must have fled with his tray of food for 8 to 10 times from one of the twin girls (same age) who constantly/relentlessly threatened him by angrily (an awful and negative facial frown) approaching him. So again and again (8–10 times) he would attempt to eat, then would flee with his tray of food at hand. Finally, she was able to steal his tray after which he chased and caught her and physically wrestled from her the unspilled tray of food.
>
> There is much milling around and much horseplay. A boy walks past others who are eating and thumps both of their ears. One of them jumped up from the table and made extremely threatening (fighting/fists raised) gestures and postures toward the thumper. A girl walking past takes a potato chip from the plate of a girl seated at the table. She jumps from the table, seizes the hand of the girl with the chip and forces her to politely replace the chip onto her plate (her face was distorted and showing much anger. Perhaps this is what seems out-of-place here, the degree to which so many of these fun pranks are responded to with anger and/or dead seriousness. An observer cannot miss the tremendous amount of hostility expressed in these hot drawn faces).
>
> Around the tables nearby there is much, much standing, hand flagging and beating the table to summon another's attention, much horseplay. Supervision by houseparents tonight seems to be minimal. A white male said to me, 'Bad girl' and pointed to a fourteen-year-old white girl. She responds, "Silly, silly, silly," as if she had taken him seriously, as if fearing I would believe him.
>
> Down the table a well-dressed black girl (age 15 or 16) signed to me, 'Will I get sick if I eat this second helping of peaches and second helping of ham sandwich?' I said, 'No, you won't get sick unless you eat too much' (using the sign 'full' to the chin). Then she speaks to a white boy across the table who had obviously kidded her by telling her she would be sick

> if she eats the seconds. She repeated (as if reporting back to him new information) to him what I had said, then looked back to me. I said, 'No. It's okay. Eat it! It's okay!' And she tells the boy, 'It's okay! It's okay.' So she ate the food. [Comment: this is, I think, an indication of the naivete, the lack of general knowledge often exhibited by these children].

There seems to be a great lack of what Berger and Luckmann (1967) call "receipe knowledge" in this student culture. Some have reported such behavior as 'immature,' including several teachers at SSD. One day Don was informally interviewing a very interesting teacher in middle school when two students rushed in. His field notes record the event:

> A fourteen-year-old boy rushed into the room, interrupted our interview and said that the pretty girl behind him spelled 'f-u-c-k' to him. The girl quickly injected, 'He kicked my bottom.' The teacher said, 'Both of you are to blame. You don't kick people and you don't use that word. Be a lady!'

This incident led our conversation to the topic of public use of 'dirty words' by these students. The teacher related a couple of stories relevant to the notion of subcultural differences, or, different recipes of knowledge.

> When I was dating a deaf boy in my college days, he was signing to me and kept using this sign [shit] again and again. I thought I would soon catch what it meant. But in a while I asked him what it meant. He was embarassed and said, 'I thought you knew!' But deaf kids use these four letter words all the time. They don't pick up the little social graces.
>
> For example, a boy will go to the restroom and stay a long time. I sent a second boy to see what is keeping him. Soon he returns to describe graphically to me and the entire class what the first boy is doing in the restroom. I tell him, 'Don't use that word [sign], just tell me if he is [legitimately] using the restroom.
>
> Don: Why do they use dirty words so freely, openly?
>
> Teacher: Because we have to teach them so very much! They don't pick up anything on their own. We have to teach them the states, the capitals, etc. Maybe we need to be teaching them social graces, etiquette. A hearing child picks up norms from many sources, but it takes more effort to teach a deaf child. You teach a hearing child offhandedly.

Social Stratification within the Student Culture

It should be very clear by now that SSD is a complex social system, complete with its own stratification systems. In this section, we will look at social stratification at SSD in general and solely within the student world. We are interested in the hierarchical arrangements which have been established by the students. These students, like human beings everywhere, have worked out social differences in terms of power and prestige. It is of interest to document what qualities are differentially valued and what categories of people inhabit or occupy the slots of any given hierarchy.

General Stratification of the School

During the past decade several social changes have altered the character of the student body at SSD as it had historically existed. First, many middle-class deaf students have been mainstreamed into public and private schools. Thus enrollment at SSD has decreased. Another factor contributing to a decrease has been the end of the Rubella epidemic which occurred some years ago in the United States. This has left lower-class, black, and more multi-handicapped deaf students to attend state institutions. An administrator described the kinds of students who now attend SSD as follows: "All kinds. I think the kind of kids we most usually miss getting in here is some of your very, very bright deaf. Some from your higher class families because they tend to try the public schools first." A middle school teacher discussed the difference between now and five years ago. "More mentally retarded kids now, more multi-handicapped kids." A high school teacher stated that the language patterns found among students at SSD are related to the fact that most students today are from the lower classes and have more multiple handicaps. "Either you're very bright or you're mentally retarded. The middle ground is not there." SSD, then, is a kind of residual place. It is where many students go for lack of acceptance elsewhere. SSD gets a preponderance of disadvantaged children who bear the scars of emotional and physical detriments besides their deafness.

Stratification Among Teachers

Deaf and hearing teachers are differentially distributed along vertical axes. First of all, deaf teachers (and administrators and staff) are greatly outnumbered by hearing teachers. In high school, for example, there were around twenty teachers, four of whom were deaf (and only one of these is a prelingually-profound deaf person). Of the middle school's ten teachers, only two were deaf (both postlinguals and one deaf aid [prelingual]). The school has successfully filled racial quotas with approximately one-third black teachers in the lower and middle schools, although no black teachers or aids were deaf.

The rural location of SSD ensures that deaf teachers will remain few in number and thus small in strength. For most deaf people, an urban setting offers more hope for a community of kindred souls. In contrast, the rural setting of SSD is a kind of deadend. Its location is a vestige of history when asylums for "strange" people were established in out of the way places. As a high school teacher noted, SSD has problems recruiting deaf teachers: "This place is the last resort. No one from a large city will come to this small town because there is nothing to do ... No balls to attend, no whisky to buy. There's nothing to do."

While it was of interest to find out how deaf and non-deaf teachers perceived one another, it was impractical to very directly inquire about this. In doing field research, it is important that local civility between researchers and respondents be maintained. Consequently, deaf/non-deaf reciprocal views were carefully and usually indirectly approached.

Several administrators indicated that the school looked "very positively" upon the idea of having more deaf teachers at SSD. They could serve as role models for students and they could keep hearing staff members aware of problems of deaf students and deaf staff members. But these are "official" definitions of the situation. Behind the facade, however, in the "backstage" (to use another Goffman term), one finds conflicts between deaf and hearing teachers. In fact, some deaf teachers were viewed as incompetent and had been removed from the classroom and placed in various staff positions which, some say, were "created" for them.

While some hearing teachers praised and supported deaf teachers, others denigrated them. Several said there should *not* be more deaf teachers at SSD, "Cause a lot of the time I think the deaf teacher is very limited in his understanding of things that go on and so is the deaf child. I mean if they [students] had *all* deaf teachers, they'd be limited to whatever that deaf teacher ... however far her education went and what she got." At the risk of overstating the case, it did seem at SSD that deaf and hearing teachers were generally not very satisfied with each other. Deaf teachers felt they were subordinates, second-class people in an institution filled with children of their own kind. They felt controlled from every angle, as if they were high school graduates instead of equally educated peers of hearing teachers. An administrative, pedagogical dilemma was apparent – deaf adults did seem somewhat less capable of teaching and "doing academics" to the standards and average expectations of their hearing colleagues; even though they were deaf (hence more ascriptively like the children), it did not seem as though they were generally as effective in the classroom as the hearing teachers. As a result they were not only dominated by the hearing majority but also filtered "down" into lesser positions. The epitome of this "placement" was a Gallaudet graduate who first worked as a counselor in an unsatisfactory way, and who works today as a houseparent.

Most deaf teachers felt powerless. This was angrily (in fact, irately) expressed by one person who was asked if deaf people had input into the decision-making process at the school. "No! Zero! None! N-o-n-e! Period! P-e-r-i-o-d! Never the deaf get what they want!" Deaf teachers (as well as some hearing administrators) felt that school policies regarding linguistic codes used at SSD were dominated by hearing people. They also complained that too many sign systems were utilized on campus. "Deaf people," said one administrator, "wish that hearing people would leave ASL alone." And a deaf teacher strongly believed that young deaf children just beginning sign language should be exposed to more deaf teachers. "I wish *all* the teachers in the primary department were deaf – all of them – all of them! Deaf teachers could give the children a basic foundation and then hearing teachers could teach them from that point on."

Sports Heroes and Academic Nonheroes: Immediate and Deferred Glory

The student subculture at SSD values and extols sports. While male students are popular because of a combination of factors such as ability to play football or basketball, friendly personality, and academic achievement, *the* single most important variable of all is whether or not one is engaged in sports. At SSD sports make the man. One teacher was asked how the high school was stratified, who the big shots on campus are? She immediately answered, "the sports heroes" (later a staff member said, "The pretty ones (the girls) and the athletes"). When told that quite a high percentage of the football players had been described as "slow students," the teacher replied,

"Well, I'd say yes." This observation was affirmed by other teachers who were interviewed. Being intellectually slow does not necessarily interfere with one's ability on the athletic field. Again, it is sports and not brains which are valued by the student culture at SSD.

While sports are the primary source of status, they are not the only one. Generally, athletic success at SSD is restricted to men – at least status occurring from participation is restricted to them. However, academic success offers a kind of alternative, albeit not as popular, ladder for prestige.

A high school teacher described two hierarchies at SSD, one of them being "intellectual" and the other being "physical." He described the physical hierarchy as something of a pecking order in which person A assigns work to person B and B passes it on to C, and so on. Down at the bottom of the pecking order, he said, there are students who are ironing clothes for those people above them as well as making up their beds or cleaning up their rooms. It is "something houseparents constantly deal with" (and was observed by us). It was quite apparent that larger and stronger males would compel smaller and weaker boys to do their washing in the dormitory at night. This stratification system of work also occurred in the girls' dormitories. In either case we see a kind of social Darwinism in which the strong survive and thrive.

One might assume that cheerleading would be a status producing activity but at SSD that is not necessarily the case. First, cheerleaders are almost exclusively hard-of-hearing and, ideally, should be able to use their voices. Second, at SSD, at least, this is accepted as more of a role to be carried out than it is an honorific act. That is, at SSD, cheerleading is simply something that occurs in conjunction with athletic events. Despite the fact that cheerleading entitles the individual to more "free time" (discussed earlier) it is not something which other students seem to envy. (Again, it could be a case of deaf students "using" the hard-of-hearing students up front – or the hard-of-hearing may form cliques which, they feel, are superior to the nonhearing, nonverbal people below.)

The intellectual hierarchy is something which is not heavily emphasized among most of the students. Instead, its prestigefulness is more emphasized by the teachers, something we discuss in more detail shortly.

Social Status and Sex: A Matriarchy

Female students at SSD achieve relatively high status in various ways. One way is to belong to different groups and organizations at the school such as the drama club, the junior National Association of the Deaf, the Explorer Scout troop or the singing signs club. When asked about the seeming female dominance of school organizations, a popular high school girl said that boys simply do not volunteer for leadership in those programs. Also, she said, the boys tend to think that the girls are smarter and therefore do not challenge them for those leadership roles.

A brief look at the *1981 Yearbook* might not clearly lead to this conclusion. Senior class officers, for example, were made up of two males and two females. But the president of that class was a very bright girl who could lip read well and speak well; she now attends a hearing college. In that same yearbook, junior class officers consisted of three boys and one girl who is, according to one high school teacher, *the power*. This girl, Cindy, became the homecoming queen during the course of this research. She is popular and percieves herself as something of a matriarch. According to one teacher, Cindy and the matriarchy work like this:

> In the senior class you have the most intelligent boy – who is just a head and shoulder above any other boy I've ever dealt with. Now Macer is a super athlete and quite intelligent, so he's a natural leader. Ted, although extremly intelligent, is not an athlete and does not have a lot of charisma. So he's not a leader except that he's sort of like an advisor. He comes up with the concepts and he throws them around and then Cindy okays them and then Macer will act on it. It's a very nifty system. Then you got under Macer two black boys and they are your sergeants in this hierarchy. They get it and take it down to the ranks and get it done.
>
> (Both black boys, incidentally, have some residual hearing.)

Better evidence that a matriarchy exists at SSD was the 1981 sophomore class officers, with four females in those positions, and the freshman class officers, with three females and one male. It must be remembered that there are more males at SSD than females in high school. Thus the number of female officers in these high school classes is disproportionately greater than would be expected by chance. As one high school teacher said about the male officer in the freshman class, "I guarantee you the boy doesn't have much power at all." This same kind of disproportional representation is clear in examining virtually all SSD coed organizations. The matriarchical character to student life at SSD was explicitly acknowledged by a teacher who said that when a bright, aggressive new girl arrived on campus, "She almost unglued the matriarchy which existed here."

Status and the Use of English

All communities are stratified and have a notion of "correct" speech (*Hochdeutsch*) and incorrect or "bad" speech (Hertzler, 1965). Deaf children, like deaf adults, are stratified along language lines. Those who can read, write and/or speak English are on top. The sole deaf administrator at SSD is a postlingually deafened person who speaks well enough to be interviewed on television. Of all the deaf teachers at SSD only one is a true (prelingual) deaf person. This is not too unlike the status distinctions drawn between users of English in the hearing world[12]. Language ability is, axiomatically, thought to be an indicator of intelligence, as a reflector of one's social position. The better one's language ability, the better his/her chances of success in life. As Jacobs (1974), a deaf author, has stated (and as testimony to our thesis):

> The better educated deaf adult ... appreciates the value of oral skills more than do the less educated adults. They go into vocations ... where oral skills become highly useful. Therefore, hard-of-hearing or deafened adults who indubitably possess more natural and understandable speech are more likely to be accepted by the hearing community than others.

Hearing, then, sets the normative boundaries for judging accomplishment in the society at large and it is hearing-related skills that are prized by the deaf community. The normative expectation for deaf people is to become "pale imitations of hearing people" (Jacobs, p. 18). It is hardly surprising, then, that among the deaf, language skills are of especial importance. As Jacobs says, "a pecking order according to the usability of their oral skills is frequently perceivable among deaf ... [and] deaf leaders" (p. 68).

This same thing is found at SSD. Most students who have English skills are clustered in the highest level grades. As one parent said of her child's classroom (9 – 1, the highest level of the 9th graders): "All of the kids in that classroom have some speech." More dramatically, a deaf teacher recalled an experience from when she had student-taught at SSD. The teacher she had worked under pointed out certain students who "were not smart;" those students worked on puzzles.

The teacher informed her that in this way she could work with the smart students on the other side of the room.

> I noticed they were hard-of-hearing and could talk, were smart. The ones who were not smart were on the other side of the room and we ignored them. Give them some work, the slow ones, keep them busy, that's all. And so the teacher and I would work with the hard-of-hearing or the deaf who could talk on the other side of the room and leave the slow ones to work by themselves.

She also recalled her own high school days at SSD where children performed in programs in the auditorium. "They always picked those who could talk." Whenever visitors came to the school, she said, they would also choose students who could talk to demonstrate to the visitors how well they were doing. "The teacher never picked the ones that couldn't talk – never. Always picked the ones that could talk."

The emphasis on language skills and making it a prerequisite for academic success leads to a self-fulfilling prophecy. Ability to use verbal and written English not only helps to place students in the highest level classroom of each grade level, but it also influences – in fact, is nearly perfectly related to – perceptions of them as leaders and college bound individuals. As one teacher said in describing the power attributed to Cindy, it is her use of "language," both signs and English. "She probably knows more idiomatic expressions than any other deaf student on campus. And I think this gives her a certain amount of clout." The high school teacher who had mentioned "two hierarchies at SSD," one physical, one intellectual, discussed why he and other teachers (although not necessarily the students) saw the supremacy of the intellectual hierarchy. "You've got a group of students who are good at language, they're pretty bright, they've been called on to be leaders from day one. And they are. They're natural born leaders. They make most of the decisions that concern the school." Thus, while he sees some students as "natural born" leaders he notes that they are good at language, a socially acquired skill.

This same theme arose during an interview with a former teacher. She was asked if the smarter students looked down on the vocational program at SSD. She said, "No, I really don't think so. They know they are college bound and they know that they're the class leaders and this kind of thing ..." But what was special about the college bound people; what did they have going for them? She replied, "there are *some* profoundly, stone deaf, that are college bound. But a lot of them have a lot of hearing and got language in those formative 1, 2, 3 years of age or just have the IQ to go with it."

At SSD it is extremely clear that among the teachers and administrators, language (English) ability is *the* critical variable in explaining student success as measured in and out of the classroom with the notable exception of athletes. And for truly deaf teachers and students, the path to success is a difficult one since some residual hearing (or postlingual deafness) is so highly associated with developing language skills. Ironically, this advantage even carries over to sign language since it can be more quickly acquired and one's vocabulary expanded if the individual can or has ever been able to hear. That is, *hearing, in and of itself, opens the cognitive doors to our minds. In its absence, all knowledge is slow to be acquired.*

Chapter VII

Deafness and the Sense of Self

> The *immediate man* ... his self or he himself is a something along with 'the other' ... the self coheres immediately with 'the other,' he manages to imitate the other men, noting how they manage to live, and so he too lives after a sort. (When he dies) ... a self he was not, and a self he did not become ... For the immediate man does not recognize his self, he recognizes himself only by his dress ... he recognizes that he has a self only by externals.
>
> Kierkegaard[13]

Thus far the analysis has focused on the objective side of life in a total institution and the world-building processes associated with it, primarily through the acquisition of language. In this chapter we turn to a more subjective consideration: the formation of self-concepts among SSD students. We consider the role played by individuals who are significant to them (i.e., "significant others" in Harry Stack Sullivan's terms) and students' own definitions of self.

Theoretical Prologue

In this study we have accorded tremendous power to the role of language. It is with language that we act upon the world. It is with language that our social self emerges and develops. Whenever these two (language and self) develop normally humars are both blessed and cursed: their dilemma stems from the fact that they not only occupy a world of matter, of stimuli (*Umwelt*), but also a world of symbols and dreams (*Welt*) where their sense of identity and self-worth is constituted symbolically (self is an "inner symbolic world of experience," "an inner landscape;" Becker, 1973:3,263). Becker (1975) virtually equates self with language. "Personality," he says, "is a locus of word possibilities" (p. 58). Similarly, Charon (1979), explaining the Symbolic Interactionist theory of self, writes, "The person as object can really only emerge when objects take on some meaning, that is, when objects are defined with words (p.65). What is the "essence" of selfhood? It is the ability to communicate with our self (with words according to the preceding sentence, [p. 79]).

Given this power, it is easy to understand one's disorientation upon entering a culture where a "foreign" language is used. The differences of which we are aware are not simply geographic ones but ones of language which serve to anchor us or give meaning to our circumstances. Without this command of language, we can no longer (to paraphrase Becker) "navigate without fear in a threatening social world" (p. 61). This is precisely the situation which confronts deaf people within their native-born cultures. They find themselves relatively powerless in acting upon their larger society including their own families of orientation.

Clearly Mead is another who gives language a central role in man's social, symbolic existence. He was especially interested in the relationship between gestures (as language), mind and self. Language is essential for the biographical development of self – something not present at birth. Lower animal life does not involve a self, a reflective, thoughtful process. In contrast, human beings tend to organize their memories upon the "string of our self" (Mead, 1977:200). The self is reflexive: it can be an object to itself. For Mead, if one cannot become an object to himself he cannot act intelligently or rationally. Persons with a severe language impairment or limitation (infants, retardates, isolates, many deaf children), then, cannot be an object to themselves, hence can have no mind, no self, and cannot act intelligently, at least by a strict interpretation of Meadian social psychology.

Against a backdrop of a hearing, speaking society, deaf people are at home and comfortable within their own communities and this is especially true for children in residential schools such as SSD. In that world, students have the power and capacity to present themselves by their language and to create and maintain strong interpersonal ties. But outside, in the larger universe of discourse, they are limited by their lack of ability to use English. The extent to which they are competent in its usage determines the level of power they will have. Less competency equals less power (something we alluded to in the previous chapter). We extend this thesis here to state: *the greater the degree of language problem a deaf student has, the greater will be problems with sense of self.* In short, we posit that *sense of self and language ability will vary directly with one another.*

From a structural point of view, it is known that as one ages from seven to twenty-five, the number of groups to which one belongs increases in volume, leading one to internalize as part of his/her self definition a large volume of such identifying statuses as age and sex, specialized occupation, family groups, association groups, and prestige rankings (Kuhn, 1960:429–434). Contemporary social psychologists proffer similar arguments about self – we come to reflect the groups to which we belong. The social interactionists' postulate for this is that man is an object to himself (Mead's position), "that his conception of his identity derives from positions he occupies in society" (Kuhn, 1960:434). A narrow or more constricted conception of self should result, then, from occupying fewer positions. As Shibutani might put it, a member of mass society with multiple and diverse reference groups would have a more segmented, multi-faceted self. At SSD, on the other hand, one experiences a *gemeinschaft* world and thus develops a more unified or unsegmented self (see Charon, 1979:68). In modern, mass, urban society, most of us interact with many different reference groups and, as a consequence, the self "is segmented to the extent that the individual's reference groups are segmented" (Charon, 1979:68). Since residents at SSD experience essentially one generalized other, one perspective (their own student body, teachers), then self has more unity and less change than non-residents.

Kando (1977) has also wondered what effects the absence of language or restrictions in linguistic proficiency would have on self. Studies on feral and blind deaf children, and on aphasics, mentally retarded and schizophrenic persons indicate that "the development of a mature, healthy, and competent self requires adequate mastery of the language used by one's significant group. Failure to adequately master a language is a major aspect of inadequate socialization" (p. 147). Kando states that feral and isolate children are not "truly human" because they are unable to communicate symbolically, to take roles and play roles; "they had no selves" (p. 147). Even Helen Keller is mentioned as not being socialized, as being (as Keller, herself, said) "a little animal."

It follows from the previous discussion that a person with a language problem has a self problem. We can imagine a continuum from "no language, no self" to "full language, full self." As Joyce Hertzler (1965:402) says: "When the individual ... is unable to talk competently to himself or to communicate readily with others, he is diminished as self to himself and to his associates." Man without language would experience "a big, booming, buzzing confusion" (a phrase attributed to William James by Hertzler, p. 41) and "could not develop even the simplest mental pictures" (p. 42). This is well illustrated by Helen Keller (1902) who tells how the mystery of language came to her at the pumphouse, how she first learned that "everything had a name, and each name gave birth to a new thought." With the power of words, typifications, categories and concepts man brings objects into existence (including self); the referents of reality are represented, signified, and categorized by man. Words enable us to avoid the feeling of "terrifying isolation in the universe" (Hertzler, p. 38).

Many of the children in our study are more like those suffering from aphasia, a situation where speech is impaired or lost; consequently, they suffer primarily from the inability to think abstractly with a regression to a more concrete holographic attitude. They cannot easily take the role of others or empathize with them, a learned skill which has been termed "social intelligence" (Charon, 1979:106). Also it is the "basis for human symbolic communication," it helps one know how to manipulate, direct and/or control others and is even necessary for love to develop (p. 104). "Their [aphasics, schizophrenics] frame of mind, as that of young children, is egocentric" (Kando, p. 148), something also found among lower class people who have recently experienced some great tragedy (see Schatzman and Strauss, 1966). We turn now to our students who demonstrate how like these people (and unlike the hearing) they are.

Teachers' and Staff Perceptions of Students' Selves

A high school teacher described his own sense of student self concepts at SSD:

> Well, they have a self-image and usually its tied up with what they're good at. You know the kids that are good athletes, they strut their stuff and that is their image ... The ones who are the brains in this school, like Ted Nostic for instance. He came in the other day and he says, 'Why is it that all the bright students are pot-bellied?' He said, 'I'm bright and look here I'm soft. Look at you, you're bright and you're soft. Look at these other people, they're bright and they're soft. But now look at the kids out here who are not very bright and they got bodies like a rock.' He asked, 'Why is that?' I said, 'I don't know.' But that's his self-image. He knows he's very bright. He knows he's head and shoulders above everybody else but he knows that physically he is no competition.

This boy (a postlingual) was one of the very few who could so articulately discuss his "self" vis-a-vis comrades. As the teacher said of this boy's comments, "These are the types of self-images which are abundant here at SSD," and students are aware of them. Rare is the person who can safely be described as both bright and athletic.

This teacher's hypothesis is that what seems like egocentrism may be an artifact of the language system used at SSD. When you are forced to speak in declarative sentences, there is little room for qualifying statements. Thus you either are one way or another, but the middle ground is simply not available. It is, as Levi-Strauss put it, an intensification of man's natural proclivity to nomize (impose order) upon aspects of nature, of his need to "convert continuous contrasts into absolute contrasts," of classifying by binary opposition (Kottack, 1982: 331).

While teachers believe that students have inflated images of themselves (for which teachers offer partial, tentative explanations), they also believe that many students have doubts about their abilities. This is particularly true when their frame of reference is normal hearing people which, by their accounting, is superior to deafness. A high school teacher mentioned how the student culture, being relatively closed, provides a very narrow reflection of what one's self is. In fact, he believes that a lot of deaf students have an inferiority complex.

> They don't feel like they're as coherent as hearing people. I often have kids come in here and tell me about their dreams. They dreamed that they can hear. Then they come in and tell me how they pray every night that tomorrow they'll wake up and they will be able to hear ... I've had some high school kids come in here and just cry ... They'll say things like 'I really wish I could hear, listen to the radio, listen to music, I'd really like to know what it is.' I've had them come in here and say, 'Well I went out and got stoned last night and I could hear.' They come back and they say, 'Man, I went to a concert. I went to a rock concert and I could hear it.' And I would say, 'What does it sound like?' and of course they cannot tell you.

This particular teacher had attempted to get at the self of individual deaf students by asking them whether they planned to marry a deaf or a hearing person. On the one hand, many deaf students tend to distrust hearing people and said they plan to marry a deaf person "because the hearing person might cheat on me or give me a hard time." On the other hand, this same teacher said that he had observed students saying that "all deaf people are stupid. I want to marry a hearing person because they are smart and they can take care of me and they can do things that I can't do and that's going to be good."

From the student's point of view "one day all deaf people are stupid and the next all hearing people are mean and vicious." It appears that deaf people, like other minority groups, may denigrate and stimatize their own kind. If there is an out-group and an in-group, they are clearly out. And in a very real sense they are looking in, watching a drama which they are poorly prepared to understand. The teacher remembers that a year ago one of the smartest students who "had everything going for her" said, "Don't worry about me, I'm just a deaf person. I'm not important." The teacher said he was really shocked, "really hit between the eyes" by that negative statement of self.

One deaf teacher at SSD expressed her own identity problems and attributed negative self-feelings to the fact that deaf people grow up with *hearing* role models and not deaf role models.

> All they [deaf] grew up looking at [were] hearing teachers. They don't have a model of the deaf teacher. Their [hearing teachers] body language, their expression is lost. They keep their bodies very rigid. Now they [deaf students] grow used to a deaf world, a lot of action, a lot of special education expression and they're [hearing teachers] straight and they [students] are lost. Deaf can't do that smooth movement; all the deaf people are more wild in movement. We are different. Am I doing right to be part of deaf or should I be part of the hearing world? Which one am I? All of us are confused. That's what I think. Many times all of us finally become part of the deaf world. That's fine. But with many struggles, many frustrations. Many deaf people have to struggle and struggle to gradually change and *become like the deaf* [emphasis added].

Note the frequency of undefined pronouns used in the passage above – something which indicates a large degree of taken-for-grantedness, that the listener understands who "they" are. From this teacher's comments confusion over self seems understandable. She expresses the agony of students whereby they look up to the superior hearing teachers and yet resent them and wish to identify with their own world of deafness. But as we have already noted, at SSD – like many other state schools for the deaf – deaf teachers are few and far between (see pp. 107–158, *American Annals of the Deaf* 127, April 1982).

The notion that deaf students distrust hearing people arose again in an interview with a deaf staff member. He was asked why students at the school were unable to respond to the statement, "Tell me five things about yourself." He replied that most students distrust hearing people, thus denying them this information which would be too personal. They tend to see hearing as superior, deafness as inferior. For them, responding to certain hearing inquiries could only increase the advantage of the hearing person (i. e., knowledge is power). The consequence of this is that they are caught between two centrifugal forces, two different role models. On the one hand there are the prestigious hearing teachers who dominate by sheer numbers and influence; on the other hand, there is the deaf peer culture. A combination of respect and deference are mixed with fear and distrust for the hearing person. Thus, one "hides one's weaknesses from the superior outsider," as the staff member put it.

Teachers and staff members report that many deaf students also have low aspirations for themselves, which is thought to reflect a poor self concept. Students are described as giving little thought to the future. One staff member said:

> The kids do not stop and think about the future. They can get SSI (Social Security benefits) and just make it along with some small low blue-collar job. They think that's doing very well as they have seen others before them who have left here just getting along. They accept that.

If this observation is accurate, then the question becomes shall we blame the dependent victim or shall we look to the system which created the victim?

A high school teacher also perceives that students do not have long-term goals, that their aspirations are relatively low. And like the staff member above, he cites the "free" handouts given to the deaf and suggests that self-esteem is lowered in the process.

> They don't have long term goals. I think that's the key to any type of positive thinking. It's the old priority of values. If the only goal you have is to appease your basic instincts, your primary needs, and if you're having trouble doing even that despite government largess, then you are going to have a very negative self-image and you are going to dislike those who are near you, those who are like you. 'My life seems to be a failure.' 'He's deaf and I'm deaf and then I don't like him either.' 'He's stupid and a liar and I'm stupid and a liar.'

In a very analytical way, though, this teacher suggested a possible relationship between language and (negative) self-concept. He believes that ASL lacks ability to express some ideas except in harsh ways. For example, he explained that in English we have many expletives; we have "shucks" and "shoot" and "gee whiz," but the deaf have only one sign that covers all of those ideas. And signing depends strictly on body language and facial expresson to present the degree of intensity for the expletive, whether "shit," "shoot," or "shucks."

Another high school teacher believes that part of the explanation for low self-esteem is in the way that students are grouped: true deaf are put in with a high percentage of mentally retarded or brain damaged deaf children. The true deaf child then feels tainted by that association because he/she is cast into a social group of which he/she is not really a part; it is confusing.

> That hurts his self-image in a lot of ways, having a lot of deaf people here who have some type of brain damage. That does in fact hurt most of the other deaf kids' self-image. They feel like: 'Well, if other people see that person and he's mentally retarded and he acts stupid then they're going to act stupid;' and that part of the self-image is definitely ugly.

A deaf teacher in high school also had similar thoughts:

> I must disagree with this Special Studies program here at this school. It is punishment for the children. They put kids together, slow kids, and some of them tell each other they are nitwits, that they are 'mentally retarded.' They put children down there whose behavior is unacceptable and I believe if they would overlook some of their behavior and leave them alone that they would outgrow it. They would outgrow this behavior but no, they place them in the special studies school with slow and mentally retarded children. If you tell a boy that he is mentally retarded or that he is a 'nitwit' and if you tell him afterwards to study, he will say to you, 'I'm a nitwit. No need to study.' We have three levels of intelligence here at SSD: (1) We have high intelligence; (2) average; (3) low. And I think they should be separated. They should not be all mixed up as they are now.

The Teacher as a Positive Influence on Self

Previous studies (e. g., see Meadow's review of the literature on self-image and deafness, 1969:431) have indicated that deaf children in residential schools exhibit a surprisingly positive self-image, perhaps unrealistically and overly positive. In part this may be the result of the praise given to them during classroom activities. More than a decade ago, Boyce Williams (1970:38) leveled a criticism at the "lavish praise" that a deaf child frequently receives for classroom work that is actually far below his true abilities. Williams called for more realistic rewards and motivation, for a heightening of the deaf child's capacity for self-evaluation. But at SSD, this seems not to have happened.

Praise of students, and especially young deaf ones, is not, of course, at all out of the ordinary in daily school life wherever it occurs. What is rather unusual, however, is the degree and intensity of praise being offered. Too, it must be remembered that classroom size at SSD is small, usually between six and ten students. In these small social situations, characterized by win or lose academic contests, students constantly seek praise and reward from their teachers.

The youngest children arrive at the lower school with little or no language. According to one teacher, once they begin to understand the symbolic system, then "they are able to prove that they understand what you are saying because they can respond to you and they feel good about themselves which makes you feel good about yourself (as a teacher)." So the child begins to have self-feelings as language is attained and as he interacts with those around him/her.

In one small lower school class, a boy hesitated again and again to write an answer to a math problem; he continually looked toward the teacher hoping for her approval. Eventually the teacher noticed his behavior, shook her head wistfully and remarked, "They hate to make a mistake." In that same classroom, on another day, a boy began to cry and whine because he was unable to spell two or three words successively after the teacher had called (signed) them out. Several teachers told how students in all grades would become upset whenever their work, filled with mistakes, was generously marked in red. One teacher said that students "seek pleasure and avoid pain." The possibility of constant failure and loss of teacher approval is a most serious matter.

At SSD exclaimed evaluations occur regularly. During the very first interview in the lower school, a teacher said, "When these children do something right, I praise the stew out of them." This type of thing was observed over and over. At the same time, primarily in the lower school, teachers often went to the other extreme. Thus one hears (or sees) "Very good! Very good!" but one also hears "Mistake!" "Mistake!" On balance, however, it seemed to be the positive side which prevailed, something which may be related to the aggrandized statements which students make about their own abilities.

In an earlier interview, a former teacher demonstrated how lavish praise and childish baby-talk are used to motivate students and in the process to create inflated selves. She told of having some difficulty motivating the children to wear their hearing aids.

> So when one person would reach and start to put on their aid I'd say, 'Great! You remembered your hearing aid. I'm so happy about that. Good girl.' Then I might go on and do something else and then, 'Hey, look, you remembered yours too.' And my peripheral vision would see hearing aids going on all over the classroom. Then finally if there was just one person without an aid I would have to deviate a little bit and I'd just say, 'I'm so sorry that Tommy forgot his aid. Just so sorry that he can't remember.' Then he'd grab that thing out and he'd hurry and put it on but it made a difference. I think the voice quality and the praise makes a big difference.

This teacher seemed to give and expect in return positive feelings – a kind of mutually reciprocal arrangement between herself and her students, with at least some divine intervention ("The Lord sent me here to work with these children," she said at one point). She described how she would walk around and praise the children, give them eye contact and make them know she loved them. When she walked past some of them she would put her arms around them or touch them on the shoulder or on the head.

> Sometimes I would go by and they'd kiss my arms all the way up. It's amazing they're just so loving. And anytime I felt that I needed to be loved or wanted or appreciated I would get on the school bus and ride to this city or that city or somewhere with them and they'd all fight to see who could sit with me.

Whether this somehow led to inflated egos seems to be of lesser importance, in this case, than the larger image of a teacher who could provide so much emotional contact for children who might otherwise experience little by way of affection.

In the lower and middle school, students who would write their names correctly would receive strong reinforcement and praise. If a student fingerspelled or wrote the correct spelling of a word he/she was generally praised very strongly. The social climate is one in which young children struggle and compete for the praise and reward given by the teacher for the smallest accomplishments. As shown above merely wearing one's hearing aid was occasion for great acclaim.

The praise found in the lower and middle schools also occurs in the high school. There, however, a kind of self-fulfilling prophecy is set in motion. For example, on one occasion three or four students were unable to use the English word "occupation" correctly. Two students did not know the word at all. Another student wrote on the blackboard, "Is your father work?" She meant to write "What is your father's occupation?" At last, the teacher asked one girl if she could write the sentence correctly. When she did, the teacher replied in sign language for all to see, "See how you can count on Sue?" Or, loosely translated, "I expected her to do it correctly and she did."

The Teacher as a Negative Influence of Self

In the previous section we have shown how teachers try to boost self image, how they make the students feel good about themselves. Clearly, many SSD teachers, staff and administrators are compassionate and sensitive toward the children. Some teachers, however, tell students they are somehow inferior, that they cannot learn, that English is too difficult for them. (Again, this in no way suggests that all teachers behave this way. As expected, most teachers are caring people engaged in rewarding but difficult work). In an unintended way, this is perpetuated by the school which stratifies and segregates students by mental, physical and scholastic criteria.

It was not unusual to have teachers say of their students, while standing in front of them, that they are not up to par, that they are inferior, that they are flawed. In fact this was so blatant as to be shocking. These comments were made in sign language with students looking on! In 1978 Moores wrote, "teachers of the deaf seem especially prone to tell visitors at length about the limitations of their students as though they had no sense of what was occurring" (p. 145). As Don entered a high school classroom, the teacher seemed somewhat excited to have an interviewer present and, therefore, was eager to converse. In the interview he signed, in front of his students, "The deaf cannot learn because they don't have (English) vocabulary. They don't understand that one English word has many meanings." Since Don was wearing hearing aids, this teacher continued to sign publicly his opinions about limitations of his slow students. "I take them outside to the lake of water and they cannot remember the name of algae in the water. They can say only 'the green growing.'"

In another high school classroom a teacher explained to Don:

> This is a very low level sign class. I teach them signs such as you would see on the street or in restaurants or stores. They must know these signs. [comment: Both Don and the teacher are signing so all students are able to see the conversation]. They have very low level ability.

Some teachers felt that the multihandicapped, the slow, the retarded deaf children cannot learn; consequently these children are stigmatized by both teachers and students. A kind of self-fulfilling prophecy occurs. Two middle-school teachers told how some teachers stigmatize Special Studies students.

> Teacher #1: Some teachers do stigmatize Special Studies students. They say, 'You don't have to teach them. Why try?'
>
> Teacher #2: And even some of the teachers in Special Studies themselves feel that way. 'Oh, these kids can't do anything. Why should I spend my time beating my head against the wall?'

But despite these negative comments, both of these teachers indicated that such children might not "hit the top of the world" but that they could learn something.

The lower school was the best place to observe how people worked with children whose attention span was very short. Problem-solving tasks had to be changed quite frequently. Competition for favorable teacher evaluations was continual. And as we have noted earlier, the use of dichotomies is very common, in fact normative.

In one classroom a TA (teacher's assistant) tried to help a young boy whose attention span seemed very, very short. The TA would place fingers on a chart while at the same time standing nose-to-nose with the child. Simultaneously, as the child made an error, the TA would hold (for several seconds) the sign "mistake" on her chin. Quickly she turned to another boy, "That's not right. Not right. That's a mistake. That's right. Good." And the little boy clapped his hands together. Nearby another little boy played at a table with his arms stretched over his head and the TA looked at him and signed "Mistake! You made the flag fall down. Place it back again." Five minutes later a little girl wriggling in her chair slipped from it and looked at the teacher who was staring at her. In anticipation the little girl spoke to herself by making the sign for "mistake" and quickly re-seated herself. The teacher noticed how the boy who had inadvertently toppled the flag was doing nothing. She spoke to him, "This work we're doing is for babies. Are you a baby?" The boy answered, "Yes." Teacher: "Do you want a bottle?" Boy: "No." Teacher: "Mistake." Soon the TA observed the restless little girl and commented that she always misses the spelling word, "doll," writing instead "ball" everytime. The teacher interjected, "This little girl confuses the 'd' and the 'b'; also she confuses the 'n' and the 'u.' That shows some kind of brain damage." Quickly the teacher turned to chastise the little girl. "I can get mad with you," said the teacher. The little girl signed, "Mistake."

For hours and hours the elementary classroom is a world of "mistakes" and "good" and "v-e-r-r-y good" events. Not only is it a world of praise and punishment linguistically, it is also a world in which children judge themselves by the criteria of their teachers. A child makes a noise or slides from the chair and looks toward the teacher, making the sign "mistake" before the teacher herself is able to make the sign. A little girl age eight, whose paper had just been corrected with red ink, turned to Don and said, "Paper (is) bad." He signed back to her, "It's alright." But slumping in her seat she nodded her head vigorously and signed, "No, no, no." Taking the role of the teacher, she evaluated and accepted the judgment that there was little good about her paper. It was another "mistake."

A standard practice at SSD is to use models from the hearing world as normative. The reference group presented, aspired to and glorified is the hearing world, not the deaf world. It is the hearing person's language which must be mastered. It is the hearing world where one will work. Even one's parents and siblings are usually hearing people. A former deaf teacher, who had taught teenage students, allowed no chewing gum in his classroom. One must remember that deaf children have to be taught not to smack their lips when they eat or when they chew gum because they are unable to hear it. Also, they are constantly taught not to drag their feet which makes noise. The message is always the same: hearing people must not be offended or intruded upon by the noises of the deaf.

On the one hand, using the hearing world as a standard for judging all behavior may seem lamentable. On the other hand, given the linguistic and spatial segregation of SSD students, it would be (and in many cases *is*) easy to acquire a distorted view of self. Some psychiatrists have wondered if deaf children – under such circumstances – could attain a degree of "healthy ethnocentrism" so characteristic of most other subcultures. Consequently, some teachers may make negative comments in an attempt to bring the deaf student closer to what is believed to be reality (his or her actual abilities). As one teacher said about student aspirations for the future: "They are not realistic when they talk about the real world." They may have laudible goals but the means to attain them are a mystery.

On the high school campus there is a reading laboratory where the "brightest" students (primarily hard-of-hearing, postlinguals and middle-class students) go to acquire intensive and additional English reading practice. One interpretation of this is that it is a form of special or favored treatment. As the laboratory teacher says, "These kids *know* they are on top." This can easily (and, perhaps, inevitably) lead to an inflated sense of self. Thus some "top" students will enter the laboratory classroom and tell the teacher that they do not need to know the lesson on the blackboard. According to the teacher, this might be a lesson that not even the brightest student would know.

> They might know some of the information on the blackboard and they would become upset if I have information there that they do not understand. Their own self-image in this case is that they know a great deal and therefore I am attempting to challenge them everyday. I am trying to show them that they do *not* know a great deal.

This teacher is intentionally trying to deflate their self-image and their self-confidence, to make them more "realistic." This may be "negative" but its intent is clearly constructive.

The Role of Parents

The material on parents is limited at best. Only a few parents were interviewed and most of the impressions were gained from indirect references, especially students talking about their own parents. Even with this limited information, a fairly clear picture of the parents of a deaf child emerges. It is a troublesome picture since these parents are caught in a very difficult bind. On the one hand, to keep the child at home may, in effect, deprive him/her of knowing other similar children and importantly, from acquiring language. On the other hand, if they turn their child over to a residential school, they may be accused of being callous and indifferent. A third choice, to mainstream the child in the local public schools, is also a possibility but it is often predicated on the child having at least partial hearing.

A very unusual situation generally exists between deaf children and their parents: they do not speak the same language. When a child lives at a residential school, child and parent may come to occupy two different worlds and the bridge between them is not an easy one to cross. It can safely be assumed that most parents wish for their children to be much like themselves (Benderly, 1980). At a minimum they want them to be healthy, including being able to hear. Having a child with a defect of some kind, then, is almost certainly a disappointment, the seriousness of which will vary by the seriousness of the defect. It can be especially difficult for the parents of a deaf child since the defect may not be immediately realized. Too, once it is, the child's language skills have already been retarded. To remedy this, either the child must learn the parent's language or the parent must learn the child's. All evidence indicates that this latter solution rarely occurs at least to any appreciable extent.

In our effort to understand the formation of self process for deaf students, students were asked to explain their own parents response to learning sign language. One very popular student was clearly bothered by responding to this query. The disappointment in his parents was evidenced by his facial expression and comments:

> I tried to teach and my mother and father tried themselves [to learn sign language] but they never did; just a very, very little bit. They improved. Just a little bit, but not much sign language. Since I started to school they encouraged me [to learn] but they never did it. I encouraged them but they never did it. [I] encouraged them ... I wanted my father to learn sign language but I'm disappointed.

As we have already noted, the deaf child-parent relationship is a potentially stressful one with plenty of room for each to be disappointed in the other. During an interview with a parent who had moved to be near the school, some of the language problems became apparent. This mother described her child's language as somewhat restricted. When asked in what way the deaf child's language was restricted, she replied in terms of his inability to use signed English:

> Mother: (He) was trying to tell me in complete English sentences and he knew he couldn't do that so he just said, 'I don't know.
>
> Don: Does that happen often?
>
> Mother: Well, when I sign to him I try to sign in complete sentences. I put in all the articles and adjectives and prepositions and everything (note: signed English) and I think that inhibits him sometimes because he thinks that I expect the same from him. But he's got to have it if he's going to learn to write sentences and communicate with people. But he'll tell me something in a phrase sometimes. Okay, if he's got that phrase backwards it's not meaning as much to me and I have to sit there and just have to work and work to *drag* it out of him sometimes. And I'll say to him, 'Tell me again. Explain again. Try another way, tell me another word.' And he'll say, 'I don't know, I don't know.' I said, 'But try to make good sentences and tell me so I can understand.' And he'll keep working and finally he'll get enough across to me that I can understand. But I have to drag it out of him because in the deaf world you don't do that. You just ... a word here, a phrase there, you know, and that's why they can't make good sentences. They don't ever sign in sentences where you can understand them.

Here we see a highly motivated, well intentioned parent; a parent who is so concerned that a home in another part ot the state had been sold so that the family could relocate to stay together when the child began at SSD. The parent realizes that signed English (not just signing) is the critical skill to be acquired. But there is a hidden message to the child in this – to be fully like me you must be able to talk like me. Your world's language (ASL) must be rejected, and the deaf community who can *only* sign must be rejected along with it.

One popular and very influential senior girl was interviewed and asked if her mother and father had tried to learn sign language. Predictably, her response was, "Yes, but they preferred me to talk (rather) than use the sign language." Again, the message is the same – you adapt to us (and by implication, our hearing world) rather than we will adapt to you (and the deaf world).

My Self, My Friends, My World

The students at SSD offer a classic example of ethnocentrism. One teacher told of the awe expressed by middle school students who learned that deaf people live in places other than this one. For these children, SSD is clearly *the* world *tout court*. Again, in the gymnasium when coaches are giving out different colored sweat shirts to play ball, young students insist that they be given tan and red colored shirts because they say tan and red are "deaf," and the blue shirts are "hearing." After a ball game between SSD and a rival school, students return to the dormitory shouting, "Deaf Won! Deaf won!" The attitude seems to be that deaf people at SSD are "the people" (akin to other groups around the world who see themselves as somehow favored). Young students will color pictures tan and red and will say "This picture is deaf. I colored it deaf," meaning that tan and red are the school colors and are therefore equated with the social system there. We mentioned in Chapter 3 how this reveals much about the cognitive processes of these deaf children; that thinking of objects in terms of concrete qualities such as a color (recall the student in Chapter 4 who described his place of employment, not with discrete or specific words [fingerspelled], but as a color: 'I work at color orange,' meaning 'Orange Bowl) as opposed to particular or specific (and more abstract) names of objects.

Deaf students at SSD strongly identify with each other. Some middle school children even expressed great awe when they learned, by observing a map of the United States, that deaf people live in places other than their own state. In their particular institutional setting the school environment is womb-like and family membership is redefined. Thus, some young children will confuse common family terms. Since they live far from family members, their confusion is understandable. A teacher's daughter may be thought of as a sister; sons become brothers; and so on. If they are from the same town they think they are kin; their shared deafness forges a bond between them offsetting all other differences. The feeling of closeness, intimacy and kinship is epitomized in one conversation with a senior boy. He was asked to tell a story about himself. He described how his parents brought him to the school and how he "looked around and was afraid," not being used to the strange environment. Afterwards he said he began to learn, to grow, to develop. His bond with SSD is especially clear in the following quote:

> A short time I will graduate and go out. Can't come to school again. Truly, I like school. That's all. Truly, I hate to leave school because I like staying many years [here] because I like to see my best friends in SSD. More interesting, friends interacting with each other ... more fun, pleasure and joy. When I leave school truly very disappointed if go to work, work, work for long time living. My friends [will be] gone out and gone away and dispersed and I can't meet them, my best friends. Maybe my friends will move to another state and I want to meet them so I know where they live. Really I'd like to stay in school. I truly want to stay in school until I die. I wish I could because I like to see my best friends, more fun, pleasure, and joy. So I want to see my old friends, I wish to see them before they die. I want to remain with friends so that I can see them every [time of] interaction [or association] with friends. So I can visit and talk and visit ... more fun, pleasure. I truly don't want them to die and to be absent [drop out] and not be able to talk. I want to be able to see my best friends. I don't want to see them drop out and can't appear again. I wish they would stay and keep living forever.

At age twenty, this boy dreads and fears the departure from his community. This is his world; this is the place where he first acquired language and the ability to establish community (and intersubjectivity to some significant extent) by means of sign language. This is the world about which he knows most. The world which awaits him on the outside is a world of strangers; like the marital pair of Berger and Kellner's (1983) essay, the deaf and hearing are strangers to each other in that they come from different face-to-face contexts, from different areas of conversation and have no shared past.

The outside is another social world characterized by a different and difficult universe of discourse. When asked, "How is the deaf world different from the hearing world?" the senior boy attempted to define the deaf world in terms of one of the relatively few social organizations which exist for the deaf adult. "[In] the deaf world [one] goes to a deaf club; it's a professional SAD (State Association of the Deaf) club. I think really [it is] very hard to explain, but I don't have any experience in the deaf world [outside the school]. I [am] late going to the deaf world." Presumably he had heard about deaf adults attending local SAD chapters in various towns and cities, but beyond that he seemed to have no conceptualization whatsoever of a deaf world in contrast to a hearing world. For him and others, SSD *is* their world. Although they are keenly aware of the larger hearing society, they seemed to actually know little about the "deaf world" of adults outside who live in pockets of various cities around the country.

Deaf students at SSD are very comfortable with each other and sometimes afraid of social interaction with hearing people. As one deaf teacher said, "I drive one thousand miles in order to be with a group of deaf people." Students frequently made the statement that hearing people do not understand the feelings of the deaf. This was bluntly stated by one girl.

> Hearing people may not understand me, and they say, 'I don't understand that [what you said].' I'm afraid. Talking people should know that deaf [are] hard to understand because they cannot hear. Hearing [people] can't understand the deaf try [efforts].

This language-communication problem often results in the feeling among deaf students that they are on the outside looking in, which helps to explain the very tight cohesion found among them. Whenever deaf students look out towards the hearing world of English speaking people, they feel shy, apprehensive and fearful. But whenever they return to their deaf peers within the confines of SSD, they feel good, comfortable and normal.

Although there are indications of this kind of "we" solidarity at SSD, deaf adolescents nevertheless exhibit some self-awareness apart from the group (in Mead's terms, the "I" vs. the "we"). In a high school classroom which had one part of a wall completely mirrored, a girl stood at the mirror during the beginning of class time looking at herself and fixing her hait. The irritated teacher commented, "That is the worst thing they ever put in this room. The first thing they do every morning is to look at themselves." As the girl finished her hair, she began to shake and shimmy and dance to the thunderous voice of the teacher who called, "Sit down!" She begrudingly walked towards her desk; looking directly at the teacher, she signed "headache," meaning, "You give me a headache." Surely the examining of one's reflection in the mirror shows some awareness of self, of the unique "you." But it was very difficult for students to talk about this.

Students Decribe Themselves

We were particularly interested in any differences we might find between the truly deaf and the hard-of-hearing. Our supposition (borne out in our analysis reported thus far) was that there would be stark contrasts between the two groups. And, indeed, this is what we found. Not only did the deaf have great difficulty with queries about self, but they were far likelier to make negative statements. In this section we report first deaf statements about self and then hard-of-hearing statements. Following this we turn to a discussion of why self-disclosure is so troublesome for deaf students.

The deaf. Max is a fourteen-year-old boy described as both bright and mean by a middle-school administrator. He is something of a fighter in the school. The following comments by him illustrate, in part, how institutional life may compliment rather than replace life experienced before coming to SSD (again, see Shover, 1979, on the notion of a life "imported" into the institution).

> Don: Tell me about yourself. I am a little bit ignorant about you. I am interested in you. Tell me five things about you.
>
> Max: 1) I live in Southtown. 2) My cousin has a car painted like the Dukes of Hazzard. (Max stalled, his eyes rolled with a pensive expression).
>
> Don: Tell me more about *you*. Tell me more.
>
> Max: 3) Mother sent me to store nearby and some man stole my money and mother got mad and then we had a fight. She got a switch and whipped me (stalled again). 4) I had a fight with Mrs. Sanders (teacher) because she wanted me to write something and I did not want to write it ...

It cannot be claimed that Max approaches his self as a socially defined and named object, at least not from the statements made above (which took considerable time to elicit from him). In fact, he makes no status identification (e. g., age, race, sex, grade level, etc), no references to social location at all. Moreover, the only associations mentioned (with mother and teacher) are negative. Furthermore, he made no self-definitions or self-evaluations, not even self labels (names).

Other students exhibited similar difficulty in talking "about" themselves. Sammy, a handsome seventeen-year-old from a slow class, had no knowledge of English terms relating to certain facial parts (chin, neck, cheek, eyebrow and eyelash). Several approaches were used in an attempt to elicit statements about himself. "Tell me about yourself. Pretend that you write a letter to me and tell me about yourself. What would you say?" There was a long silence during which Sammy stared thoughtfully into space, eyes squinting. Once more, "Just tell me five different things – just *five* things about yourself." Don began to count for him, "Okay, first ..." (pause for response). At last he signed:

> 1) Yesterday (I) saw (a) basketball (game). 2) Last night, play, play, play. 3) (I) want (to) swim. 4) Last night, (I) watch(ed) TV, HBO.

At this point he stalled again so Don asked, "Tell me about your personality." He replied, "(I) fuss with girl friend." Why? He simply pointed to a small scratch on his nose.

The boy seemed so normal (not retarded, not multihandicapped, not poorly dressed, etc.) that one final approach was tried. A deaf instructor was called over and told about the questions being asked. The instructor agreed to ask, in his own way, questions which would elicit self-statements. Soon, however, it was clear that the boy could think of nothing more to say. Thus, the instructor tried to lead him easily, gradually, one question at a time:

> Teacher: What are your hobbies? Do you like camping?
>
> Student: What does that ['camping'] mean?
>
> Teacher [Using much mime and gesture] You go into the woods and set up camp. You throw out [a] fishing line [and] you sit back in your chair and you relax, etc.

(Getting no response, the deaf teacher shifted his approach and tried to tell Sammy how to explain things about himself).

> Teacher: What is your name? What is your hobby (again)?
>
> Student: Swim. Like girls. Like (to) help people.

Don interjected, "How do you help people?" After a long silence, Sammy finally answered, "I don't know."

A few days later, after being told of the difficulty students were having with self-disclosure attempts, an administrator suggested an experiment. We would talk to (presumably) some of his best students. He wanted to see for himself just what would happen. Thus, we sat down with a fourteen-year-old, postlingually deafened boy (which means he had an English advantage over others). After some preliminary questions, Don said, "You know some people write books about themselves. If *you* wrote a book about yourself, what would you say?" His answer came in the familiar and brief one-sign responses: "1) Science; 2) SS (social studies); 3) language. (What do you mean, 'language')? Verbs, nouns." The administrator interrupted and said the boy did not understand the question. It was suggested that he be given some examples (which amounted to rehearsing him). After the administrator and Don signed some things, the boy followed: "I am age 14; I love to pet animal; my weight is 85; I will go home Friday, December 18; I like to work math in school." (Each statement of his was made after the administrator and Don had made their single statements).

The question is why do bright students (even this postlingual one) need to be rehearsed or led before they can make statements about themselves? Whenever one repeats a question in sign language – signing it first this way and then another – why are students either puzzled or prone to talk about their daily school activities? Does this suggest that the self is socially anchored and embedded in the school context to the extent that these are the "natural" responses to give? Or it could be argued, perhaps, that the setting of the interview (with the administrator present) was not ideal. However, this "experimental" boy behaved precisely like other students who were interviewed in more ideal settings. On two other occasions seemingly bright, postlingually deafened students were interviewed. On both occasions the results were the same – first, references were to school and subsequent references were oblique at best.

The hard-of-hearing. Given the results with deaf students, there was a certain amount of trepidation upon beginning similar talks with the hard-of-hearing. But in this case the contrast that was anticipated was, in fact, found. First, these students uniformly described themselves as "hard-of-hearing" not "deaf" ("deaf" being a less preferred label or category than the former). Second, their command of English is much better, as a whole, than the deaf group; thus they were able to tell (or even write) better stories about themselves. Third, as a group they are non-marginal persons. That is, while SSD is their school, sign language is *one* of their languages, and the deaf culture and social organization at the school was adopted as their own. In general, they "love SSD," and feel very positive about themselves and their futures. They have more status and prestige at SSD then they did in regular schools. That they find so much comfort and satisfaction by changing social worlds says much about the human need for community *and* communication. Further, it suggests a different sense of self than might otherwise occur.

The interplay between English skills and the superior ability to talk about one's self is well illustrated in the following exchange (note the vivid description of regimented life at SSD). Don: If you wrote a book about your life, what would you write?

> Student: I don't know. A long time ago when I was a little boy, my mother asked the boss of the school, 'Can my son join the school?' So I went to class and had good friends and talked and sat with them. I sat with a friend side by side and we wrote math and science and different things. And we finished. Then we had recess and we went out and played, played, and played.
>
> Time to go eat, then we line up ... lined up and we marched like soldiers. We marched to eat ... we marched ... and then we sat down in straight lines. Rows and rows of lines, finished. We put up our dishes and we went outside to play, play, play.
>
> The bus leaves home (from SSD) and we arrive in (the capitol city) and we sit (there) til seven o'clock on the bus. We get a ticket and we arrive home. My mama gets me up and takes me home and puts me down and I go outside and play with my dog. Then I play and play and my mama goes out and does things and my father is working on the job. And me and my sister we just go and do different things. We go fishing, shooting the gun and playing. Then we go to sleep – myself alone – I sleep.

The richness and diversity of this boy's experiences, told in sign language (and very choppy English), is far superior to the brief stories told by deaf students. No other interview so dramatically captures life at school and at home for a deaf child. Real parents allocate authority for the child to the school: "Can my son join the school?" The spontaneity of life outside the school was found inside it: "we went out and played, played and played." But the spontaneity of life was joined by life's institutional, regimented side: "we lined up and we marched like soldiers." Finally, a day away from the school, at home, is concluded in poetic isolation: "myself, alone – I sleep."

Another boy, age 14, who identifies himself as "hard-of-hearing" (as opposed to "deaf") came to SSD after only one year at a public school. His response to 'writing a book about himself' is choppy but expressive.

> I am tall. Tall and thin. Skilled in basketball. Some boy is short. The short boy runs, runs. Expert. But that boy plays football. Plays. That's all. I play basketball, skill. Short boy, Mitch is the short boy. I'm tall.

Don: Do people love or hate you? [An attempt to elicit his lovable traits]

Student: Friends, me. Friends, good. Nice.

Don: Who is nice?

Student: Me.

Don: Do you have a girl friend?

Student: Yes. Her name is Barbie. She is a talking girl. She's from my hometown.

Don: Does she love you?

Student: Yes.

Don: [Trying to elicit statements about his lovable qualities] Why does she love you?

Student: Long time ago, bad trouble for girl. Sweetheart wants me. They love me. Sad, sad, sad, me.

Outside SSD many of the hard-of-hearing students were marginal persons. However, once they moved into the deaf world, learned signs and adjusted to their new surroundings, they found forms of acceptance previously unknown to them. In a sense they went from the bottom rung to the top – a little hearing at SSD can carry one a long way (but the stratification system is complicated – the hard-of-hearings are not "truly" deaf and may yet stand outside the true community). Their enhanced sense of self (which we confess must be assumed since this was not an experiment with pre- and post-measures) seemed clear in the interviews.

Don: If you wrote a book about yourself, what would you say?

Student: I would say I'm a good worker. I am a good worker. I am a brilliant (bright) student. I am the best favorite in the class. I am the best cheerleader. I want to be vice-president in my class ... I want to be a good player on the basketball team. I have many good friends here. I am popular.

A pretty fourteen-year-old girl (also a cheerleader) came to SSD in the seventh grade and worked her way into the highest level of grade 9 (i. e., 9–1). Clearly, it was the pain of marginality associated with a hearing loss which pushed her toward the deaf world:

> In public school I couldn't really understand when the teacher explained ... it just was really hard for me to understand and to be around with them (hearing students). I was afraid they would get impatient with me because I couldn't hear. My mother and daddy wanted me to come over here and I joined it (SSD).

When asked if it hurt when she moved from the talking world to the deaf world, she described herself as "satisfied." The general sense of satisfaction occurred in other interviews as well.

Student 1: I miss my family very much but I love SSD and I love all the teachers.

Student 2: I feel comfortable better here than I did outside. People are friendlier here and I have always dreamed of being a cheerleader.

Student 3: At first I didn't like school here. One year later I quit school here and joined school at my home, but I never liked my new school, too. I told my parents that I want to go back to SSD again, SSD really chance [changed] everything like a big fun ... I am really going to miss SSD a lot when I leave to college ... SSD is really a great school for any deaf student.

Many of these hard-of-hearing students not only identify themselves with the institution (SSD), but they also reveal a placement of themselves in the deaf social world, in that language community. This is indicated by their responses to queries about their future spouses and children – whether they would, preferably, be hearing or deaf people.

Don: [to a pretty high school cheerleader with good speech] Do you want to get married?

Cheerleader: I wouldn't mind that, but not this soon. Maybe in the future about four or five or six years from now.

Don: Do you want to marry a deaf or hard-of-hearing or talking person?

Cheerleader: Maybe a deaf. I feel more comfortable around a deaf person because. . . I don't know, it's just better.

[Another younger cheerleader said she wanted to marry a deaf person and Don asked why. She bluntly stated:

Girl: Because I don't like talking people. I love the deaf. I want to go straight on with the deaf. I want to marry a deaf person and teach him something so he can hear.

Don: Why do you prefer a deaf husband? Why?

Girl: He needs some help when people knock on his door. He probably cannot hear, so I am going to go there and help him. I can call him on the alarm. I can call him on the TTY, teach him how to write checks, teach him how to get a job.

Earlier we mentioned a deaf boy who said he did not want a hearing girl friend because she might lie to him and run around on him. A hard-of-hearing girl expressed an even greater fear of hearing people.

Don: When you graduate, do you want to marry a deaf boy or a hearing boy?

Girl: A deaf boy.

Don: Why?

Girl: We'll both be deaf. A hearing boy killed a deaf girl in a nearby town ... I don't want a hearing boy.

One hard-of-hearing girl, Lena, had just moved this year to SSD and not unexpectedly, her identity differs. About her preference of spouses she replied, "Talking or deaf, no matter is my favorite." In contrast, the deaf homecoming queen, Cindy, first said it made no difference whether she marries a deaf or hearing person. Later, she was asked what is wrong with a hearing husband to which she replied, "My fear is he might leave me out of the group of his friends and he might not know how to sign and he might not understand the feelings of the deaf."

Finally, we asked a younger hard-of-hearing boy (in middle school), Angel, about his preferences. "Maybe a hearing girl or a deaf. I don't know. Deaf maybe."

For these hard-of-hearing students, SSD really is a "big fun" (an expression used by several SSD students) and a "great school." SSD provides more freedom and prestige for them than they might enjoy in the outside culture. In particular there is freedom from isolation and communication problems. But more than that, "big fun" is also a vivid description of the social climate (the collective orientations, values and attitudes) at SSD. A heavy strain of anti-schooling (academics) runs deep at SSD. Life in the classroom is said to be "boring" (a sign used very, very often by students) and physical horseplay is common. At this point in their lives they do not seem "sorry" about their deafness nor do they see themselves as deficient in any very serious way. Quite the contrary, as many of them recognize, they are special people at SSD.

Problems of Self-Disclosure With the Deaf

Several techniques were used in an attempt to get deaf students to talk about their selves. These included the Twenty Statements Test (TST; Kuhn and McPartland, 1978), having students tell five things about themselves (something suggested by the school superintendent) and asking them to tell a story about themselves. In every instance the technique employed was an introspective, projective one. No matter what technique was used, getting intelligible responses was nearly impossible. Some students would stare into space for a long time and finally say, "I don't know." On the other hand, some students would immediately begin to tell about their daily activities such as going to English class, chemistry class, social studies class, and so on. Only one or two students mentioned their hearing status. Apparently, at least as reflected with these techniques, hearing ability is taken-for-granted for them just as it is for hearing students.

We wondered why students were unable to respond to queries about the self. Teachers and administrators were quick to suggest that language was part of the problem. One high school teacher, for example, explained "They have communication problems and limitations. They begin language late ... The deaf child starts school with zero vocabulary and he never catches up with the hearing child in terms of language." But if deaf students utilize ASL, a real language, shouldn't they be able to respond to questions in that language? The teacher suggested that "students learn about tangible things and have problems with abstractions."

The 'problems with abstractions' was something we had theorized would be problematic about sign language. Quite serendipitously this problem arose in trying to discuss the one constant in all social interaction – the participants' selves. As a point of curiosity, we simply wondered what deaf children would say about themselves. In particular we wondered if they might mention their hearing status. Instead of pursuing that, however, we turned toward gaining more information on why they could not talk about themselves.

A middle school administrator said, "the word (sign), 'thing,' is too abstract for students to handle ... it is quite an abstract concept." A high school teacher agreed. "If you give the question, 'Tell me five things about yourself,' it means nothing to deaf people. The word, (sign) 'about' means nothing to deaf people." On the same day SSD's communication specialist expressed precisely the same view: "I think your question is too abstract ... the word (sign) 'about' means nothing to deaf kids."

Not only was language offered as an explanation but so, too, was its corrolary, experiential deprivation (one top administrator especially emphasized again and again the factor of experiential deprivation). In this case their language prevented them from conceptually understanding what it meant to have a self. The Cartesian certitude becomes most uncertain when applied to these deaf children. What we mean when we discuss the power of mind to think – as in, "I am, therefore I think I am" – is called into question.

An administrator who has excellent sign language skills attributed lack of response on self queries to experiential deprivation, specifically symbolic deprivation. The students, he felt, had never heard such a question. He argued that asking deaf students, "Who am I?", was equivalent to asking most people to talk about Einstein's theory of relativity. For him, the truncated symbolic universe of the deaf means that some questions (like "Who am I?") never arise.

A high school teacher was especially puzzled that Sammy, a high school student, was unable to give a single reasonable response. The teacher, who knew Sammy very well, remarked, "What I don't understand is why a kid like Sammy, basically a bright kid, has never grasped the concept 'about.'" The teacher was convinced that Sammy had a concept of self although it "may not be as developed as most hearing people's concept would be at his age." But why? "Well, the lack of experience ... lack of reflection ... self is based on reflection." He clarified the latter notion by pointing out that if one's parents, relatives, or neighbors cannot reflect to you *what you are,* then your self image will be very narrow and undeveloped. Again, this is partly a language problem, but more than that, it is a problem having to do with experiential deprivation – a deprivation tied directly to an inability to fully communicate with diverse, significant and generalized others.

Earlier another high school teacher had discussed the self-disclosure problem. She believes that

> [The] students can give you back what they have been exposed to. Maybe they never had the opportunity to give a description of themselves. It is a question they have never encountered. The kids should have been asked questions like that down in the lower schools.

By sheer luck a teacher from the lower school overheard this conversation and stopped to give her own explanation. She, too, located the problem not only within the language itself, but within the style *and* the very socialization process which takes place within that social world. She speculated, "Perhaps the students cannot answer the statement, 'Tell me five things about yourself,' because we have brainwashed them and taught them to give one single answer to one single question and your asking them for five things at one time is too much." She suggested a better approach might be to ask one question, then another question, and so on. The superintendent offered a similar view of the differential learning process which usually begins so late for these children. Normal hearing children acquire a broad base of knowledge (several blocks or bricks) and build subsequent knowledge onto that base. In contrast, deaf children begin with a small restricted base (one block/brick) of knowledge

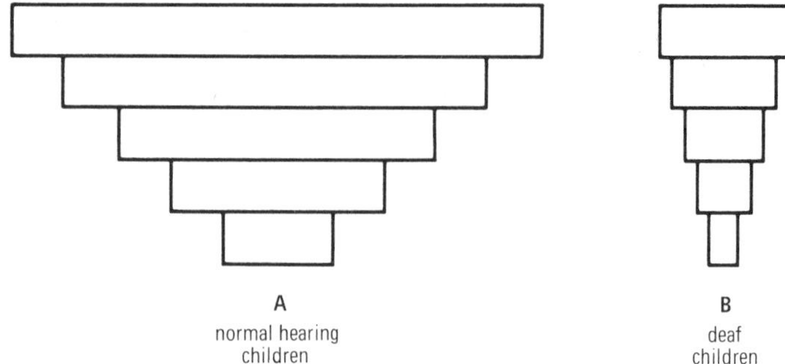

Figure 4. Differential broad (A) and restricted (B) bases of early and subsequent knowledge for normal hearing children and for deaf children.

and accumulate other restricted blocks of information to that base (in a columnar fashion). He depicted his idea of these two funds of knowledge as follows (see figure 4).

Having "one answer for one question" was echoed by a former teacher who is now a staff member. She said, "I let students see that they can each and individually have a different thought, and that two or three of them can still have a perfectly acceptable answer and not be afraid. That it's not straight down the road, one single answer." Yet, the students themselves belie that. For them, it is more often one question, one solution. It is a rigid mode of thinking typical of deaf people generally. The deaf are used to concrete, specific concepts and their applications. Anything abstract is immediately troublesome.

A middle school teacher with excellent signing skills and energetic classroom teaching style describes the problem this way:

> We tell them what to do, what time to do it. Do this, do that – out of necessity. This puts them in a lockstep pattern. I find the deaf very patterned. Many of them don't develop language to think abstractly. They never get a vocabulary that a hearing child has and so they can't use abstractions. They think in facts [she could not define nor expand that idea].
>
> I wonder if there are characteristics that go along with deafness. A deaf child who goes to public school performs just like these. The kids are rigid, intolerant. If I sign differently from some other teacher, or have them put their names at the top or bottom of the page, they say, 'Wrong!'
>
> Different is wrong! So I tell them how our book shows some cultures having three, four wives. The kids say, 'Wrong!' and I try to say, 'No, it is just different. Or some people, nomads move every day and they say, 'Wrong.'

> Along these lines, deaf children are so persecuting of other handicapped children. They will giggle and make fun of a disfigured or deformed kid. I find deaf kids to be very intolerant. They do everything in groups and have so much supervision. Thus, when they have a chance they jump to the other end (other extreme) and neck in public. Sometimes they think holding hands is wrong. They see things as black or white.

Reference to the use of polar or binary oppositions also reappeared. As one staff member put it, "their choices at the school are limited to either-or choices. For them, things [concepts] must be tangible." In that context, we discussed the peculiar way in which deaf students will sign "I have touched California" meaning "I have visited" or "I have been to California." The staff member referred to a test consisting of twenty pictures given to hearing students who frequently and literally said, "I feel ..." i.e., they would self-disclose upon seeing a picture. When this same test was administered to twenty deaf males, there were only three self-disclosures. Why are deaf students so stymied? Because, said this woman, they use ASL, signed English, and other forms of manual language which affect one's ability to express oneself (and, we might add, one's "self").

This staff member talked about administering a set of picture tests (different from those cited above) to get at the "self" of deaf students. Students are shown faces smiling at one end of a continuum while other faces change slowly until there is a sad face at the other end. Other pictures, similar to the happy-sad ones, deal with strengths and weaknesses, and various degrees of anger, again moving from left to right on a continuum. How did students at SSD react to these tests?

> They never use the middle section. They're never in between, they're either-or .. out of thirty students we did not get any midliners. They are either happy and they're smart or they're unhappy or they're sad and they're not smart or they're really pretty ... it's just either-or.

The resulting pattern on these tests is always "an extreme," she said.

Several teachers and the communications specialist related student reticence (when asked about self) to traditional distrust and/or hostility between deaf and hearing people. First, they may try to hide their (deaf) identity because they do not want any possible weaknesses to be known. Second, deaf students have a normative side to their peer group behavior which is rather secretive and, by extension, protective. One teacher stated this very succinctly:

> You ask them a question and they'll tell you it's not your business (a second teacher who was present pointed out that this is more often the case in high school). Just that quick. 'My business. It's not your business.'

Similarly, when another teacher asked a girl to write an autobiography, she was accused of being "nosey." Generally, however, SSD students seemed remarkably open. Problems with self-disclosure seemed more often due to inability than unwillingness to be cooperative or choosing to be secretive.

Through Rose-Colored Glasses

Ernest Becker (1975) has commented that "if we put our self-esteem on the block in society, we also need society to add to that self-esteem. Our identity can only be validated in the social encounter." By referring to Cooley and Mead, Becker states that the eternal question, "Who am I?" can only be answered by the society in which one is anchored. "Every social encounter is a potential life source for self-aggrandizement" (p. 65). Nowhere can this be better demonstrated than at SSD.

Much of the literature in the last ten to fifteen years has described deaf adults as being immature and somewhat egocentric (see Moores', 1978, summary of the literature at that time). In very recent years, there has been much criticism of this. One might expect "handicapped" children to be depressed about their shortcomings, but that is not what we found. Our findings, clearly support the older studies – deaf students do have incredibly inflated egos.

The following is intended as a collage of quotes from students interviewed about themselves. While all of the quotes are removed from comments made before and/or after them, in no case has the intent of their statements been altered. That is, each is quite understandable on its own. In this presentation, each student comment is preceded by the question which prompted the response cited.

> Who is the smartest person in your class? "I am."
>
> Who is the smartest person that you know? "Me."
>
> Who is a girl in your class liked by many people? "Me and Louise."
>
> Who are the most popular students in middle school? (After naming two students, this boy said) "and me."
>
> Who are some popular students on campus? (After naming students in different classes, this girl said) "The [popular] juniors include me."

Who is nice around here? "Me."

When the homecoming queen was asked about a popular boy, she stated,"He is nice to people, understands people, not in trouble, almost same as me."

Who is the smartest person that you know? "Me."

How do you know that you are the smartest one?

"Because I'm always studying every night and it makes me understand. I make many 100's in class ... I never made an F."

You told me you were popular. Can you tell me why people like you?

"I wonder why! I'm the best popular cheerleader. They love me because I use my voice all the time. I holler to win."

Who is the smartest person in your class?

"Me." (Why do you think so?) "Because I understand the English and I write it and I can do it by myself without help. I can read a story and I can write a story. I have made A's and just one C and I can write good stories.

[Some students who were asked to write about themselves, i. e., answer the question, "Who am I?" wrote]:

'I am a good boy.'

'I am pretty.'

'I am pretty' (written by a very fat girl [over 200 pounds] with crossed eyes).

As Kurt Vonnegut says, "and so it goes." These students have a very intriguing sense of worth. This is found not only in the domains of intelligence and popularity but also in more physical activities (such as athletics and cheerleading) and more monetaristic considerations. The findings there more clearly demonstrate the possibly distorted view of the world (and themselves in it) that these students have. Who is rich? "I am." Who will own a beautiful car? "I will."

When the daughter of a wealthy attorney began to attend (high school) SSD, it seemed like a good opportunity to inquire about student perception of social class. While our own theoretical orientation was heavily influenced by Bernstein, hence already sensitive to possible social class aspects of life at SSD, the students themselves had most peculiar views of money (and things associated with it). Many of them named themselves or their friends as "rich." One girl was asked how much money she had. "Much!" How much? "Ten dollars," she answered. On another occasion some boys asked Don about his old, small automobile. One of the boys volunteered that he was going to buy a Cadillac after graduation. Had he saved money for this? "I am rich." His friend, standing nearby, intensely supported him with his own testimony. "He *is* rich." How much money did he have? "In the bank I have $168.42." This is going to be a very old Cadillac!

Having not bought a car, $ 168.42 may seem like a sufficient amount. Not having ever experienced large sums of money, $ 10.00 may seem like a fortune. But three staff members said they easily understood the Cadillac story. "These kids don't understand math nor money," a former teacher of many years explained. "If a Cadillac costs $ 15,000 (a figure cited by the deaf boy) and he has $ 168.42 saved up, he probably thinks the two sets of numbers, each having five digits, are close. They don't understand numbers like that." The other staff member further emphasized the point. Around Christmas time, he said, the school bused children to a K-Mart for holiday shopping. Each student had $ 3.00 to spend but whenever they reached the checkout counter many (some are "slow" students) had piled up $ 60.00 worth of goods. "We do this year after year," the former teacher exclaimed with dismay. "You'd think they'd learn the value of $ 3.00 and what it will buy." Don asked, "Learn such a lesson from once a year experiences?" The staff member agreed it was not enough.

One day Don was talking with a high school boy (Tippy) down at the vocational school. Tippy, who has just returned to SSD from a suspension home, said he wanted to be a farmer (after graduation). "I can earn $ 1,000 or $ 1500 per month. But the hours are too long. Last summer I worked with wood and logs." [Both Don and the teacher marvelled over such figures and agreed verbally that it was not possible to earn such money with logs].

These children see and understand things not as they are but as they must imagine them to be. A top administrator emphasized this with a lucid example of the way they fail to understand that "what appears is not always real."

> A student might observe (not hear) me making an appointment with a physician on the telephone. He misses the vital fact that the accomplishment is three weeks later (how easily accomplished, it seems). Eventually the student wants me to phone the doctor for an appointment *today*! Three weeks from now? Never! 'I want the appointment now!'

Alas, the notorious "real" world stands outside the campus like a kind of grim reaper, waiting for these children as part of its harvest. Given the large amount of time they spend watching television, one might expect that some of "life's lessons" (to include financial ones) would have been learned via this medium. But television has never been been known for its deftness at articulating means-ends relationships (even if students could hear television). Just as these students simply are deaf (and even many of the older ones have a poor understanding of exactly why this is their fate), just as they simply receive "SSI" (Social Security benefits), just as they simply are at SSD, so, too, some of them imagine that they will "simply" have success away from SSD just as they have had success while there.

They can have somewhat unrealistic images of themselves with inflated sense of worth because they live an isolated, insular existence. Competition among themselves is hardly the equivalent of competition in the larger society. The problem of how to "best" educate these children is an extremely difficult one. Part of the case for mainstreaming these children is to preclude their sense of isolation. Similar to the Supreme Court's ruling in Brown v. Board of Education of Topeka, one cannot but wonder how damaging such a segregated experience is to the "hearts and minds of (deaf) children." At the same time, to take them out of places like SSD may be more harmful than helpful. Many of them would be unable to effectively communicate with parents, siblings and neighbors on the outside. Special education departments in public schools do not have skilled signers. How would they learn in a soundless and signless classroom? Who would they talk to during the day? Play with? The larger point remains: somehow, someway these children have to develop healthy, positive self concepts, *but* grounded in some consideration for reality as it will be experienced after leaving the world constructed for them at SSD.

Chapter VIII

Theoretical Lessons

> Imagine the condition of men living in a sort of cavernous chamber underground, with an entrance open to the light and a long passage all down the cave. Here they have been from childhood, chained by the leg and also by the neck, so that they cannot move and can see only what is in front of them ... At some distance higher up is the light of a fire burning behind them; and between the prisoners and the fire is a track with a parapet built along it, like the screen at a puppet-show ... .
>
> In every way, then, such prisoners would recognize as reality nothing but the shadows of those artifical objects.
>
> "The Allegory of the Cave" (Plato)

> Yet by any name those institutions that have total or near-total control over their inhabitants' lives are abominations to humanity. Once the absolute corruption of absolute power has come to dominate an institution, even the most benign establishments brutalize everyone in their midst. Hospitals cease to care for the ill and become huge boarding homes for the unwanted. Prisons mirror the worst features of the underworld community ... Students are trained in conformity to meaningless rules rather than educated.
>
> Samuel E. Wallace, 1973

The previous analytical chapters have provided a wealth of detailed information on life at a state school for the deaf. These chapters have focused on language, self, student culture, and the total institution. Each has drawn upon a somewhat different theoretical orientation – some two chapters relying heavily on Mead and, to a lesser degree, Bernstein, two chapters relying more heavily upon Goffman. Given the large number of analytical observations made in these chapters, the task of now giving some theoretical coherence to them is overwhelming. Rather than spend very much time (and space) on any one chapter's findings, the present chapter will highlight some of the key findings from the overall study. In a philosophy of science manner a series of hypotheses will be stated in such a way that the empirical findings are restated into a more formalized, theoretical format. We close the chapter with a brief section on theoretical implications to be drawn from our study.

It has been the position throughout this study that SSD and other similar institutions offer a vast arena of research possibilities. These institutions house children who arrive with little or no formal language. The researcher is afforded the opportunity of observing children as they acquire language in a step-by-step, moment-by-moment process. It is impressive drama, an unfolding before one's eyes of humanization, of movement from *umwelt* to *welt*, from diadic to triadic worlds. In a larger sense, it is an opportunity to watch the social construction of reality at its origins, to witness symbolization of (near) blank slates. Here, a researcher can observe the processes, the techniques used by teachers as they segment continuous holistic reality into labeled bits and pieces. Prior to stating any specific theoretical statements, a brief overview of the study's principal questions is given.

Following the conceptual lead of Bernstein (1977), one of the theses of this study has been that American Sign Language (ASL) is a restricted code, since it is relatively undeveloped (Vernon, 1974; Benderly, 1980). As Sternberg (1981) says, "The first and most striking difference (from English) is vocabulary size." Sign language often has "a single sign to express what English has a whole series of words for" (p. xxxv). And, we are told, since the meaning of a sign can be altered by changing size, speed, tension, precision and duration of movement, there seems to be no need for large numbers of synonyms.

Again, Bernstein's distinctions between restricted and elaborated codes of communication (and the social conditions which give rise to such codes) are conceptually useful in a study of deaf people with their dependence upon sign language. This allows for empiricaly testing whether or not ASL is a restricted code. Of course for Bernstein, restricted codes of communication are associated closely with the working class. At issue in the present study has been exploring to what degree ASL (a type of restricted code) is dependent upon class factors versus questions about the very nature of the small tight-knit (relatively isolated) group and its language (its global iconicity). An extension of this is to observe deaf persons of different social class origins to see if differing forms of sign language are used by them.

Another interesting problem for social scientists arises. Anthropologists and linguists have argued that no language is inferior to any other language and the deficit theory is generally rejected. Hymes (1972: xx) forcefully claims (as noted earlier) that "... it is scientifically absurd to describe children as coming to school 'linguistically deprived,' so far as the presence of regular grammar and the capacity for creative use of language in social life are concerned." There are no superior languages. Is that true also for manual forms of communication? If ASL is a language which has survived and continues to be perpetuated by children from one generation to another can it develop as fully as languages which flow through adult brains? Is it possible that deaf groups are so sharply separated socially and linguistically from all other sound-based language groups that ASL develops and fits (in terms of lexical repertoires) their own relatively simple niches/worlds (*gemeinschaft*) but not the more complex *gesellschaft*? As Hymes so pointedly declares, "The key to understanding language in context is to start, not with language, but with context" (1972: xviii).

Writers like Hertzler and Farb are not reluctant to refer to "The shortcomings of a language" which can have a "limiting effect upon the kinds and range of thinking occasioned by new individuals and social awarenesses, conditions and needs" (Hertzler) or to an Indian language which is "stubbornly literal" (Farb). If ASL lacks conventional signs for many everyday objects and events, is it equal to other languages? Why are so many different sign language books for sale – books which provide vocabularies in common areas like religious signs, legal signs, academic signs and sexual signs? If ASL, a physical-gestural-spatial language, does not effectively teach English, a word language, should it continue to be used to whatever degree in academic institutions? What happens to students who graduate from high school unable to read and write English well enough (literacy) to find good jobs in their own English-speaking society? Why do state schools and deaf people continue along this path? Why not strive for bilingual competence? Or is the fundamental problem late language acquisition which prevents most deaf children from ever using manual and written English well? Again, we do not argue that these children must learn to actually use *speech* which seems out of reach for the majority of them. We mean that 'bilingual competence' includes (1) ASL and (2) reading and writing English (and, of course, manual English).

A third area of inquiry (and we are linking and expanding some preceding categories) relates to the triad: language/self/social interaction (usually considered in dyadic pairs). First of all we cannot research the self-social interaction relationship if no language is present. That is, in order to get at self adequately we must be able to use language with our subjects. We must be able to talk to interviewees about themselves, to ask them questions and to convey to them our own intentions, meanings and inquiries. Nevertheless, since many levels of language skills exist among deaf children, SSD and other sister schools do afford us opportunities to see more clearly how language and self are related. We can discover whether or not students with restricted and limited language abilities (but not too limited) also have limited selves as suggested by some writers (Hertzler, 1965; Charon, 1979).

While Mead's (1977) theory argues that language is a prerequisite to self, that without language one has no self, (see Charon, 1979 who makes the very same claim) this is initially difficult to imagine or to accept. And yet one way that individuals define, describe and talk about themselves is in terms of status concepts (I am a boy, a student, a girl scout, etc.). It seems important, at this point, to strongly emphasize the distinction between self as a *social* object – an object with a name, with consensual definitions, valuations (good, bad, dumb, smart) and demographic/hierarchical labels (the Baptist, the student, the poor boy) – and self as a *physical* object. Of course one without language can learn to recognize his/her own reflection in a mirror but only as a physical object. As Charon (1979:45) felicitously points out: without language Charles Mole, the man, the teacher, the moral person would be merely a physical object and not "Charles Mole" because "we approach reality with the symbol." Do language-impaired deaf children have no social selves *or* does their language difficulty simply make it less possible to express a sense of self? And if you say they *do* have a self, how can it be? What definitions, valuations, names, etc. have they been able to internalize?

The self/social interaction nexus has been of great interest to sociologists for a long time. Goffman, in his classic work on stigma (1963), analyzes the physically disabled as "tainted." But many deaf children in residential schools do not see themselves that way. Quite the contrary, many of them hold extremely positive views of themselves. Several writers (cited earlier) relate these feelings to the fact that lavish praise is often given to deaf students whenever they accomplish very minor tasks. At SSD, the significant others (with a few exceptions) of the school constitute a very positive "looking glass" (Cooley, 1964), consequently we find the opposite of what Goffman (1963) described in *Stigma*. For deaf children (the prelinguals in particular) there is a taken-for-grantedness about deafness. In a sense it is normal, it is okay (many say it is "better") and not at all negative. For those born deaf there never was sound nor speech. How can one miss or even understand something one never had? One deaf staff member told a remarkable story about her first childhood years at SSD. As she acquired sign language and gradually entered that linguistic universe, she (and other children) began to wonder what was "wrong" with adults who did not sign to each other, but faced each other constantly moving their lips.

Finally, there are questions about the institutional side of life at SSD. For Goffman (1961) the "totalness" of an institution is indicated by the extent of isolation from outside society. As we have argued throughout, deaf children in residential schools are doubly removed from the outside culture by space and language. Some arrive at the school with little or no language and eventually acquire a language (ASL) foreign to the natives on the outside. This may result in worlds which are literally languages apart.

Having little or no language deaf children initially arrive at the school with little culture. Here they grow up under salaried surrogate parents employed by a department of "home life." To avoid confusion, their office doors are labeled "parents." But these "parents" are strange substitutes. Often they are of another race, another social class and, more importantly, may or may not speak the language of "their children." Odd parents, these. But SSD is "home" for many. During summer months children write letters back to SSD. They are lonely and want to return. And once each year many generations of adults make their pilgrimage back for the "homecoming" weekend.

At the institution *group life* is touted above all else. According to Bernstein (1977) this condition favors the emergence of a restricted code of communication. Part of the rationale for undertaking this study was that insight into types of relationships and codes of communication could be gained by studying the linguistic communities at SSD – communities tightly knit together, thoroughly separated from the larger world, which ensures the emergence and perpetuation of a subculture, an argot, and a distinct sign repertoire.

Further, schools for the deaf – as total institutions – permit investigations of Goffman's (1961) "underlife," the ways in which individuals attempt to preserve self from the long tenacles of the social order. Do deaf children, under processes of "total enculturation" (which tends to inspire great loyalty), attempt to circumvent the system of authority and rules to lesser (or, perhaps, greater) degrees than inmates in prison? In a setting where many teachers and houseparents are not highly skilled with the students' language, will patterns of "secondary adjustments" differ from those found in other institutions?

As an organizational entity, SSD is threatened by policies which could alter its constituency or worse (from an organizational point of view) put it out of business. Mainstreaming, for example, threatens the life and security of the school employees. It changes the face of the student body, taking away middle-class students and retaining (and increasing in number and proportion) lower-class students as well as multiple handicapped people. What happens, then, to self-images of "normal deaf" when grouped with physically handicapped, retarded, blind, etc. deaf peers? Do they get along or do "normal deaf" tend to stigmatize these other people? Too, what happens to those students who are mainstreamed? Administratively, what happens to social relationships in a school where administrators and staff are frightened of losing their jobs? When funds are being cut, enrollment is down and classrooms are over (or under) staffed?

The research findings reported in the analytical chapters of this study suggest numerous theoretical hypotheses. In the following, certain of these are specified. In all cases the statements flow from empirical findings of the study. Additionally, the statements represent a combination of Glaser and Strauss' (1967) "grounded" theory and a more formal theory presented in a bivariate fashion.

Hypotheses About Language and Reality

As Berger and Luckmann (1967) observe, for the child, the parents' world "becomes *the* world" in a most massive and unchanging way. But this is not necessarily the case for deaf children. Although not stated by them Berger and Luckmann assume a normal, hearing child is the one learning (being socialized into) his parent's culture. For the deaf child, however, it is generally the school and its actors not the family which provides for a sense of "the world." Since most parents of deaf children are poorly skilled – if at all – in sign language, the deaf child learns little of symbolic significance from his family. Instead, it is school officials and student peers who both provide and participate in constructing his social world. In this way, the deaf child will become more of a reflection of the school world than his own family's world. He/she must learn to be a deaf person primarily from other deaf children rather than from adults. This leads to three related hypotheses:

> H1: The more restricted (undeveloped) a child's language system is at home, the more restricted (impoverished) is his knowledge of the world (intersubjectively known signs and symbols).
>
> H2: The more restricted a child's knowledge upon entering a residential school, the greater the degree of "total enculturation" experienced at the school.
>
> H3: The greater the impact of "total enculturation" at the residential school, the greater the discrepancy between the worlds (cultures) of child and parent (and child and society).

H1 posits that for a child born with no hearing, his knowledge of the world is severely truncated from birth until such time as he has a symboling system with which to "understand" his surroundings. If language is a map, to use Korzybski's metaphor, which describes the territory we call "reality," then the child inhabits an unsegmented plain dotted only occasionally with rudimentary social objects, a world of gaps. From Mead and Weber, to understand is predicated on shared symbols – in Weber's term, it is the experience of intersubjectivity whereby two individuals mutually define into existence and agree upon the meaning of some object or event. And all knowledge, says Hertzler, is related to language; we definitely agree with Postman and Weingartner (1969:102) that almost all knowledge *is* language. In the humanizing process, of course, the absence of language precludes any form of understanding as we commonly think of it; precludes the acquisition of everyday "recipe knowledge" (Berger and Luckmann, 1967). Technically, the deaf child is "in" but not "of" his own family. He is more of an appendage than full participant in family life.

H1 in its broadest application builds on the work of Bernstein, for it says nothing about deafness. Instead, it focuses on the style and degree to which language is experienced in the home. For Bernstein (and Hertzler) this relationship was largely the result of class background – the lower the class, the poorer would be one's facility with universalistic codes of language. Thus this would result in one's using fewer words (i. e., having a more limited vocabulary), and being likely to speak more often with condensed utterances (intrinsic meanings) than with complicated sentences which evince some clarity and development to a thought. We do not herewith espouse a deficit theory for hearing children whatever their social class. We do claim the deficit theory of language applies to our deaf children. The magnitude of this problem is amplified drastically when you introduce the element of a child with no hearing. Now one is presented with a situation in which even a poor vocabulary accompanied by poor syntax is made largely inaccessible.

However, at the same time that most writers (as in previous references to Berger and Luckmann) assume hearing as an attribute that the individual will possess, in reversing this assumption we cannot assume that all deaf children will suffer a total hearing loss. Deaf children, then, may – and in fact do – differ in both degree and kind. That is, hearing loss may range from total to only partial. In the most axiomatic way and having the greatest inclusiveness of any of our theoretical statements is the hypothesis that:

> H4: The greater the degree of hearing loss, the greater are all "social" relationships (c.f., acquiring language, family-child interaction, general "understanding," and so on) made problematic.

This hypothesis ties in directly to H1–H3. In fact, it in a certain way subsumes each of its predecessors since it focuses so specifically on hearing itself as the crucial variable. It posits that from degree of hearing loss all other things flow. Note, this is not to say that innate capabilities (e.g., "native" intelligence defined in terms of ability to learn) disappear or take on less importance than they otherwise would. It is to say, however, that all things being equal, the degree to which one's hearing is impaired may be *the* key determinant for much else which occurs in one's life. For example, the prelingually deafened earn less income than the postlinguals (Benderly, 1980:18). Thus we return to hypotheses 1–3.

As we already noted about H1, for the deaf child, knowledge of the world is "truncated." The world simply cannot be experienced in all of its complexity because the individual's sense perception and thus early language is diminished. Deafness automatically means (or equals) reduced reality. *If* the child's experiences at home result in a severely reduced base of knowledge by virtue of the absence of language, *then* it follows that the child's acquisition of "culture" must be accomplished in part via other mediums. Thus the less the child brings into the school with him (in the form of language and general knowledge of the culture), the greater will be the impact of the school upon him, something we stated in H2.

In George Herbert Mead's terms, the preclusion of language from consciousness can only result in a rather undirected form of activity, a relative lack of self-control on the part of the child. For Mead, the normal child moves from the play to the game stage; in this way the child more and more learns to grapple with the world in terms of social rules and roles and these are made available primarily by means of language. And in the extension of Mead by Berger and Luckmann, much importance is given to reciprocity as social life is lived out in a kind of ebb and flow (give and take) quality. But how is this possible for the young deaf child? It isn't. Deafness necessitates for a young child the ability to encounter one's world as a series of charades in which, more often than not, he/she is the only player.

Of course the enculturation experience at the residential school is more beneficial than not since it initially provides the child with a formalized, structural (and accessible) culture where none or little previously existed. At a comparatively late point in time the child begins to learn the definitions and meanings of social objects and events. Human reality (Berger's "world construction") slowly and awkwardly emerges via hand shapes and motions. The child moves from dyadic to triadic behavior, from direct to indirect experiences of things, from physical to social objects.

In some extreme cases the child arrives at the residential school virtually a "cultureless" individual. In fact, we believe research should move quickly to the intriguing question: How much culture, how many symbols – if any – can be learned at home without language?

But the school itself does little by its day-to-day example to build upon what the child had previously known (barring the child having already developed some mastery of language). The new world which he now faces is almost exclusively one of signs (ideograms), rather than oral expressions (words). He must, to a certain degree, unlearn what he previously "knew." Again, reference to Berger and Luckmann is helpful since they refer to knowledge as the certainty that things are real – that they are what they seem. And one's culture, as acted out by those around him, provides assurance that individual perception and reality are more-or-less isomorphic.

As stated in H3, the more the school norms and culture are subscribed to, the greater will be the discrepancy between whatever was learned at home and whatever one comes to see as "normal" at school. The point was repeatedly made throughout our analysis that learning the culture at the school was not necessarily the same as learning how to cope in the society and culture-at-large, a point to which we return shortly. It was the disjuncture between the two which would create the sense of discrepant or somewhat contradictory world views.

This contradiction for the individual is not without its cost. And, again, this cost can be traced, in part, to the lack of language for whether at home or away, the languageless individual is cast adrift in a kind of sociological "no man's land." It is, as Percy (1983:108) graphically writes, a form of nakedness – an absence of a "permanent semiotic habiliment." As noted above, this, at the same time, can also lead to a type of "marginal man" (Stonequist) status since the individual can conceivably have a foot in two different worlds at the same time. Here, however, our concern is more with the potentially anomic state in which an individual may find him/herself.

If *a* culture is not clearly understood as *the* world for the child, it is understandable then why it would present a confusing picture of things to the child. The order which is so easily taken-for-granted by the hearing world is replaced by a possible chaotic terror in the mind of the deaf child. Berger and Luckmann refer to the taken-for-grantedness of everyday life as presenting a "self-evident, massive facticity." Its 'massive' quality means that it "cannot be wished away." Having been in this social factlike world for a long enough period of time, one learns its ways – one comes to identify as being "in" and "of" his world.

But if language is sufficiently impaired at the outset of one's life, it is likely to be difficult to sort out potentially discrepant world views. This leads to the following hypothesis

> H5: The less formal language one has to help organize his sense of the world, the less *any* culture will confront him in a coherent, massive way and the more likely he will engage in some form of deviant (anomic) behavior.

This hypothesis also brings to mind the issue of cognition, or thought as it may occur in the mind of the deaf child. The term "charades" was used earlier to refer to the acting out which deaf children must do to make themselves understood. In Meadian parlance, this means that much of what passes for "language" among deaf children is conveyed by mimetic "gestures." These gestures must somehow convey to the observer an intended meaning.

This physical side to deaf life was frequently commented upon in the analytical text. Miming, touching and a generally more tactile form of communication is commonplace. Lacking English terms or standardized signs for things, one must constantly improvise to express him/herself. Too, this often requires that two people share in close temporal proximity some object or event so that the iconic nature of improvised language is understandable. For example, several children watched a television program in which two kangaroos were boxing. Later, two teenage boys discussed the program. Every reference to the kangaroos required that fists be made and held to the chest accompanied by hopping up and down. Clearly, this is one example of an undeveloped (or localized) sign language's problem with conveying phenomenological "essences" or less abstractly, the "meanings" of things as opposed to the things themselves. Too, it further demonstrates Cicourel and Boese's (1972) point that sign language is often context bound. This leads to the following hypothesis:

> H6: The lower one's level of language development, the more physical are one's communication acts (play, mime, etc.).

This observation for deaf children has a counterpart in the hearing world. Hess and Shipman (1970) found that working class mothers use more nonverbal teaching methods with their children than did middle-class mothers. For the boys in the example above, then, arbitrary words (or signs) are simply replaced by iconic gestures, and these are often (as in the case above) context or situationally bound. In that sense, then, the undeveloped language is a restricted code of communication being highly concrete in its referent, as discussed by Bernstein (1977). As Piaget would say, a child with normal language cognitively moves from the simple to the complex, from the physical/concrete to the ideational/abstract (Boocock, 1980:10). And at an even more macro level mind must have emerged under evolutionary pressure in order to handle "an order of complexity in behavior greater than that of any other form of life" and it must have devised language to maintain that complexity in equilibrium with the world (Caws, 1970:213). But these very transitions from the restricted to the elaborated are clearly problematic for deaf children.

Hypotheses About Language and Self

Following Mead (1977) we assume deaf children are not born with a self; self is not the same thing as one's body. The self is a social object which emerges within social interaction and, we insist, the most important aspect of social interaction is talk. Language, says Mead (p. 199) is "essential for the development of the self." Of all the traits, it is man's capacity to become an object to himself, i. e., a *social* object with a name and a set of definitions/evaluations, which distinguish him from all other life forms.

Becker is another for whom language and self are entangled. Language is a form of power and without it one faces a threatening world. As Berger and Luckmann (1967; and Hertzler, 1965) say repeatedly, interruptions of one's languaging process create a nightmare of "terror," and yet these statements are not supported by our findings. Instead, our young deaf children (with the exception of Sachmo) seem more like Percy's (1983:124) scientists and artists who are able to transcend self and thereby experience the "semiotic Eden when the self explored the world through signs before falling into self-consciousness."

These "innocent" young deaf children have never heard any sound at all and do not know sound (nor language) exists. Nevertheless, it follows that those with a serious language problem will have a self problem. As Hertzler (1965:402) notes, inadequate language results in a "truncated personality and an incompletely socialized individual ... he is diminished as a self to himself and to his associates."

One explanation of the difficulty students had telling stories about themselves is directly tied to language. First, it is possible for a deaf student to be lodged so tightly, as Goffman might say, into the walls of his social world (the tribe) that he cannot extract himself as an individual. He/she resembles Levi-Strauss' primitive who "is in the fortunate condition of not knowing that he has a self, and therefore of not being worried about it" (Caws, 1970:204). But, secondly, low level language skills may be related to this inability to talk about oneself. In this frame the following hypothesis seems logical:

> H7: The lower the level of language development (or acquisition), the more difficult it is to self-disclose.

In H7 we see a close relationship between certain concepts of Mead's and those of Bernstein. "Self," by virtually all admissions, is a highly abstract concept. Certainly its empirical referent can only be derived by very indirect methods; it is clear in the old debate between the Chicago and Iowa schools of symbolic interaction that there is much disagreement about how self can be assessed. Given its abstractness, then, disclosing and/or discussing one's self may be difficult even for a very bright, articulate individual. When this is coupled with a fundamental language problem such that the individual is required to more often than not act out ideas to express himself as opposed to communicating in words (as a symbolic alternative to gestures or signs), the plausibility of H7 becomes quite clear. Rephrased, we could say that it is axiomatic that individuals who depend upon restricted codes of communication will find it most difficult to express all abstractions including notions of "selfness."

We noted in H4 that the greater the degree of one's hearing loss, the more problematic will all aspects of life (and knowledge) be. Earlier (in our first chapter), we noted that not all deaf people are equally deaf. Deafness is not a discrete variable providing either/or states of itself. Rather, deafness is a continuous quality running from the extremes of totally deaf to totally non-deaf. Additionally, deaf children may have parents with or without a hearing loss.

Understanding of this point is critically important in terms of both language acquisition and self-disclosure, two things which we have already seen must be understood in relation to one another. This leads to a series of hypotheses (some of which could just as easily be placed in the previous section):

> H8: The time at which hearing loss is experienced and the degree of the loss will vary directly with language acquisition. The earlier and greater the loss, the greater will be the difficulty of learning language.

Given that H8 posits that later onset and less hearing loss will enable individuals to more easily learn language, it follows that:

> H9: The later and less the hearing impairment, the more likely will the individual be to self disclose.

H8 and H9 are direct corrolaries of one another. Our argument has been that self disclosure is nigh on to impossible if language acquisition has been severely impaired. The more severe the impairment, the more restricted will one's codes of communication be. But since we know that there is a potential intergenerational component to deafness and language ability, it is also necessary to state two hypotheses for those individuals who have one or both deaf parents.

H10: Deaf children with deaf parents will more quickly learn a useable language than will deaf children with hearing parents (especially where the degree of hearing loss is profound).

Given that deaf children with deaf parents will have something of a language advantage, hence acquire it sooner and likely be more skilled in it by virtue of their complete (early) dependency on it, it follows that:

H11: Deaf children with deaf parents will be more able to self-disclose than deaf children with hearing parents.

Although we did not interview enough deaf children of deaf parents (DD's) at SSD to indicate their abilities (or lack of) to self-disclose, numerous studies throughout the 1960's and 1970's compared children with deaf parents (DD's) to those with hearing parents (DH's). These studies consistently found that DD's "exhibit educational, social, and communicative superiority" over DH's in spite of the fact that the latter had more preschool experience, tutoring and higher social class backgrounds (Moores, 1978:180).

Hypotheses H7, H9 and H11 require some further comment because to a certain degree they may appear to stand in opposition to classical Meadian social psychology. In the analytical text there was cited the case of a teenage boy who simply could not understand queries about his "self." Even when a deaf teacher was called upon to help, the boy's responses remained largely irrelevant to the questions being posed. His case illustrates that for deaf children, Cooley's "looking glass" reflection may be observed in an opaque mirror. Unable to freely and competently communicate with his "significant others," the near languageless child may apprehend vague, distorted and restricted reflections from others.

On a daily basis, those around the child do have some occasion to recognize him, even if in no more than a perfunctory way. In their recognitions, positive and negative images are presented to the child by gestures, facial expressions, rewards and punishments, and so on. We make it clear in our "self" hypotheses that individuals will have greater or lesser difficulty with self-disclosure in part dependent upon the timing and severity of their hearing loss.

But it is necessary to qualify this position by speaking of a "primitive self," or a "preself" (Charon, 1979:69, 99). That is, self-recognition as a physical object is not the same as knowing one's self as a *social* object whose origin is tied to significant others and reference groups (with whom one talks). The physical self is similar to Charon's "preself" in that a basis for self exists but may not be developed to the point where a more well-defined, articulated "sense" of self as a social being occurs. And as we note in H11, it is likely that deaf children with deaf parents will be able to self-disclose earlier and better than their peers with hearing parents. Thus, language qualities and quantities must be conceptualized in a broad sense (as a system not based solely on sound) when it is related to awareness of self. In fact, the very concept of self may be as much a product of a particular socio-historical epoch and culture as it is any language peculiar to those things.

H10 is a direct extension of work by Furth and by Cicourel and Boese. They, too, argue that deaf children born to deaf parents would not only acquire a useable language early but for Cicourel and Boese, this would occur as a "natural" or "native" thing. In the absence of hearing and easily acquired oral skills, signing is what one would do to make him/herself known.

We have made it very clear that restricted codes of communication engender restricted worlds in which individuals live. If the world was conceived of as a pie, the analogy here would be the greater one's language abilities, the greater the share of the pie would be. Conversely, the less the language, the smaller the share. One of our empirical findings was that many deaf children evinced a high degree of egocentrism. While they often had great difficulty in describing their "selves," they were very quick to make comments about their smartness, richness, popularity, and so on.

No empirical finding has presented a greater paradox in this study than this one. Here we have children for whom self-disclosure is difficult. Not only are they language impoverished (in the relative absence of vocabulary and abstract concepts) but they are often anchored to a group. Thus language and groupness in combination may strongly affect the vague responses to self. At the same time, however, they are egotistical. Why? Our posited answer is expressed in the following:

> H12: The lower one's level of language skills, the more one's behavior is hedonistic and ego-centered.

We believe language is the medium par excellence which enables a human being to move from ego to the social, from "I" to "us," from maximal to minimal self-seeking behavior. It is the principle conduit to others by which one is normatively pulled from egoism to altruism.

One must always be mindful when dealing with these deaf children that to a very large degree, theirs is a world of dichotomies – there is black and white, good and bad, smart and dumb, and so on. Remember our discussion about "Mistake!" Wrong was definitively wrong. In the later years of school, of course, subtlety and differentiation are more easily accomplished. The odd thing remains though – these children are often prone to see themselves in very aggrandized terms. Even when having relatively little money either on them or in the bank, they are "rich." Again, if words symbolize reality ("words are to reality what a map is to territory") then we have here a classic example of "map-territory disjuncture" (Wagner and Radner, 1974). Likewise when asked about the brightest person in the class, the answer is easy, "me." These inflated expressions of self worth are helped along by teachers who, by their own admission, are quick to praise deaf students for doing even the easiest problems correctly.

One final note on this paradox. By reversing the emphasis and wording of H12, we would be saying that the greater one's language skills, the less hedonistic and egotistical his behavior would be. Our reasoning for this is that language ability allows one to more fully understand his circumstances. Thus "others," both significant and generalized, can and do have a more dramatic impact on the individual's sense of things. Intersubjectivity can only be "inter" when two or more individuals are on the same cognitive wave length. If language is sufficiently impaired, then arriving at shared meanings is made difficult if not impossible. Where language is not terribly impaired, however, it seems far likelier to result in a more well-rounded, well-integrated individual who more easily and fully understands what others' expectations for him are. Thus one's focus may be less on a truncated or fragmented self and more on a self that is understood with both strengths *and* weaknesses.

Hypotheses About Total Institutions

A working hypothesis of this study was that in the total institution setting of SSD, student "underlife" would be a very important phenomenon for investigation. And, indeed, this was found to be the case. As noted in the analysis, the older the children got, the more inventive they were at circumventing the "official culture" of the school. That is, the rules and norms of the school were frequently replaced or altered by the rules and norms of the student culture. The overwhelming side to this is readily understood since as a residential school, many children spend much of their lives within its confines. Too, as Berger and Luckmann say about normal socialization, adults made the rules up and their game is the only one in town. So, too, is this true at SSD. However, as we have alluded to previously, there may in fact be two games – one sponsored and organized by adults, the other by the children – with two conflicting sets of rules.

Above all else, total institutions are characterized by their generation of and dependence on rules. In turn, enforcement of these rules serves to regularly remind one and all that there are supposed to be two groups of people in the institution – those with power and those without. In short, the controlled and the controllers. And there are even two (or more) language modalities at SSD and these, too, conflict and compete with each other. As Weber (1964) showed about bureaucracies generally, and as Goffman and others have shown about total institutions, despite their rule-reliance for their existence, there are always ways for creative individuals and groups to find ways to soften-up the impact of the rules. This leads to

H13: The greater the number of rules enforced and the greater the sanctions for violating them, the greater the perceived disparity between residents and staff in the total institution.

H14: The greater the perceived disparity between residents and staff, the greater the creativity of those seeking to circumvent the "official" rules of the total institution.

What is recognized in H13 and H14 is that rules create classes of people based on authority relations (Dahrendorf, 1959). In this way power becomes a zero-sum game – for some to have it, someone else must be doing without or giving up something. The more strictly this is enforced, the more likely those disaffected are likely to see a gulf between themselves and those in power. And unless those disaffected completely acquiesce, they are likely to seek out ways to make their rule-guided lives as pleasant as possible (see Willis' "lads," 1977).

For children in institutional settings (as was empirically shown at SSD), this often takes the form of "conning" the system by following the spirit but not the letter of the law. For example, recall how children would tell a teacher or houseparent that they were going from one place to another (thereby satisfying the institutional requirement that someone "in charge" know where his "charges" were going to be) then, they would go somewhere else. Or, the girls who went to the dispensary ostensibly for medical attention when in fact they were going there to have some privacy for their own conversation. The most vivid, graphic illustrations of H14 deal with sexual behavior. Sexual encounters were achieved in the relative privacy of a room, woods or car but also in the bold public of a school bus with children on it – children who knew of a sexual liaison occurring and, in fact, helped to see that those engaged were given the opportunity to do so (a practice also found in prison where homosexual encounters are common and must often occur in publically-confined circumstances).

The "totalness" of the total institution refers not only to the peculiar culture which pervades it, but to the extent of isolation from other groups. Goffman emphasizes the regimentation of everyday life and its collective character which results in little privacy. The net effect of this for the individual is that Mead's innovative and creative "I" is effectively suppressed. But this process of I-stunting is complicated by the fact that relative language deprivation can also arrest the development of the social "me" for many deaf. As Hegel allegedly said, in order to become a person one "must 'ingest' the history of the race, become a We in order to become an I" (Zimmerman, 1970:215). To put it in simple terms, two powerful social factors work to create the "deaf person:" separatism with its group character and linguistic deprivation.

The more massively real total enculturation has been, the more likely individuals are to subscribe to the institution's rules and regulations; in Berger and Luckmann's terms, the more the "truly social self" will dominate. Translated into Mead's terms, we may characterize the deaf social system at SSD as a "me" (public/social/institutional) society (as opposed to an "I"/individualistic/segmented) society in the sense that tribal life tends to stifle individual expression (with the exception of the egocentrism mentioned above). In this homogeneous society one is socialized to conform not create, to cooperate not compete. Like children in other collective environs (Israeli Kibbutzim, for example) deaf youth at SSD are "literally afraid to find themselves different from the group" (Kenkel, 1977:161). They are like Becker's "inauthentic men who avoid developing their own uniqueness; they follow out the styles of automatic and uncritical living in which they were conditioned as children ... tribal men locked up in tradition ... " (1973:73).

Also in this closed society there is a leveling process through which average academic performance is produced in school (within a social climate of mediocrity). Experientially, the daily pull for any individual is toward the central axis, toward fusion and sameness with the "deaf way" (not the hearing way: *they* say study, *they* say English, *they* say no sex, no booze, no ... etc. But *we* know "deaf is better"). So totally enculturated members (tribal men) make less attempts to express "I" because the social me dominates their conforming behavior. This results in

> H15: The greater the degree of "totalness" (as isolation from the outside and pervasiveness of socialization within the institution), the less tolerance there will be for individualism (creative expression, deviance).
>
> H16: The more enculturated the individual, the less individualistic he is likely to be.

These two hypotheses suggest not only overtones of Meadian social psychology but more structurally they evince a certain lineage to Emile Durkheim's concern for social solidarity. Of course for Durkheim the relationship between the individual and the group was always a dialectic one – each existed in part because of the other (a point amplified into a book by Berger and Luckmann). In the total institution, normative loyalty was often to the system of authority (despite the daily attempts to circumvent it at many points in the road). In the plaintive words of a deaf man, "It is a microcosm that unmercifully tries your individuality" (Mow, 1974). Thus students often expressed no anger when punished for committing some wrong.

For the very young children, the total institution provided a form of total enculturation (see H2 and H3), providing a sense of culture where none may have previously existed. On the other hand, older deaf students who come from other schools may, in fact, experience a process of "disculturation," a term Goffman (1961) uses to refer to cultural disruption. The consequence of this for newcomers is that they must conform and fit into their new surroundings – and at SSD this is exactly what happens. But not entirely. Consequently, we see two related theoretical statements:

> H17: The younger one is at time of initial residency in the total institution, the greater the impact of the institution will be.
>
> H18: The older one is at time of initial residency, the greater is the likelihood of active participation in the institution's underlife.

Those whose entire lives are more-or-less lived out within the institution's walls experience the institution as a relatively homogeneous, consistent life world. This stands in sharp opposition to latecomers (cosmopolitans) who may have much first-hand experience with a broader range and diversity of social groups – ranging from family ties, other schools (perhaps including other deaf schools), and so on. It seems very plausible, then, to suggest that older children who first attend the school will have a larger number of experiences to draw upon in evaluating the school (approximating Berger's "cosmopolitan" motif) thus their reactions to it may be of a more varied nature (i. e., in ways unlike those whose whole lives have been spent there and for whom the school is very much in the "natural" order of things).

The total institution's cloistered life style is also likely to produce a particular style of interaction unique to it. As already shown, the very form of sign language often results in improvisation and unique localized iconic gestures for objects and events for which no word is known. Also reflecting this restricted code of communication is the sharp bluntness with which individuals address each other – and this includes, as shown in the text, not only relationships among students but also among students and teachers. In a kind of parody of ghetto life, deaf students often "do the dozens" with each other. They not only one-up each other (as shown in the ego-centered nature of many of their comments) but they deal with one another in an interpersonal style which would be shocking to those in the hearing world. They call each other "stupid," "whore," "fat," "ugly," "sloppy," "nitwit," and so on. Lacking the ability to be subtle in their interpersonal dealings (by virtue of signing which is a public act), bluntness is the rule not the exception.

> H19: In the total institution where everyday life is of a public/group nature, interpersonal communication will be characterized by a public, open, blunt and (in the norms of the larger, outside culture) tactless style.

Finally, we consider Berger and Luckmann's (1967:163) notions about successful and unsuccessful socialization. For Berger and Luckmann, successful socialization occurs when the objective, structural circumstances and the individual's sense of those circumstances fit closely together – i. e., when they are more-or-less isomorphic or symmetrical. From Durkheim on, the sociological principle here has been that the simpler the society, the more easily successful the socialization experience is.

One of the avowed purposes of SSD is the socialization of deaf children to live in the larger hearing society, to make them full participants in it. SSD (as with other residential schools for the deaf) does not intend to give its students skills which work only within the deaf community (although preparation for life in that "home" community is definitely an important goal of the school, and according to Nash and Nash [1981] and Higgins [1980] this sense of deaf community is critically important for deaf individuals).

What has been discovered in this study, however, is that SSD's students are well socialized for the deaf world but poorly socialized for the hearing world. One of the papers obtained from the superintendent's office at SSD listed the "social problem" of deaf people as "the subculture problem" within which "they are cut off from normal sources of information and are unaware of events which may have great significance for them." As shown throughout the analysis, many of the students have very distorted views about the "outside" world. The total institution provides for a cloistered, isolated and overly protective life world. As one teacher stated, "They are not realistic when they talk about the real (hearing) world." Similar comments were made by bicultural hard-of-hearing students whose grasp of both hearing and deaf worlds was superior to long time SSD students. One of these students said she was "worried about the deaf" because they had little knowledge of the larger world.

School-supported efforts to enable the children to more fully understand the outside world are made difficult by deaf students and deaf adults, for both of these groups demand ASL (or, total communication). Of course if too much emphasis is put on ASL or total communication, skills in English may suffer which is exactly what happens at the school. In turn, a self-fulfilling prophecy is set in motion in which teachers and others often find themselves utilizing non-English sign language because that is the "children's language." This generally isolated, institutionally-unique growing up experience leads to our final two hypotheses:

H20: The greater the degree of spatial, linguistic and interactional segregation from the society at large, the less successful is the socialization process (in terms of the larger society's norms).

H21: The greater the degree of spatial, linguistic and interactional segregation from the society at large, the more successful is the socialization process in producing a subcultural native.

These final hypotheses recognize two important points about spending most of one's formative years in a residential school, and the accuracy of our statements should hold whether the "school" is for deaf children, juvenile delinquents or any other group isolated from society. The first point is that it is difficult to learn to be a member of society if most of your life is spent apart from the society. This is like saying that you can not be "in" it if you are not also "of" it. The second point is that the more the individual is held apart from the society, and finds an institutional culture as more of a substitute than supplement to the larger society's culture, then the greater is the likelihood that the individual will be a "native" of a somewhat unique and – in the larger society's scheme of things – peculiar culture. In a sense, such a person sits in Plato's cave looking not at real things but only their shadows. Recall that for Berger and Luckmann (1967) "successful socialization" means a "high degree of symmetry between objective and subjective reality." For us "successful socialization" of deaf children is to establish a high degree of symmetry (isomorphism) between the institutional world and the world outside.

Chapter IX

Conclusions

> ... reality as evidenced is not something visible, tangible or in any sensuous way perceptible. Its framework is something intellectual, capable of being apprehended only through symbols ...
>
> Effective reality is, for us, essentially a language-made affair: we catch it and encircle it comprehensively by means of words.
>
> Joyce Hertzler

> In group discussions where you alone are deaf, you do not exist. Because you cannot present your ideas through a medium everyone is accustomed to, you are not expected, much less asked, to contribute them. Because you are deaf, they turn deaf.
>
> The day you lost your hearing your universe shrank many times over; your power of choice in a world of sound is drastically reduced. Thrown in the storm of silence, you seek refuge among your own kind and become part of a microcosm which you are not sure you want. It is a closed society whose bond among members is founded not on mutual interests or intellectual equality but on a common desire for escape from the "cruel outside world," for communication frequently turns out to be an illusion. It breeds dependence, stagnation, pettiness, and finally boredom. It is a microcosm that unmercifully tries your individuality. You either surrender to tribal conformity or return to the other world.
>
> Shanny Mow

Since sociology has "late touched" the deaf, much work remains. Our general understanding of the social world of deaf people has been greatly advanced by such authors as Benderly, Higgins, and Nash and Nash. In every case we have been allowed to look into ("up close," as the ethnographers say) a world about which most of us know very little. Our own work has, we hope, added to this literature. In our case this has been done by focusing specifically on the lives of deaf children and in particular deaf children who reside away from their parents in an institutional setting.

In this closing chapter we turn our attention to a brief agenda. First, we return to our major theses – the sociology of language can be used as an overarching framework for sociological research *and* language, as a sociological phenomenon, must be conceptualized in dialectical terms. Second, we address some of the ethical issues involved in doing this kind of ethnographic study. There is always the risk of misrepresenting the views of individual participants and the groups and institution of which they are a part. Third, we close by commenting on the need for a certain pedagogical stance toward deaf people generally, and deaf children especially.

The Dialectics of Language Colonization

In the foreword to his book, *The Language of Dialectics and the Dialectics of Language*, (1979) Israel states: "I argue for the thesis that the sharp dualistic distinction between knowledge of language, and knowledge of reality, has to be abandoned. Knowledge of language is knowledge of reality. Language itself is part of reality." (p. xiv, emphasis in the original; Hertzler too sees language and knowledge as "always related," 1965:134). But while calling throughout his text for a more wholistic, "totality" oriented view of language, he nonetheless also recognizes the need for some conceptual format for distinguishing between dialectical provinces (e. g., subject and object). That is, he sees the "interrelatedness" of things and from that view rejects attempts at "monism" or relatively simple cause and effect statements. Having worked through our theoretical position, our analytical text, and the theoretical propositions we draw from our work, it should be patently obvious that we agree with Israel.

To talk about knowledge *is* to talk about language since without it little can be "known." The point was made long ago by Korzybski that the medium *is* the message (Postman and Weingartner, 1969); knowing is inseparable from languaging (p. 122). If little can be known without language, what "reality" can be apprehended by one's naked mind? Indeed, in what sense can mind even be said to exist? To us it seems necessary to temper certain tenets of Meadian social psychology and symbolic interactionism. Mead, for example, claimed that language is the vehicle for thought (mind); that language is a prerequisite to thought; and that language is necessary for self to develop. Likewise, Charon (1979:65) says a person as object can only emerge "when objects are defined with words." Where does this leave the young, languageless deaf child? Is he capable of thinking? Has he no self?

We believe that a deaf child without language does have mental processes (logic, rationale). Mead has underestimated the power of the brain to imitate others, even without formal symbols. Young deaf children view themselves in mirrors and "know" (in some sense) that they are physical objects – even before acquiring any language (see Furth, 1966). In some rudimentary way a deaf child can be socially defined without words. He can be praised, patted, petted, smiled at, etc. (positive communciation) or either scowled at, beaten, scolded, etc. (negative communication) and there is no reason to believe that he is without any evaluative feelings about himself. Perhaps we should follow Charon (1979) and call it the presymbolic child's "preself." Again, *the* proper question may be whether or not one can become a *social* self without language (a social object with labels/names, and status definitions, etc.) as opposed to a physical object with positive-negative self "feelings."

While it makes sense to argue that language (especially the naming of objects in one's surroundings) does greatly enhance one's ability to structure reality and his experience of it, it is also true that young deaf children (prelinguals) are able to structure the world, to nomize it to some extent by observing those around them. They dress each morning, line up, get served cafeteria style and eat with utensils. Simply put, they have a modicum of order and structure without a formal symbol system; they are not wallowing in a fury of pandemonium. And this is precisely a problem for sociological researchers: to what extent is social structure possible without language? The structuralists have already given their position: ". . . the very archtype of structure . . . [is] language itself" (Caws, 1970:210). Thus, for us, the relationship between language and self is relative and not absolute: the more language one receives, the more fully developed one's self and the more able one is to express feelings (as indicators) about self. It is simply too strong an assertion to state, as Mead did, that without language there absolutely is no "mind" or "self."

Whereas we wish to modify a Meadian view of the world, our findings seem to offer further credence to the general argument set out by Bernstein. His elaborated and restricted codes (with their respective abstract or concrete-particularistic meanings) were clearly evident at SSD in the various languages in use. And unfortunately, it would seem that the more restricted code (viz., undeveloped and poorly standardized sign language) is the dominant one. At SSD, language replaces Bernstein's social class as the key indicator of prestige and acceptance. It is language (of whatever type) that gives one entree to peer groups and classroom assignments (reflecting various levels of difficulty).

We repeatedly found the meanings of sign language to be cryptic, situated and context-bound. For example, a student said "My favorite teacher is BK." Who is that? "I forgot his name," the student replied. Or, "I will get married next year." To whom? "SW," the boy said. When asked to spell her name, the boy shrugged uncomfortably and said, "I don't know the spelling (of her name)." Nearby towns are initialized. Where are you from? Student, "M," the letter M moved from shoulder to shoulder as if everyone would know what town "M" represents.

In colorful and stylistic narratives, the condensed and compacted quality of ASL was shown, much like the findings of Cicourel and Boese. One boy was asked if he had a girlfriend. "Poor," he signed (a teacher had commented one time that students said "poor" about things or conditions that were bad). The boy meant that there were poor girlfriend choices at SSD, not that someone was economically poor. In vocational school, one teacher laughed and marveled at the way boys would say a truck (or anything old) was "country." One student said his favorite teacher was "Mrs. CF." Why? His response, "Body." The only way to understand his response was by being familiar with the local scene. The boy was not speaking of a teacher's beautiful body but instead he was referring to the fact that Mrs. CF taught the health course about human bodies. In Bernstein's (1979b:475) words, these people are "in the grip of the contextual constraints which determine (one's) speech act."

SSD students have colonized into a language community. They accept the "total" institution (Goffman) as "home" where a shared language, community and friends are to be found. Either through enculturation (for younger students) or disculturation (for older, first-time students), SSD becomes one's normative basis for experiencing the world. It is where one learns to be deaf; to act like a deaf person; to ontologically *be deaf.* As many say, "Deaf is better."

As Benderly notes few deaf people learn "how to be culturally deaf in their parental homes; they must learn to be the adults they become from others, in other places, and often without their parents' knowledge or approval" (1980:12–13). And perhaps there is no more lucid example of learning to be deaf than what happened in the following incident:

> In a strange inversion of the usual situation, a boy who had always signed and never spoken was found, upon entering a school for the deaf at age six, to hear perfectly. But he had learned his home language from his deaf parents and two congenitally deaf siblings, and had never considered that he might differ from them. He immediately entered regular school, spoke normally, and made good progress (p. 47).

A type of "labeling" (Goffman) occurs which seems to socially define the individual apart, *as deaf*. At SSD a person almost unquestionably experiences the greatest sense of community he will ever find. SSD is an oasis (of symbols) in the middle of a (linguistic) desert. Breakfast, bus rides, classroom hours, free time, etc., all are spent in the company of "like situated" people. Acceptance is total; stigma (at least due to deafness) is unknown.

It is our position that in each instance cited above, language is *the* paramount issue. This is tempered only to the degree that it is language in conjunction with experience which gives shape to one's view of the world. In nearly every case, it is language as a dialectically constructed, maintained, and altered phenomenon that guides discourses and our understanding of things. As Israel says, "Knowledge of language is knowledge of reality." The sociology of language, then, must be dually focused – on language as process *and* product. Berger and Luckmann assert that man constructs himself. Man is dialectically interwoven with his own construct; in a peculiar way he gives birth (as a social creature) to himself. And it is primarily some form of language which hastens or deters this dialectical process. As we stated in the last chapter, the more language one knows, the greater is his ability to grasp and grapple with his world. For those whose primary language is signing, however, the social callipers provided will ensnare only fragments of what is available to the speaking world.

ASL as an Undeveloped Language

This brings us to our rather thorny concept of ASL as an "undeveloped" language. This notion that a language, any language, is "undeveloped" flies the face of the widely accepted tenet that all languages are somehow equal. That is, there are no "superior" nor "inferior" languages, no "good" nor "bad" languages; there are merely different languages!

What, then, do we mean when we say that ASL is an "undeveloped" language? Is Navajo language undeveloped because it is an ancient tongue whose vocabulary lacks (some percentage of) terms for urban and/or technological objects and events? Hardly anyone would argue this case since Navajos collectively have well developed vocabularies (classifications, categories) for objects and processes extant in their own rural environment (having, for example, more than five hundred plants identified; Levi-Strauss, 1966: 5). Nor would we argue that a normal hearing child, age 5, uses an "undeveloped" language. What is undeveloped is his repertoire, his vocabulary (at this point in time) and not his symbol system (English).

But deaf society and deaf language differ significantly (and sociologically) from all others. First, deaf people (in any given city or town) do not live in "deaf town" as, say, Chinese people who live in a "China town." Instead, they are sprinkled all around the city as couples (or more) and rub shoulders in their neighborhoods with people who speak a foreign (English) language. In short, they are a linguistic group, but not necessarily a *linguistic community* (if 'community' means living close together in large numbers). This isolation and fragmentation is not conducive to development of standardized lexical items. Indeed, the opposite is the norm: numerous pockets of localized/situated (and thus limited) signs are rampant. As Cicourel (1973) says, this diminishes the power of sign language.

Secondly, ASL is a language of children. As children *most* signers learned *most* of their signs from other children in a state school. And, again, most of them were unable to learn the native language of their own parents, of their own community/neighborhood. Worst of all, most of them learned language (signs) very late – past the optimal period of time for language acquisition and many writers believe they never "catch up."

Finally, and more to the point, ASL has an undeveloped vocabulary, a small vocabulary. Unlike Levi-Strauss' (1966) primitive people who have generated and accumulated numerous fine classificatory schemes for plants and animals (some *individuals* being able to identify two hundred and fifty species and varieties of plants; p. 5) ASL has yet to divide the generic sign "meat" into subcategories. And many high school students have no specific terms (signs) at all for facial regions like chin, cheek, forehead; no vocabulary for automobile parts (fender, hood, trunk) other than identification by pointing.

Limitations and Ethical Issues

Ethnographies, like other qualitative studies, are always subject to criticism because no parameters (in a statistical sense) can be known. Too (and likewise a statistical caveat), no hypotheses as such can be tested; statistical probability theory is simply not applicable. The reader must always trust the veracity of what has been presented.

As we stated at the outset, we pursued a form of grounded theory without *a priori* theorizing in any logico-deductive way. Our approach and data have (to our satisfaction) "internal validity" by virtue of the extent of agreement among our participants about crucial points in the analysis. For example, *all* teachers interviewed said that deaf students are concrete minded and have difficulty with abstractions. Similarly, language ability was repeatedly mentioned as critical for deaf students' better understanding of the world around them. The degree to which our findings have "external validity" remains to be tested; but our citations to Cicourel and Boese, Nash and Nash, Benderly, and Higgins (i. e., all major sociological works on the deaf thus far) continually support the case we have presented. And we suspect that our findings are generally reliable although we realize that there will inevitably be between-school variations whether the schools are for the deaf or the general population.

Our greatest concern is not with such research issues as validity and reliability but, rather, with a more personal problem – ethics. We have tried to provide as much anonymity as possible for the school and its members. Often this has been nearly impossible because content, status position, and/or philosophies (or even attitudes) of participants will be recognizable by some members of staff who read this report. With so few deaf teachers at SSD, for example, some of their statements *may* be easy to identify. This is truly an ethical problem since most deaf teachers and staff were very trusting and open in participating in the study.

Another ethical problem lies in the fact that certain administrators cooperated fully in making this study possible. In fact without the superintendent's initial interest, encouragement and acceptance, the study would have been aborted. It is difficult, then, to report negative events or situations which may cause any administrators to "look bad" in some way. And yet we are scientifically obligated to report as accurate a picture as possible, even when parts of that picture are negative. It is our sincere hope that the study is not read in this context, however; what we do hope is that it is read as an analytical description of one school which has its successes and failures just like all other schools. It was never our intention to make any one person or group look either good or bad, although we admit that SSD teachers, staff and administrators face a difficult and not easily met challenge.

Pedagogies of the Deaf

In his important work, *Pedagogies of the Oppressed,* Paolo Freire's (1979) thesis is that education is not so much liberating as enslaving. If education does not totally open you to new vistas, it certainly prevents or controls access to them. In a related and largely unintended way, this is what happens at SSD. We have no belief in any kind of conspiracy at SSD; we do not believe that there is any joy in seeing successive generations of deaf individuals who face a life of restricted opportunities. But this, in fact, is the net effect of the educational experience at SSD and we suspect that the results are not too dissimilar at other, similar institutions. "The system fails deaf workers not once but twice. They get less education than the hearing, and they don't get jobs that fully exploit the schooling they have" (Benderly, 1980:17).

It is undeniable that schools such as SSD offer their students an experience they would not find elsewhere (at least not in any schools near their homes). And this experience is a wholistic one – it includes their acquisition of a language and a culture. The rub is that (a) the language they become most proficient at is not the one used in the larger culture and (b) "their" culture, itself, is so much at variance with the larger culture. They are local Americans who cannot speak the language of their own parents nor read and comprehend (very well) the newspaper of their land. In a very real sense deafness itself acts as a "total institution" which, in this case, is a condition and not a place. In deafness one is isolated and cut-off from the wider society – and this includes parents, siblings, television, the printed media and on and on.

The sign languages found at SSD are many and varied in their levels of sophistication. Any given student is confronted by various codes, styles and types of signs. Teachers, houseparents, staff and administrators use the core language of the student body with varying degrees of skill. In the course of a day, from dormitory to infirmary to classroom to the gym, one meets TC, ASL, signed English, fingerspelling, newly invented signs (in the form of initialized old signs), and pidgin English. *We do not mean* that students are lost in a maze of unknown language systems, they are not. *What we are saying* is that the lack of standardization of one language system, and the various flavors or styles or signs which proliferate, add to the problems of clear communication at the school. As we know, communication even with a single standardized language is confusing enough. But at SSD there are signs in lower school not known by students in high school. One staff member demonstrated three different signs for "has" used on campus. He told how teachers say that a *poor* standardized system would be better than existing non-standardized systems.

One of the most important findings of this study is that SSD does not give maximum priority to the teaching and learning of English – which is the language needed on the outside. English is the language which one must use skillfully in order to rise above poverty and menial work. Literacy is related to life chances (87 percent of the deaf but less than 50 percent of the hearing engage in manual labor; Jacobs: 1974). But teachers and administrators say it is most important to communicate ideas – by any means possible (whether one uses English or mime). The point here is *not* that children should be forced to verbalize English. Instead, they must be given every chance to graduate with a command of written English. If they could learn to verbalize some English that, too, would be helpful.

What we wish to suggest is that SSD's strength – its giving the children a place of their own – can be built upon. This will not, however, be accomplished by a continual contrast with the outside world in which deaf students are the odd ones out; instead they must be sensitized to (a) their identity as deaf persons and (b) their ability to merge themselves with the world outside. This latter theme was frequently expressed by teachers and staff; the children at SSD (as is probably universally true of other "handicapped," institutionalized children) must develop better skills for existing after they leave SSD.

In its *en loco parentis* status, SSD must tread a fine line between protecting the child *and* making him aware (as much as possible) of the larger society of which he is a part. We are suggesting that an important part of the "hidden curriculum" at SSD should be made more explicit and given comparatively greater emphasis – deaf children should be schooled for the real world not just for a world of the deaf. And to do this requires above all else that they develop some mastery of English. No matter how "equal" any legislation tries to make things, it is the deaf who will continue to suffer in society's stratification system. The deaf must develop skills in English for it is surely the case that the larger society is not going to willy-nilly learn sign language.

Footnotes

1 This is true only for the "manual" deaf community which uses sign language. Some "oral" deaf do not use sign language at all.

2 For more details on our methods, see Don's unpublished dissertation, *The Social Construction of Reality in a Total Institution: An Ethnography of a Residential School for the Deaf.* Lousiana State University, 1982.

3 But Joyce Hertzler (1965:29) argues that man is the only creature with symbol-forming power which makes complex [human] culture possible. It is not that man is simply a great tool maker because we know that the great apes use and even modify tools. White (1949) and Farb (1973) agree that *Homo loquens* is qualitatively different from other animals: Man alone creates, establishes, institutionalizes and uses language. Only man has the tremendous range in the kind and quality of communication across space and time that language makes possible ... What is epochal is not *Homo fabricans* (tool maker) but *Homo loquens* (speaker or verbalizer; Hertzler, 1965:31).

4 For a good discussion of the private vs. the public spheres of life, see Berger and Kellner (1983). They view the public sphere as "an immensely powerful and alien world, incomprehensible in its inner workings, anonymous in its human character" (p. 311). It is within the private sphere where the individual seeks self-realization, power, intelligibility – a place where he/she is somebody.

5 It can be anticipated that signers will object to Don's presumption that he is "such an expert" as to make assessments of this type. His response to that objection is (1) signers generally are able to quickly rate one another within a few minutes of observing one's use of sign language; i. e., sign skills can be judged and classified; (2) Don has signed since 1964 and has taught the language at the university level since 1971. Further, deaf people consistently remark to him that his signs are "expert/skilled."

Poor signing is defined as signing which is halting, jerky, and rough. It is unclear because of its poor form and slouchy articulation (either in the movement of the sign, the hand configuration or in the place of articulation – these may be corrupted by lazy or mere incorrect presentations of one or more of these parameters). In short, a poor signer's language might be comparable to an immigrant's heavily accented and choppy use of English.

Fair signing may be described as smoother but slow and often lacking sign vocabulary which necessitates much fingerspelling (more English, and more ambivalence for the deaf reader of fingerspelling).

Good signing refers to smooth, fluent and fairly rapid (i. e., not dragging) presentations of messages more typical of ASL syntactical structure; fingerspelling is easy and not jerky.

6 Taken from a mimeograph paper (p. 130) which is available to SSD staff in great stacks. The paper is almost certainly a reproduction of some journal article and its title is "Dormitory Personnel – Preparation and Functions." Neither author's name nor publisher was given.

7 Taken from another nimeographed paper (see footnote 6 above) entitled, "From a Residential Child's Point of View," by William Tipton.

8 See Joshua A. Fishman's (1982) call for research on "language loyalty/language nationalism" among the deaf.

9 Jayne Greenstein, "Sounds of Silence," in *Atlanta Weekly*, August 31, 1980, pp. 14–17; 28–29.

10 As an aside, it has been observed in the Israeli Kibbutz that whenever children visit their parents they too become happy about returning to the Kibbutz, to their group (see Melford Spiro, *Children of the Kibbutz*, 1971). It is as if the children have two families: a bio-kinship group and a sociological (kibbutz) "family group." In other words, deaf children may wish *not* to go home because of their strong interpersonal attachment to the surrogate family (the school dorm) *as well as* the facility of communication which is found there.

11 Some who have researched sign language would disagree. They would argue that signs, too, have "intonation" in the form of body posture, intensity of movement, facial expression, etc.

12 Especially is this true in England itself. There, the first words you speak to someone may determine the kind of reception you get. The "Queen's English" or "RP" (regional pronunciation) are rarely intermingled with a "Cockney" accent or a "Yorkshire" dialect. In the U.S., of course, this same thing is found although its effects may not be quite so drastic.

13 Cited by Becker in *The Denial of Death* (1973:73–74).

Bibliography

Allport, Gordon
1958 *The Nature of Prejudice.* New York: Doubleday.
Anastasiow, Nicholas, J. and Michael L. Hanes
1976 *Language Patterns of Poverty Children.* Springfield: Charles C. Thomas, Publisher.
Ashworth, P. D.
1979 *Social Interaction and Consciousness.* New York; John Wiley and Sons.
Auel, Jean M.
1980 *Clan of the Cave Bear.* New York: Crown Publishers, Inc.
Becker, Ernest
1962 *The Birth and Death of Meaning.* Glencoe: The Free Press.
1973 *The Denial of Death.* New York: The Free Press.
1975 "The Self as a Locus of Linguistic Causality." In *Life as Theater: A Dramaturgical Sourcebook*, pp. 58–76. Edited by Dennis Brisset and Charles Edgley. Chicago: Aldine Publishing Company.
Benderly, Beryl Lieff
1980 *Dancing Without Music.* New York: Anchor Press.
Bereiter, Carl and Siegfried Englemann
1966 *Teaching Disadvantaged Children in the Preschool.* Englewood Cliffs: Prentice-Hall, Inc.
Berger, Peter
1963 *Invitation to Sociology: A Humanistic Perspective.* Garden City: Anchor Books.
1969 *The Sacred Canopy.* New York: Doubleday and Company, Inc.
1975 "Religion and World Construction." In *Life as Theater*, pp. 234–242. Edited by Dennis Brissett and Charles Edgley. Chicago: Aldine Publishing Company.
Berger, Peter and Brigitte Berger
1967 "Becoming a Member of Society." In *Socialization and the Life Cycle*, pp. 4–20. Edited by Peter I. Rose. New York: St. Martin's Press.
Berger, Peter and Hansfried Kellner
1983 "Marriage and the Construction of Reality." In *Social Interaction: Readings in Sociology*, pp. 392–404. Edited by Howard Robboy and Candace Clark. New York: St. Martin's Press.
Berger, Peter and Thomas Luckmann
1967 *The Social Construction of Reality.* New York: Penguin Books.
Bernstein, Basil
1973 "The Limits of My Language Are Social." In *Rules and Meanings*, pp. 203–206. Edited by Mary Douglas. New York: Penguin Books.
1977 "Social Class, Language and Socialization." In *Power and Ideology in Education*, pp. 473–486. Edited by Jerome Karabel and A. H. Halsey. New York; Oxford University Press.

Boocock, Sarane S.
1980 *Sociology of Education: An Introduction.* Boston: Houghton Mifflin Company.

Bossert, Steven T.
1979 *Tasks and Social Relationships in Classrooms.* New York: Cambridge University Press.

Bourdieu, Pierre and Jean-Claude Passeron
1977 *Reproduction in Education, Society, and Culture.* London: Sage Publishers.

Bowker, Lee H.
1982 *Corrections: the Science and the Art.* New York: Macmillan Publishing Company, Inc.

Burr, Wesley R. et al (eds).
1979 *Contemporary Theories About the Family: Volume 1.* New York: The Free Press.

Capra, Fritjof
1983 *The Turning Point: Science, Society, and the Rising Culture.* New York: Bantam Books

Caws, Peter
1970 "What is Structualism?" In *Claude Levi-Strauss: the Anthropologist as Hero*, pp. 197–214. Edited by Nelson Hayes and Tanya Hayes. Cambridge: The M.I.T. Press.

Charon, Joel M.
1979 *Symbolic Interactionism: An Introduction, An Interpretation, An Integration.* Englewood Cliffs: Prentice-Hall, Incorporation.

Cicourel, Aaron
1973 *Cognitive Sociology.* Baltimore, Penguin Books, Inc.

Cicourel, Aaron V. and Robert J. Boese
1972 "Sign Language Acquisition and the Teaching of Deaf Children." In *Functions of Language in the Classroom*, pp. 32–62. Edited by Courtney Cazden, Vera P. John and Dell Hymes. New York: Teacher's College, Columbia.

Cicourel, Aaron and John J. Kitsuse
1963 *The Educational Decision-Makers.* New York: The Bobbs-Merrill Company.

Coleman, James S.
1961 *The Adolescent Society.* New York: The Free Press.

Collins, Randall
1975 *Conflict Sociology.* New York: Academic Press.
1985 *Sociology of Marriage & The Family: Gender, Love and Property.* Chicago: Nelson-Hall.

Cooley, Charles Horton
1964 *Human Nature and the Social Order.* New York: Schrocken.

Dahrendorf, Ralf
1959 *Class and Class Conflict in Industrial Society.* Stanford: Stanford University Press.

1969 "Toward a Theory of Social Conflict." In *Sociological Theory*, pp. 213–226. Edited by Walter Wallace. New York: Aldine Publishing Company.

de Saussure, Ferdinand

1970 "On the Nature of Language" In *Introduction to Structuralism*, pp. 43–56. Edited by Michael Lane. New York: Basic Books.

Eastman, Carol M.

1980 *Aspects of Language and Culture*. Novata, California: Chandler and Sharp Publishers, Inc.

Evans, Don

1975 "Experiential Deprivation: Unresolved Factor in the Impoverished Socialization of Deaf School Children in Residence." *American Annals of the Deaf* 120 (December): 545–552.

Fant, Louie J., Jr.

1972 *Ameslan: An Introduction to American Sign Language*. Silver Spring: National Association of the Deaf.

Farb, Peter

1973 *Word Play: What Happens When People Talk*. New York Bantam Books.

Fishman, Joshua

1982 "A Critique of Six Papers on the Socialization of the Deaf Child." In *Conference Highlights: National Research Conference on the Social Aspects of Deafness*, pp. 6–20. Prepared by John B. Christiansen et. al. Washington, D. C.: Gallaudet College.

Fishman, Joshua A. and Erika Lueders-Salmon

1972 "What Has the Sociology of Language to Say to the Teacher? Or Teaching the Standard Variety to Speakers of Dialectal or Sociolectal Varieties." In *Functions of Language in the Classroom*, pp. 67–83. Edited by Courtney B. Cazden et al. New York: Teachers College Press.

Fleming, Joyce D.

1979 "Field Report: The State of the Apes," (pp. 123–134). In *Anthropology: Contemporary Perspectives*. Edited by David E. Hunter and Phillip Whitten. Boston: Little, Brown and Co.

Friedman, Lyn A.

1977 *On the Other Hand: New Perspectives on American Sign Language*. New York: The Free Press.

Freire, Paolo

1970 *Pedagogies of the Oppressed*. New York: Herder and Herder.

Furth, Hans G.

1966 *Thinking Without Language*. New York: The Free Press.

Garfinkel, Harold

1972 "Conditions of Successful Degradation Ceremonies." In *Symbolic Interaction*, pp. 201–207. Edited by Jerome G. Manis and Bernard N. Meltzer. Boston; Allyn and Bacon, Inc.

Gecas, Viktor

1979 "The Influence of Social Class on Socialization." In *Contemporary Theories About the Family*, pp. 365–404. Edited by Wesley R. Burr, R. Hill, F. D. Nye and I. L. Reiss. New York: The Free Press.

Glaser, Barney and Anselm Strauss
1967 *The Discovery of Grounded Theory.* Chicago: Aldine Publishing Company.

Goffman, Ervin
1961 *Asylums: Essays on the Social Situation of Mental Patients and Other Inmates.* New York: Doubleday and Company, Inc.
1963 *Stigma: Notes on the Management of Spoiled Identity.* Englewood Cliffs: Prentice-Hall.

Goody, J. and I. Watt
1972 "The Consequences of Literacy." In *Language and Social Context*, pp. 311–357. Edited by Pier Paolo Giglioli. New York: Penguin Books.

Gouldner, Alvin
1970 *The Coming Crisis of Western Sociology.* New York: Basic Books, Inc. Publishers.

Gumperz, John J.
1972 "The Speech Community." In *Language and Social Context.* Edited by Pier Paolo Giglioli. Baltimore: Penguin Books.

Gumperz, John J. and Dell Hymes (eds.)
1972 *Directions in Sociolinguistics: The Ethnography of Communication.* New York: Holt, Rinehart and Winston, Inc.

Harris, Marvin
1975 *Culture, People, Nature: An Introduction to General Anthropology.* New York: Thomas Y. Crowell Company.

Hertzler, Joyce O.
1965 *A Sociology of Language.* New York: Random House.

Hess, Robert D. and Virginia C. Shipman
1970 "Early Experience and the Socialization of Cognitive Modes in Children." In *Black Americans and White Racism*, pp. 125–137. Edited by Marcel L. Goldschmid. New York: Holt, Rinehart and Winston, Inc.

Higgins, Paul C.
1980 *Outsiders in a Hearing World: A Sociology of Deafness.* Beverly Hills: Sage Publishers.

Highwater, Jamake
1981 *The Primal Mind: Vision and Reality in Indian America.* New York: Harper & Row, Publishers.

Howell, Richard W. and Harold J. Vetter
1976 *Language in Behavior.* New York: Human Sciences Press.

Huxley, Aldous
1962 "Words and Their Meanings." In *The Importance of Language.* Edited by Max Black. Englewoods: Prentice-Hall, Inc.

Hymes, Dell
1972 "Introduction." In *Functions of Language in the Classroom*, pp. xi–lvii. Edited by Courtney Casden. New York: Teachers College Press.

Israel, Joachin
1979 *The Language of Dialectics and the Dialectics of Language.* Atlantic Highlands: Humanities Press.

Jackson, Philip W.
1968 *Life in Classrooms*. New York: Holt, Rinehart and Winston, Inc.

Jacobs, Leo M.
1974 *A Deaf Adult Speaks Out*. Washington: Gallaudet College Press.

Kando, Thomas M.
1977 *Social Interaction*. St. Louis: The C. V. Mosby Company.

Karabel, Jerome and A. H. Halsey (eds.)
1977 *Power and Ideology in Education*. New York: Oxford University Press.

Kearney, Michael
1984 *World View*. Novato, California: Chandler & Sharp Publishers, Inc.

Keller, Helen
1902 *The Story of My Life*. New York: Dell Publishing Co.

Kerckoff, Alan C.
1972 *Socialization and Social Class*. Englewood Cliffs: Prentice-Hall, Inc.

Kenkel, William
1977 *The Family in Perspective*. Santa Monica: Goodyear Publishing Company, Inc.

Klima, Edward and Ursula Bellugi
1979 *The Signs of Language*. Cambridge: Harvard University Press.

Kottack, Conrad P.
1982 *Anthropology: The Exploration of Human Diversity*. New York: Random House.

Kuhn, Manford H.
1960 "Self-Attitudes by Age, Sex, and Professional Training." *Sociological Quarterly* I (January): 39–55.

Kuhn, Manford H. and Thomas S. McPartland
1978 "An Empirical Investigation of Self Attitudes." In *Symbolic Interaction: A Reader in Social Psychology*, Third edition, pp. 83–90. Edited by Jerome G. Manis and Bernard N. Meltzer. Boston: Allyn and Bacon, Inc.

Labov, William
1972a *Language in the Inner City*. Philadelphia: University of Pennsylvania Press.
1972b "The Logic of Nonstandard English." In *Language and Cultural Diversity in American Education*, pp. 225–261. Edited by Roger D. Abrahams and Rudolph C. Troike. New Jersey: Prentice-Hall, Inc.

Levi-Strauss, Claude
1966 *The Savage Mind*. Chicago: The University of Chicago Press.

Le Premier: L.C.I.W.
1972 "Bells-Bells." Unpublished prison paper. Louisiana Correctional Institute for Women. St Gabriel, Louisiana.

Lofland, John
1971 *Analyzing Social Settings*. Belmont: Wadsworth Publishing Company.

Luckmann, Thomas
1975 *The Sociology of Language*. Indianapolis: The Bobbs-Merrill Company.

McLuhan, Marshall

1965 *Understanding Media: The Extensions of Man*. New York: McGraw-Hill Book Company.

Mead, George Herbert

1977 *George Herbert Mead: On Social Psychology*. Edited by Anselm Strauss. Chicago: The University of Chicago Press.

Meadow, Kathryn P.

1968 "Early Manual Communications in Relation to the Deaf Child's Intellectual, Social and Communicative Functioning." *American Annals of the Deaf* 113: 21–41.

1969 "Self-Image, Family Climate and Deafness." *Social Forces* 47 (June): 428–438.

Mehan, Hugh and Houston Wood

1975 *The Reality of Ethnomethodology*. New York: John Wiley and Sons.

Meltzer, Bernard N.

1978 "Mead's Social Psychology." In *Symbolic Interaction: A Reader in Social Psychology*. Edited by Jerome; G. Manis and Bernard N. Meltzer. Boston: Allyn and Bacon, Inc.

Merton, Robert

1968 *Social Theory and Social Structure*. New York: the Free Press.

Moores, Donald

1978 *Educating the Deaf: Psychology, Principles, and Practices*. Boston: Houghton-Mifflin.

Mow, Shanny

1974 "How Do You Dance Without Music?" In *A Deaf Adult Speaks Out* by Leo Jacobs. Washington: Gallaudet College Press.

Nash, Jeffrey E.

1976 "Some Sociolinguistic Aspects of Deaf Educational Policy." *Sociological Focus* 9 (October): pp. 349–360.

Nash, Jeffrey E. and Anedith Nash

1981 *Deafness in Society*. Lexington: Lexington Books.

Northern, Jerry L. and Marion P. Downs.

1974 *Hearing in Children*. Baltimore: The Williams and Wilkins Company.

Percy, Walker

1983 *Lost in the Cosmos: The Last Self-Help Book*. New York: Farrar, Straus and Giroux.

Postman, Neil and Charles Weingartner

1969 *Teaching as a Subversive Activity*. New York: Dell Publishing Company.

Richer, Stephen

1975 "School Effects: The Case for Grounded Theory." *The Sociology of Education* 48 (Fall): 383–399.

Rosenbaum, James E.

1976 *Making Inequality: The Hidden Curriculum of High School Tracking*. New York: John Wiley and Sons.

Rosenthal, Robert and Lenore Jacobson

1966 "Teachers' Expectancies: Determinants of Pupils' I.Q. Gains." *Psychological Reports* 19: 115–118.

Raskin, Marcus G.
1975 "The Channeling Colony." In *Schooling in a Corporate Society*. Edited by Martin Carnoy. New York: David McCay Co.

Russell, Bertrand
1943 *Human Knowledge*. New York: Simon and Schuster.

Russo, Anthony
1975 *The God of the Deaf Adolescent: An Inside View*. New York: The Paulist Press.

Sapir, Edward
1949 *Culture, Language and Personality: Selected Essays*. Berkeley: University of California Press.

Schatzman, Leonard and Anselm Strauss
1966 "Social Class and Modes of Communication." In *Communication and Culture*, pp. 442–454. Edited by Alfred G.Smith. New York: Holt, Rinehart and Winston.

Scherer, Jacqueline and Edward J. Slawski
1979 "Color, Class, Social Control in a Desegregated School." In *Desegregated Schools: An Appraisal of an American Experiment*, pp. 117–154. Edited by Ray C. Rist. New York; Academic Press.

Schildroth, Arthur N.
1980 "Public Residential Schools for Deaf Students in the United States." *American Annals of the Deaf*, a reprint (April): 80–91.

Schlesinger, Hilde S. and Kathryn P. Meadow
1972 *Sound and Sign: Childhood Deafness and Mental Health*. Berkeley: University of California Press.

Schutz, Alfred
1964 *The Phenomenology of the Social World*. Evanston: Northwestern University Press.
1970 *Reflections on the Problem of Relevance*. New Haven: Yale University Press.
1973 "The Frame of Unquestioned Constructs." In *Rules and Meaning*, pp. 18–20. Edited by Mary Douglas. New York: Penguin Books.

Scott, Marvin B. and Stanford M. Lyman
1975 "Accounts." In *Life as Theater*, pp. 171–191. Edited by Dennis Brisset and Charles Edgley. Chicago: Aldine Publishing Company.

Shibutani, Tamotsu
1978 "Reference Groups as Perspectives." In *Symbolic Interaction: A Reader in Social Psychology*, pp. 108–115. Edited by Jerome G. Manis and Bernard N. Meltzer. Boston: Allyn and Bacon, Inc.

Shover, Neal
1979 *A Sociology of American Corrections*. Homewood: The Dorsey Press.

Spiro, Melford
1971 *Children of the Kibbutz: A Study in Child Training and Personality*. New York: Schocken Books.

Spitzer, Stephan P.
1982 "Is Language Really Necessary for the Development of Self-Awareness?" Unpublished paper presented at the annual meeting of the Midwest Sociological Society. Des Moines, Iowa. April 7–9, 1982.

Sternberg, Martin
1981 *American Sign Language: A Comprehensive Signed English Dictionary*. Washington: Gallaudet College Press.

Strauss, Anselm (editor)
1977 *George Herbert Mead on Social Psychology*. Chicago: The University of Chicago Press.

Strong, Samuel
1943 "Social Types in a Minority Group: Formulation of a Method." *American Journal of Sociology* 48 (March): 563–573.

Sullivan, Mercer L.
1979 "Contacts Among Cultures; School Desegregation in a Polytechnic New York City High School." In *Desegregated Schools: An Appraisal of an American Experiment*, pp. 201–240. Edited by Ray C. Rist. New York: Academic Press.

Sussman, Marvin
1965 "Sociological Theory and Deafness: Problems and Prospects." In *Research of Behavioral Aspects of Deafness: Proceedings of a National Research Conference on Behavioral Aspects of Deafness*. Washington: U.S. Department of Health, Education and Welfare.

Taylor, Charles
1976 "Hermeneutics and Politics." In *Critical Sociology*, pp. 153–193. Edited by Paul Connerton. New York: Penguin Books.

Tucker, Charles W.
1978 "Some Methodological Problems of Kuhn's Self Theory." In *Symbolic Interaction; A Reader in Social Psychology*, pp. 232–241. Edited by Jerome G. Manis and Bernard Meltzer. Boston: Allyn and Bacon, Inc.

Vernon, McCay
1974 "Editoral." *American Annals of the Deaf*. 119 (December): 691.

Vernon, McCay and Hugh Prickett, Jr.
1976 "Mainstreaming: Issues and a Model Plan." *Audiology and Hearing Education*. February/March: 5–6, 10–11.

Vernon, McCay and S. D. Koh
1970 "Effects of Early Manual Communication on Achievement of Deaf Children." *American Annals of the Deaf* 115: 527–536.

Wagner, Geoffrey and Sanford R. Radner
1974 *Language and Reality: A Semantics Approach to Writing*. New York: Thomas Y. Crowell, Company.

Wallace, Samuel E., (editor)
1973 *Total Institutions*. New Brunswick: Transaction Books.

Weber, Max
1964 *The Theory of Social and Economic Organization*. New York: Free Press.

White, Leslie
1949 *The Science of Culture*. New York: Grove Press.

Whorf, Benjamin Lee
1962 *Language, Thought and Reality: Selected Writings of Benjamin Lee Whorf*. Edited by John B. Carroll. Cambridge; The M.I.T. Press.

Williams, Boyce R.
1970 "Journey into Mental Health for the Deaf." Rehabilitation Record. (September and October): 34–36.

Willis, Paul E.
1977 *Learning to Labour: How Working Class Kids Get Working Class Jobs*. Farnborough: Saxon House.

Winch, Peter
1959 *The Idea of a Social Science and its Relation to Philosophy*. London: Routlege & Kegan Paul.

Wittgenstein, Ludwig
1973 "The Limits of My Language Mean the Limits of My World." In *Rules of Meaning*, pp. 201–202. Edited by Mary Douglas. New York: Penguin Books.

Zimbardo, Philip
1982 In *Corrections: The Science and the Art* by Lee H. Bowker. New York; Macmillan Publishing Company, Inc.

Zimmerman, Robert L.
1970 "Levi-Strauss and the Primitive." In *Claude Levi-Strauss: Anthropologist as Hero*, pp. 215–234. Edited by Nelson Hayes and Tanya Hayes. Cambridge: The M.I.T. Press.

Index of Names

Subject Index